CONTESTATIONS

A series edited by
WILLIAM CONNOLLY

*The Anxiety of Freedom: Imagination and Individuality in
   Locke's Political Thought* by Uday Singh Mehta

*The Inner Ocean: Individualism and
   Democratic Culture* by George Kateb

Also by George Kateb:

Hannah Arendt: Politics, Conscience, Evil
Political Theory: Its Nature and Uses
Utopia and Its Enemies

The Inner Ocean

Individualism and Democratic Culture

George Kateb

Cornell University Press

Ithaca and London

First published 1992 by Cornell University Press.

International Standard Book Number 0-8014-2735-5
Library of Congress Catalog Card Number 92-52764
Printed in the United States of America
Librarians: Library of Congress cataloging information appears
on the last page of the book.

To Jack Cameron
and Kim Townsend

Contents

Preface

This book deals with individualism sympathetically. Yet I have tried in the Introduction and recurrently in the chapters to look at a few of the criticisms made of individualism, especially of its core, the doctrine of individual rights. I hope to suggest that when the theory of individualism is associated with democracy, individualism does not promote what its critics say it does—self-seeking and deracination—but instead furthers an aspiration toward a self and a society that stand for something good and that may even enhance existence.

Related matters are explored in some other work not collected here, especially in "On the 'Legitimation Crisis,'" *Social Research* 46 (Winter 1979), 695–727; "Democratic Individuality and the Meaning of Rights," in Nancy L. Rosenblum, ed., *Liberalism and the Moral Life* (Cambridge: Harvard University Press, 1989), 183–206; and "Hobbes and the Irrationality of Politics," *Political Theory* 17 (August 1989), 355–91.

I thank persons for their help in particular chapters, but I have other acknowledgments to make. I owe a special debt to William Connolly for the example of his work, and also for suggesting that these essays be collected and then providing advice on those that are published here for the first time. Chapters 4, 5, and 6 are the revised texts of lectures given at the Christian Gauss Seminars in Criticism, Princeton University, under the title "Human Extinction and Moral Philosophy," in the spring of 1985. I thank Victor Brombert and the Gauss committee for their invitation, and the members of the seminar for their challenging criticisms. My thanks for their steady responses and questions go to David Bromwich, Thomas Dumm, Jean Elshtain, Amy Gutmann, John Hollander, Leo Marx, Donald Moon, Barry O'Connell, Richard Poirier,

Peter Pouncey, Nancy Rosenblum, Austin Sarat, Morton Schoolman, Judith Shklar, Tracy Strong, Michael Walzer, and Sheldon Wolin. Marilyn Sale, the copy editor, asked me probing questions, for which I am indebted. I am grateful to Stephanie Jinks for her skill and patience in wordprocessing several drafts of chapters and in preparing the manuscript for publication. I am very appreciative of the sabbatical leaves made possible by the trustees of Amherst College and Princeton University.

Previously published essays are reprinted here by permission, with some changes. They originally appeared as follows: "The Moral Distinctiveness of Representative Democracy," *Ethics* 91 (April 1981), 357–74 (© 1981 by the University of Chicago); "Remarks on the Procedures of Constitutional Democracy," in J. Roland Pennock and John W. Chapman, eds., *Nomos XX: Constitutionalism* (New York: New York University Press, 1979), 215–37; "Democratic Individuality and the Claims of Politics," *Political Theory* 12 (August 1984), 331–60, © 1984 Sage Publications, Inc., reprinted by permission; "Thinking about Human Extinction: Nuclear Weapons and Individual Rights," *Dissent* 33 (Spring 1986), 161–72; "Thinking about Human Extinction: Nietzsche and Heidegger" and "Thinking about Human Extinction: Emerson and Whitman," both reprinted by permission from *Raritan: A Quarterly Review* 6 (Fall 1986, no. 2: 1–28; Winter 1987, no. 3: 1–22), copyright © 1986, 1987 by *Raritan*, 31 Mine St., New Brunswick, N.J. 08903; "Individualism, Communitarianism, and Docility," *Social Research* 56 (Winter 1989), 921–42; "Walt Whitman and the Culture of Democracy," *Political Theory* 18 (November 1990), 545–71, © 1990 Sage Publications, Inc., reprinted by permission.

G.K.

Princeton, New Jersey

The Inner Ocean

Individual Rights and Democratic Individuality

The moral basis of this book is the belief that respect for individual rights is the best way of honoring human dignity, by which I mean the equal dignity of every individual. The core of these rights is explicit in the U.S. Bill of Rights (and in articles of the original Constitution), generously construed—as construed by the Warren Court, not by its successors. Such rights are rights against government—against the state, as we now commonly say. The theory of individual rights assumes that government as such, government in any form, has its own power interest which inclines it to deny that rights exist or to encroach on those it recognizes. Perhaps there are rights against other social concentrations of power, especially when implicated in governance or financially dependent on government; but on that matter, I think, one must proceed cautiously. In any case, someone with an individualist commitment has the state most in mind, the state as the formally vested agency of coercive power. (To be sure, sometimes government does the worst things as an agent of private interests or sentiments. Private persons, not governments, owned most slaves in the United States. Also, there was no governmental interest in the disfranchisement of women.) Even in its best modern form—constitutional representative democracy—government is always under suspicion for those who believe in individual rights. It is the best modern form because it is the form that suspicion politically takes. This kind of suspicion is memorably concentrated by John Stuart Mill in *On Liberty* and *Considerations on Representative Government*,[1] even though he tries to avoid talk of rights. Rights are thus claims to certain kinds of actions or abstentions by the state, whatever its form.

[1] See especially the closing section of chap. 5 of *On Liberty* and of chap. 4 of *Considerations on Representative Government*.

The background assumption is that most people in a society of rights are disposed to be law-abiding and that government's mere existence sustains their disposition. But because some persons inevitably transgress against their fellow citizens, government can never lose the status of protector; in particular, protector of life and property, the usual objects of transgression. If, then, rights are rights against the state, the theory of rights does not ignore the obvious fact that the state exists to prevent, deter, or punish crime or mayhem. (I prefer to see crime not as a denial of the victim's rights but, instead, as legally culpable immorality; nevertheless, it is sometimes sensible to speak of individuals violating one another's rights.) Government exists to preserve individuals. The point is that it must do this work, and its other work, in a way that does not violate rights, including the rights of transgressors and those accused of transgression.

If the Bill of Rights is the core, its silences and deliberate omissions required that it be supplemented over time. Freedom of speech, press, religion, and association; due-process rights for suspects, defendants, and the legally guilty; and respect for a person's freedom from arbitrary invasions of security and privacy—all go far in protecting the dignity (or integrity) of individuals. But their dignity needs more—above all, three further rights: first, the right to vote and take part in politics; second, the right to be spared from utter degradation or to be saved from material misery; and third, the right to equal protection of the laws (in the language of the Fourteenth Amendment). The two last-named rights do not call for mere governmental abstention, as do the rights of speech, press, religion, association, security, and privacy. Nor do they call for only procedural justice, as do some other main rights in the Bill of Rights. Rather, the right to be free of degradation and misery answers to a minimal samaritanism as morally obligatory on society and looks to government to carry it out. It is a right to be given something, to be enabled to begin to live a life. Samaritanism is obligatory on society, and obligatory samaritanism would be the foundation of a right to life which was expanded beyond its present constitutional interpretation in the United States. I believe that this right, more than any other, stands in need of expansion through positive governmental action, despite all the serious risks involved in charging governments with the task of fostering life. And the equal protection of the laws may necessitate governmental action against, say, official or social racial discrimination. Naturally, in saying that the state, which must always be kept under suspicion, must also be entrusted not only with the fundamental task of preserving individuals against transgressors but also with the positive function of promoting some of the rights that are indispensable to human dignity, one admits that there will be an inevitable ambivalence toward the state. It is an enemy, the worst enemy, but it is not the only enemy and it is not only an enemy. My emphasis, however, is on the antagonism that government shows to rights by its initiatives rather than by its neglect. Throughout this book I rarely refer to rights that need government's positive contribution. The latter rights, no matter how fundamental, cannot be the norm in a society devoted to individual rights.

Different individuals may use or need the several rights variably, but when government refuses to respect rights, it not only makes people suffer, it injures everyone's human dignity.

My main reason for beginning with the Bill of Rights rather than with some other charter of equal individual rights is that it makes rights against government the norm. Another reason is that the Bill has been in effect continuously for two centuries. If its protections have sometimes been violated systematically or in episodes, and if they have been narrowly construed too frequently, still the mere existence of the Bill has both symbolized and energized a country's formal and long-standing commitment to individual rights. The words have been lived, though with a lamentable imperfection. Furthermore, there have been two centuries of judicial interpretations of these rights. I do not think that there is another literature on individual rights which is comparable in richness, subtlety, and ingenuity. When we then add the political effort to realize the three other rights I just mentioned, and the political and judicial reasoning that has aided their realization, we find a unique contribution to the meaning of human dignity.

Especially noteworthy in American life is the way judicial review allows individuals to take on the government and sometimes win; and, by winning, establish an enhanced understanding of a right for any, which is then confirmed by the government's compliance with the authority of the courts. Judicial supremacy is, ideally, the individual's supremacy: the rights of one person (or class of persons) prevailing over the policy of the state or society.

These facts (an old Bill, judicial review, and a constant struggle for rights) do not, in themselves, mean that the United States is the country in which human dignity is best achieved. I am not even sure that a calculation could ever be properly made which ranked various constitutional democracies: the same right receives different degrees of protection in different countries and some rights are not recognized by all countries. We can say that the right to life, the right not to be enslaved, and the right to be free of degradation or material misery are the most basic rights: they pertain to the prevention or remedy of great pain and the utter diminishment of human dignity. Equally basic are the rights of free speech and press because they are the key to defending all rights. By disregarding these basic rights government does not show even a minimal respect for human dignity. Other rights are not secondary, but have less meaning, or are compromised, unless the more fundamental ones are respected. These other rights are also less uniform in their presence. The presence of one such right cannot be weighed against the absence of another. We could be reduced to comparing the number of these other rights present in various countries. Nevertheless, whatever may be shown about the actuality of rights in the United States and elsewhere, the historical record of theoretical interpretation in the United States is uniquely valuable. I say all this to explain why the arguments I have tried to present in this book are guided by the American experience of rights, even though the theory of rights is now universal, or nearly so.

Why make so much of individual personal and political rights? The answer, as I have said, is that respect for rights is the best way of honoring human dignity. Why make so much of human dignity? I do not find much to say. I am not even sure that much should be said. Suppose we carry on at length about why governments should treat people in certain ways (by actions and abstentions), and in these ways unconditionally and as a matter of course, and should do so because people deserve and are entitled to such treatment, rather than because governments may find it prudent to treat people in these ways in the spirit of extending revocable privileges. I am afraid that we may jeopardize human dignity by laboring to defend it. What sort of attack would merit an answer? Is a long and elaborate theory needed to establish the point that people should not be treated by the state as if they were masses, or obstacles or instruments to higher purposes, or subjects for experiments, or pieces in a game, or wayward children in need of protection against themselves, or patients in need of perpetual care, or beasts in need of the stick? With what right does anyone maintain that people may be regarded or used in these nonhuman or subhuman ways? With what truth? Unabused and undegraded, people have always shown that they deserve better. They deserve guaranteed rights. When their rights are respected, all that their dignity, their human status, requires is achieved. People are enabled to lead lives that are free, modest, and decent—provided, of course, socioeconomic circumstances are not hopeless.

To tie dignity to rights is therefore to say that governments have the absolute duty to treat people (by actions and abstentions) in certain ways, and in certain ways only. The state's characteristic domination and insolence are to be curbed for the sake of rights. Public and formal respect for rights registers and strengthens awareness of three constitutive facts of being human: every person is a creature capable of feeling pain, and is a free agent capable of having a free being, of living a life that is one's own and not somebody else's idea of how a life should be lived, and is a moral agent capable of acknowledging that what one claims for oneself as a right one can claim only as an equal to everyone else (and relatedly that what one wants done to oneself one should do to others). Respect for rights recognizes these capacities and thus honors human dignity.

I know that adequate recognition of these human capabilities does not *entail* respect for rights as the sole and necessary conclusion. This respect is not a matter of logical inference. Rather, given initial sentiments—say, fellow feeling or special sensitivity to pain or dislike of power—recognition can lead to or add up to a theoretical affirmation of rights. The most important sentiment by far is for the idea that every individual is equally a world, an infinity, a being who is irreplaceable.

At the same time, there are other theories that seem to affirm human dignity yet give rights only a lesser or probationary or instrumental role. Examples are utilitarianism, recent communitarianism, recent republicanism, and radical egalitarianism. The first and last I will return to shortly; my response to the others appears here and there in this volume. All I wish to say now is that unless rights come first they are not rights. They will tend to be sacrificed to some purpose deemed higher than the equal dignity of every individual. There will be little if any concept of the integrity or inviolability of each individual. The group or the majority or the good or the sacred or the vague future will be preferred. The beneficiaries will be victimized along with the victims because no one is being treated as a person who is irreplaceable and beyond value. To make rights anything but primary, even though in the name of human dignity, is to injure human dignity.

I do not wish to say much, then, in defending the idea of human dignity and in defending universal personal and political rights as the political acknowledgment of human dignity. The idea is simple enough. From it flows the assertion that even when people are the moral and actual source of the power and authority of government they ideally retain an adversarial stance toward it. Their moral identity consists, in part, in making claims against it, expecting those claims to be honored, yet also expecting that these claims, these rights, will tend to suffer periodic erosion and an almost constant probing for weakness, so to speak, at the hands of the state.

Yet I know that John Rawls, in the great work on rights-based individualism in the twentieth century, makes a tremendous and continuously illuminating attempt to justify personal and political rights (or "liberties," as he usually calls them) against theories that challenge them. He wants to show that devising them (together with certain economic and opportunity rules) would be the necessary result of impartial reasoning among imaginary equals who are ignorant of all their future cultural, social, and economic traits and hence are self-interestedly constrained to fairness. Actual people, on the other hand, would arrive at the same result if they had a cultivated sense of fairness, of justice as fairness; if they could adopt "the perspective of eternity . . . within the world" and attain "purity of heart."[2]

I admire Rawls's war on utilitarianism, and the keen sense animating his work that to demand that rights serve some social purposes valued apart from and as more worthy than the equal human dignity of every individual is systematically unfair and hence unacceptable. But I do not absorb Rawls's method into these essays; I prefer to think that I can keep the matter brief and plain. I worry that even when philosophical argument in behalf of rights is powerfully anti-utilitarian and antiperfectionist the mere implication that rights need an elaborate defense can jeopardize them. This worry is continuous with the one that pertains to the defense of human dignity itself. Respect for the equal rights and hence the human dignity of every individual may therefore tend to appear only optional or properly amenable to dispute or skepticism. As it is, Rawls's

---

[2] John Rawls, *A Theory of Justice* (Cambridge: Harvard University Press, 1971), 587. Also of great importance for the understanding of rights and their justification is the work of Ronald Dworkin; see his *Taking Rights Seriously* (Cambridge: Harvard University Press, 1978), especially chaps. 7, 12; and *A Matter of Principle* (Cambridge: Harvard University Press, 1985), especially pt. 6. See also Richard Flathman, *The Practice of Rights* (Cambridge: Cambridge University Press, 1976), especially chap. 7. A valuable critique of rights has been mounted by John Gray and is concentrated in his review of Joel Feinberg's book *The Moral Limits of the Criminal Law* in the TLS, January 12–18, 1990, 31–32.

theoretical work becomes most distinctive and most controversial when it deals with the second principle of justice, which comprises rules relating to economic conditions and career opportunities, not when it deals with the first principle, personal and political rights. I do not want criticisms of the second principle to have an easy contagious effect on the first principle.

Though I am given pause by what Rawls says in the very last section of his book, I am not persuaded. He takes up the charge that he should have derived his two principles of justice from a view of human dignity (or respect for persons and their inherent worth). He says, "I believe, however, that while the principles of justice will be effective only if men have a sense of justice and do therefore respect one another, the notion of respect or of the inherent worth of persons is not a suitable basis for arriving at these principles. . . . The theory of justice provides a rendering of these ideas but we cannot start out from them."[3] It may be that a philosopher as scrupulous as Rawls must take little for granted, must start almost without presuppositions, even a minimal one like human dignity. In initiating his theory, he allows "ethical constraints" but not "any ethical motivation."[4] He wants to build a political theory, step by step, starting from something like a state of nature. I choose, instead, to start inside a mode of thinking in which individuals and their rights are assumed as primary because all competing matters urged as primary can be seen as lesser, even when not fictional or unreal. The reasons for caring about human dignity lie partly in sentiments, especially a sense of every individual's irreplaceability; but also in facts. As I have said, the especially relevant facts are that each person is a creature and is capable of being a free agent and a moral agent. What could matter more than a society or a world in which these facts (enriched by sentiments) are suitably accommodated by a political system of individual rights? The human dignity of each is the rock.

In some of the pages that follow, I do make conceptual use of a state of nature as a hypothetical condition in which no government exists, but not as a literally or historically prepolitical or presocial condition. My main use of the notion, however, is to theorize it as a recurrent reality in a stable society. I mean, as one example, that a state of nature exists in society whenever government compels persons to risk or sacrifice their lives for some purpose other than resisting their own threatened death or

[3] Rawls, 586.
[4] Rawls, 584.

slavery or utter degradation or misery. The theory of rights, as I have interpreted it, would suggest that these persons are being subjected to illegitimate force and hence may rightly assert a prudential wish not to be sacrificed. The theorist—that is, anyone committed to rights, in a thoughtful moment—will see that rights are a special kind of self-interest. When rights are under attack, they become claims that one makes, first of all, in one's own behalf. But when anyone insists on rights against the state, those of everyone else are also being demanded. In exigent circumstances brought on by the state, an individual's universalizable prudence can promote a moral end.

Nevertheless, anyone committed to rights in a thoughtful moment will also know, as Rawls says, that universal prudence is not the normal sentiment in a rights-based society because "the principles of justice will be effective only if men have a sense of justice and do therefore respect one another."[5] A person does not believe in rights who thinks that he or she alone (or some few like oneself) have them. The sentiment of equal human dignity must be widely shared, not felt only by the observer, if rights are to be sustained against the state, even as the state is pressed to sustain them. Whoever believes in rights must also be interested in how one's government affects the rights of those in other societies. Rights are universal. The protector of them at home must be condemned and resisted for violating them abroad.

A brief and unrigorous defense of individual rights, then, can perhaps suffice. The protection of personal and political rights is the only true protection of everybody's human dignity. But a religious rejection of human dignity as the highest standard in favor of the superior dignity of the more-than-human is always possible. Undeniably, the theory of rights with which I work issued from religious people in England. Yet they were heterodox and they were intent on freeing society from religious superintendence and making unsectarian political morality the rule for society. They were politically secular, even if their political theory had some religious inspiration. The framers of American rights were even more heterodox, if they were religious at all. These days, if religious views are politically introduced, debate becomes impossible

[5] Rawls, 586.

after a while. Everyday reasoning runs up against belief or faith and becomes futile. The advocate of rights cannot persist in discussion but must try to blunt any religiously inspired attack on individual rights.

In sum, there seems to be no generally credible foundation for a critique of rights. Rights emerge as the only or best way of protecting human dignity, and human dignity remains the highest standard. This is not to deny that there will be strenuous differences of interpretation of various rights and quarrels over the comparative importance of various rights. But by now even some anti-individualists, whether secular or religious, accept the idea of rights as useful or even as an indispensable ingredient in their own thinking about politics and society.

To say it again: the theory of equal individual rights (personal and political) is now almost universally professed. We should remember, however, that it did not crystallize until the seventeenth century. Though fed from many earlier sources, the theory together with the heightened sentiments that had to inspire and accompany it may be said to have got its start in England among radical Protestants. Within the Independents (also named Congregationalists) a certain group, derisively called Levellers, practically originated the modern theory of rights in almost its entirety.[6] Though the theory is now nearly universal, it had a temporally identifiable beginning, and a recent one at that; and those who formulated it and tried to promote it in their own country were a small, marginal, and unsuccessful band of dissenters. To mention these considerations is to deny that the theory has always existed or that it had to exist. Its origins are obscure and perfectly contingent. Yet, owing to a large extent to American experience and its overpowering influence, the theory, in some form or other, is now everywhere an official doctrine or a common aspiration.

We might say that once the theory appeared it was likely to spread. A drastic eruption in imagination was needed to create it; but once it was manifest its good sense was seen after a while, and people may have wondered why so much time passed without it. The feeling deepened that, of course, all persons deserve to be treated in ways adequate to their

[6] For speeches and writings of the Levellers, see A. S. P. Woodhouse, ed., *Puritanism and Liberty* (Chicago: University of Chicago Press, 1951).

dignity as human beings, despite all resistance from states and associated elites.

Must the theory and practice of individual rights therefore last forever? Clearly not. Extraordinary events, catastrophes of many sorts, some unforeseeable mutation in the human condition, could shatter the conception of human dignity as the supreme value, could make the individual appear irrelevant and individual rights profoundly injurious. But the loss of this idea would itself be a catastrophe, even if not felt. If lost, would the idea necessarily come back? Who can say? But we should probably assume that though it may come back it need not. The world went on for quite a while without it, and could do so again. The pity is that individuals can be, and are, and have been raised and then treated in ways not adequate to their dignity as human beings and that although they feel pain and may resent subordination, they may nevertheless accept their situation as destined or not correctable, and not even grasp their situation as an assault on their dignity because the very idea of rights is not available.

Rights-based individualism is the ground of this book. If it is a recent and far from inevitable idea, it is also, once established, fragile. It sometimes seems especially fragile in the country most identified with it, the United States. I do not have in mind only the numerous incursions on rights that the Supreme Court of Warren Burger and the frightening Supreme Court of William H. Rehnquist have ratified (or subtly encouraged). Their interpretations have hurt individuals in their rights and hurt the overall political commitment to rights. But there are also other (and sometimes related) tendencies: the steady growth of the state's activities, for good reasons and bad, has a regularly diminishing effect on rights. The very ease with which people in the United States use the word "state" is symptomatic. We have the warfare state, the disciplinary state, the welfare state. We have, in sum, the administrative state with a ravenous appetite for intervening and regulating, for initiating and determining, for helping and being relied on. These tendencies are not likely to abate, even though particular events or policies seem to work, now and then, toward diminishing the state's activities. Every sector, almost every detail of life, is marked by the state's involvement. It is now practically impossible to say with Thoreau after his release from prison that the state is nowhere to be seen. The state covers everything: the holes in its fabric allow only a glimpse of the unprocessed or untouched. The entire population has become its wards, and the psychology of dependence on it increases. In matter after matter, democratic institutions seem to authorize their own abdication or enfeeblement. The situation will not be altered by any logic, whether of reasoning or of events. There can be only efforts to ameliorate it here and there and to preserve the vigor of individual rights wherever possible—against the state, but also against democratic institutions when they are delinquent.

Yet even if circumstances were more favorable to the vigor of rights, an advocate of rights-based individualism would have to acknowledge that the theory of rights is not a complete system of political morality. A society without the susceptibilities or pretexts or genuine needs that magnify the state would nevertheless require some other principles to supplement the theory of rights. One must say that human dignity is the rock. But a social life that was less crowded and less developed than most modern democracies could still not be dealt with solely by reference to the protection of individual rights.

I do not mean to take seriously the idea that utilitarianism is a satisfactory replacement for the theory of rights. The well-being (or mere preferences) of the majority cannot override the rightful claims of individuals. In a time when the theory of rights is global it is noteworthy that some moral philosophers disparage the theory of rights. The political experience of this century should be enough to make them hesitate: it is not clear that, say, some version of utilitarianism could not justify totalitarian evil. It also could be fairly easy for some utilitarians to justify any war and any dictatorship, and very easy to justify any kind of ruthlessness even in societies that pay some attention to rights. There is no end to the immoral permissions that one or another type of utilitarianism grants. Everything is permitted, if the calculation is right. No, an advocate of rights cannot take utilitarianism seriously as a competing general theory of political morality, nor any other competing general theory. Rather, particular principles or considerations must be given a place. A theory of rights may simply leave many decisions undetermined or have to admit that rights may have to be overridden (but never for the sake of social well-being or mere policy preference). Also, kinds of rights may sometimes conflict, and it is not always possible to end that conflict either by an elaboration of the theory of rights or by an appeal to some other principle.

What does a theory of rights leave undecided? Many issues of public policy do not affect individual rights, despite frequent ingenious efforts to claim that they do. Such issues pertain to the promotion of a better life, whether for the disadvantaged or for everyone, or involve the clash of interests. So long as rights are not in play, advocates of rights can rightly allow a loose utilitarianism as the proper guide to public policy, though they should be always eager to keep the state's energy under suspicion. One can even think, against utilitarianism, that any substantive outcome achieved by morally proper procedure is morally right and hence accept- able (so long as rights are not in play). The main point, however, is that utilitarianism has a necessary place in any democratic country's normal political deliberations. But its advocates must know its place, which ordinarily is only to help to decide what the theory of rights leaves alone.

When may rights be overridden by government? I have two sorts of cases in mind: overriding a particular right of some persons for the sake of preserving the same right of others, and overriding the same right of everyone for the sake of what I will clumsily call "civilization values." An advocate of rights could countenance, perhaps must countenance, the state's overriding of rights for these two reasons. The subject is painful and liable to dispute every step of the way.

For the state to override—that is, sacrifice—a right of some so that others may keep it, the situation must be desperate. I have in mind, say, circumstances in which the choice is between sacrificing a right of some and letting a right of all be lost. The state (or some other agent) may kill some (or allow them to be killed), if the only alternative is letting every- one die.[7] It is the right to life which most prominently figures in thinking about desperate situations. I cannot see any resolution but to heed the precept that "numbers count." Just as one may prefer saving one's own life to saving that of another when both cannot be saved, so a third party—let us say, the state—can (perhaps must) choose to save the greater number of lives and at the cost of the lesser number, when there is otherwise no hope for either group. That choice does not mean that those to be sacrificed are immoral if they resist being sacrificed. It follows, of course, that if a third party is right to risk or sacrifice the lives of the lesser for the lives of the greater number when the lesser would otherwise live, the lesser are also not wrong if they resist being sacrificed.

I suppose that permitting numbers to count in desperate situations is

[7] A full and nuanced discussion appears in Frances Kamm, *Morality, Mortality* (forth- coming). She makes crucial the distinction between taking life and allowing to die. For an instructive account written from a perspective that combines utilitarianism and respect for autonomy, see Jonathan Glover, *Causing Death and Saving Lives* (New York: Penguin, 1977).

to accept utilitarianism (in some loose sense) as a necessary supplement. It thus should function when rights are not at stake and when they are most cruelly at stake; it should function innocently, or when all hope of innocence is gone. I emphasize, above all, however, that every care must be taken to ensure that the precept that numbers of lives count does not become a license for vaguely conjectural decisions about inflicting death and saving life and that desperation be as strictly and narrowly understood as possible. (But total numbers killed do not count if members of one group have to kill members of another group to save themselves from threatened massacre or enslavement or utter degradation or misery; they may kill their attackers in the attempt to end the threat.)

"Civilization values" are abridgments of the right to engage in activities that affect only oneself, injuriously or not, or that affect others, injuriously or not, but with their consent. Rights-based individualism has a prima facie commitment to the greatest possible amount of such legally allowed "self-regarding" activity because this activity is a major part of what I have called free agency. When the Supreme Court speaks of a substantive due-process right to liberty and of a right to privacy, part of the reason is to conceptualize freedom of self-regarding activity. Mill defends this kind of freedom, this individual sovereignty, absolutely, even though (especially in chapters 2 and 3 of *On Liberty*) he tends to make its value only instrumental. I doubt, however, that Mill would have remained absolute had he taken up certain cases that unawareness or decorum prevented him from discussing. A line has to be drawn, and not just to have a line. Where to draw it is, of course, open to dispute. An incomplete list of prohibited self-regarding activities would include, in my judgment, consensual incest between adults, the use of addictive drugs, voluntary slavery, extreme sadomasochism, nonhomicidal cannibalism, necrophilia, bestiality, and voluntary acceptance of one's own ritual sacrifice. One may fairly ask for the reasons for prohibiting any of these activities because they may all be pleasurable and meaningful. None lacks voluntariness, reciprocal or solitary. What then is wrong with these exercises of free agency?

We can say in regard to the relevant examples that no one has the right to enslave or mutilate or ritually kill another, even with the other's permission. There is no right to accept another's renunciation of a right. One cannot cooperate with or take advantage of another person's abdication of human dignity. We can also say, for other activities, that one has no right to use one's freedom to abandon it altogether (as with drug addiction) or alienate it (as with voluntary slavery), for freedom is meaningless when it becomes the instrument of bondage. All these arguments are true but do not reach the deepest level of objection, for all these activities arouse deep and widespread disgust and revulsion. To be guided by these feelings, however, is risky because many activities once thought disgusting and horrible are now allowed and sometimes welcomed and celebrated, at least in some democratic societies. Also, we cannot say that the feelings hostile to these activities are instinctual; though common, such feelings are culturally deposited.

I can understand the wish to say that these activities injure the human dignity of people who do them. It can be argued that the injury results not merely because (in some cases) they are renouncing a right and (in other cases) using their rights in ways never contemplated by advocates of rights. Rather, these free or consensual activities degrade people who do them below the level of decent humanity. The practitioners forfeit respect: that is the reason they must be controlled. I do not think, however, that I can follow this line because I do not associate human dignity with any teleology or reason for being, or even with a more bounded perfectionism. As I understand the theory of rights-based individualism, it disallows universal and enforceable answers to the questions, Why do we live? What is the point of living? I am therefore reluctant to rest a case for control on the notion of human dignity itself.

Let us say that a society of rights-based individualism encourages these and other crepuscular activities to become topics for open and popular discussion; that that fact can be taken as a paradoxical sign of the moral grandness of such a society, for practically every desire can be honestly admitted and talked about despite shame or without shame; that a society devoted to rights has no absolutely compelling arguments, in every case, to prohibit them; and that, nevertheless, civilization (democratic or not) as we are trained to understand it commits us to continue to condemn and prohibit them. The issue must be raised in dismay, and I am not able to deal with it adequately.

Can rights conflict? It is not agreeable to admit that a particular right of one person may apparently conflict with a different right of someone else. Familiar antagonisms include that between the right to a fair trial unprejudiced by excessive publicity and the right of the press to report a story and its background fully, or that between the right to privacy and, again, the right of the press to do what it thinks is its work. Though I believe, as I have said, that some rights (including freedom of the press) are more fundamental than others, in some conflicts no clear priority is likely to be established and only ad hoc adjustments are desirable. To be sure, although these conflicts may be less frequent or stark than is claimed by those who are impatient with the rights in question, conflicts nevertheless take place. This is a fact of life which no appeal to an elaborated theory of rights can eliminate. If it is a shortcoming in the theory of rights, it is also a shortcoming that no supplementary principle such as utilitarianism can make good.

I briefly discuss below the conflict between the right of ownership and other rights.

It is possible that under the heading of the conflict of rights we could take up the common case in which some are legally required (by means of conscription) to sacrifice their lives to preserve the rights of others (but not necessarily others' lives or freedom from slavery, degradation, or misery). I discuss this general matter in a chapter in this book. I want to say here only that, in my understanding, the theory of rights does not see this as a genuine case of rights in conflict. No one has the right to the self-sacrifice of another.

At this point I shall make more explicit what may be only implied in the chapters that follow. Rights-based individualism, as I understand it, is intrinsically opposed to the political quest for socioeconomic equality. I distinguish this quest from two other aims: the relief of material misery (which I consider a basic right against society and its government) and, beyond that, the welfarist attempt, undertaken by government, to improve the condition of the poor, the disadvantaged, the disabled. The quest for socioeconomic equality is a different enterprise. Its aim is to efface, to the fullest degree possible, differences between people: differences of wealth and power and, consequently, differences in life possibilities and the scope of experiences, in hopes and aspirations, in intensities of pleasure and pain. The end state is equality as brotherhood and sisterhood.

What are the sentiments that push the quest? To deny some citizens a disproportionate power to influence or even to determine the fate of the rest, and thus to make democratic citizenship truly equal. To end the insolence of some and the envy of the rest. To end class struggles on the right terms. To spread a feeling of solidarity which comes from everyone's sharing a common fate, experiencing pleasure and pain from the same sources, and being affected in the same way by events. To respect the equal human dignity of each person. Most important, perhaps, to compensate for the arbitrariness and unfairness of nature and luck in the bestowal of talents, inheritances, and opportunities, and thus to realize justice.

Any single one of these sentiments deserves more careful consideration than I am able to give. They certainly all deserve moral respect: some amelioration of the human condition has occurred owing to them. Yet I think that it must be said that no theorist of individual rights until after Marx held that socioeconomic equality is mandatory if individual personal and political rights are to be secured and if rights-based individualism is to flourish. (Tom Paine's agrarian justice did not go nearly this far.) The apparent exception is Rousseau. I say "apparent" for the reason that he does not really project an ideal society in which rights against political agencies have any practical reality. Rights seem to have a more potent reality in conjectured prepolitical conditions than in the good society. To be sure, he makes much of civil liberty, which is equivalent to the protection of many rights. But these protections are not politically guaranteed. The culture that is supposed to grow out of the initial arrangements is not the culture worked out of rights-based individualism but a republicanism that does not favor any sort of individualism. As it is, Rousseau advocates a limited inequality, not a perfect socioeconomic equality. But he seems to move, in theory, as close to it as he can. Really, he is, and he is not, a theorist of rights. He is much too perfectionist for a modern theory of rights.

Thanks in significant part to Marxism and other radicalisms, the project of socioeconomic equality became a theoretically urgent matter. Rawls's effort to show that justice as fairness requires a limited inequality is powerful and influential. We have already referred to his second principle of justice. The idea that any socioeconomic inequality must be justified by the contribution it makes to improving the lives of the least well situated has strengthened conscientious disquiet with gross inequality of every kind. And Rawls is not alone among non-Marxists in challenging the acceptability of socioeconomic inequality precisely in the name of the theory of rights.

What can be said in answer? Plainly put, the perspective of rights-based individualism is not the same as the perspective of radical socioeconomic egalitarianism. The passion for honoring human dignity may be common to both, and egalitarianism can find some rights acceptable or necessary. But most theorists of rights-based individualism expect socioeconomic inequality to exist and even to find it an outcome that is at least compatible with justice, but probably derivative from it. Then, too, their greatest aversion is state power. On the other hand, advocates of radical egalitarianism (or of a greatly reduced inequality) cannot bear the thought that morally equal human beings should not be equal in all the powers and advantages that make life decent, pleasurable, and free. Perhaps a few of them even think that it is better for no one to be well off if all cannot be. Their pity is great; the theorists are not envious for themselves. And they fear the state less than rights theorists do. So, let us say that there is at the root of each perspective a cluster of passions and inclinations which forbids a reconciliation with the other perspective.

Yet there are arguments on both sides, not just feelings. The historical record seems to show that socioeconomic equality (or severely limited inequality) is impossible except in the most rudimentary or desperate circumstances. Otherwise it exists only in such utopias as Morelly's *Code de la Nature* or Rousseau's *Social Contract* or Marx's *Economic and Philosophic Manuscripts of 1844*. Rousseau himself knows how contrary to human experience it is, and he conceived of its possibility only in a society in which the Lawgiver's prescriptions had induced an almost complete transformation of the human character. The critique of the possibility of socioeconomic equality goes back at least to Aristotle's analysis of the egalitarianism of Phaleas of Chalcedon.[8] Everything in life militates against it. Economic misery can be abolished in modern societies if there is a will to do so; poverty can be diminished; some further measure of equality can be introduced. But in any society of complexity, whether free or despotic, people will be unequal socioeconomically. And the harder the state tries to create genuine equality, the more ruthlessly it must act, the more continuously intrusive and regulative it must become, the more intolerant of resistance. The project need not go the lengths of Stalin, Mao, or Pol Pot—all of them fanatics of equality and all of them practitioners of evil for that very reason—but it will nevertheless suffocate freedom and energy. It will erode or destroy rights; it will not honor human dignity.

But does not justice require the effort? That would be the case only if the idea that there is desert or merit is entirely false. Then we could say that luck is everything, that no one deserves superior or inferior advantages, and that any society, even (or especially) a rights-based one, is morally obliged to try to equalize as fully as possible. But how is a human

[8] Aristotle, *Politics*, bk. 2, chap. 7.

life livable without some idea of desert or merit, as Isaiah Berlin has powerfully asked?[9] It adheres to the merest sense of self. Without it the self is ruined. If seriously believed under an anti-individualist inspiration, the thought that no one deserves anything or is responsible for anything, turns oneself and anyone in one's power into a blind force or passive object. The thought is, from the perspective of rights-based individualism, poison. But is it true?

It is true if belief in free will is false. Has any philosopher said enough to show that this belief is false or true? The mere fact that we are not born as adults makes the subject elusive, probably forever. Consciousness lives in us in stages, and we have no direct access to our first stages, which are incapable of representing themselves to themselves or to others except with a gross and intermittent approximation. No grown-up can therefore be transparent to self or others. The subject of free will seems forever intractable because the larger subject of human nature, of which it is an integral part, is so. Perhaps in that apparent philosophical failure lies a continuing guaranteed preservation of the idea of desert or merit. Uncertainty permits belief to go either way, yet some evidence points in the direction of free will in the most relevant sense—self-control. (Free will in the sense of spontaneity, creativity, or unpredictability, for which the record of historical change and cultural variety provides unmistakable evidence, does not seem relevant to discussion of socioeconomic equality, though it is relevant to the general subject of individualism.)

Of course, scarcely any idea lends itself more easily than does desert or merit to the rationalization of abuse, punishment, neglect, and cruelty. But the idea at its worst may still be better than a practiced rejection of it. As long as it remains out of the power of reason to decide the question of free will, then it is better for the sake of human dignity to continue to accept free will and, along with it, the idea of desert or merit. That acceptance could mean, in turn, that justice does not require radical socioeconomic equality but that, to the contrary, justice is, even if reluctantly, on the side of inequality. Desert or merit has its claims: some people deserve more than others. They have a right to get and keep more, and the right is a large part of the right of property or ownership. I do not mean to suggest that a market economy is a perfect indicator of the comparative moral worth of people. It does not bestow distributive

[9] Isaiah Berlin, *Historical Inevitability* (London: Oxford University Press, 1954), especially 27–34, 46–50, 58–66, 71–79. See also the recent instructive work by George Sher, *Desert* (Princeton: Princeton University Press, 1987), especially chaps. 2, 7, 8, 9, 11.

justice. But it does often give greater rewards to greater energy, skill, or cleverness, not only to blind luck or the human vices. Only if it could be shown that the system in which people get and keep is wholly or mostly fraudulent, exploitative, or discriminatory would this argument fail of application. The Marxist or radical case to this effect, however, is not proved.

I grant—I wish to insist—that a defense of desert or merit can only be uncertain because of the philosophical difficulties. For moral reasons it is good that it be uncertain. The right of ownership is not abridged when the samaritan duty to relieve material misery is publicly enforced, no matter how hard one tries to show that the miserable deserve their misery because of sloth, self-indulgence, or incompetence. To reject the project of ever greater socioeconomic equality is, to repeat, not to ignore misery or even to ignore bare poverty. And to sustain the sentiments of samaritanism, which can be supplemented by arguments that trace misery and poverty to structural causes that are the fault of neither the advantaged nor the disadvantaged, one may appeal to the very consideration used by advocates of strict socioeconomic equality. Only, that consideration must not be made exclusive or overpowering. I refer, of course, to the brute fact that one did not ask to be born, did not choose one's parents, one's endowment, one's upbringing, one's time or place. One begins as an accidental confluence; one's whole life is at the mercy of contingency. Furthermore, because one is first an infant and a child, free will could be an acquisition only from time and growth and is probably indissociable from mastery of one's language. In sum, free will is rooted in the darkness of early dependence, just as it is rooted in the chances of identity.

To keep the idea of desert or merit within sane bounds, we can also say that even those who have done the best or the most are debtors infinitely more than they are creditors. We can build on the great words from Emerson's "Experience": "When I receive a new gift, I do not macerate my body to make the account square, for if I should die I could not make the account square. The benefit overran the merit the first day, and has overrun the merit ever since. The merit itself, so-called, I reckon part of the receiving."[10] Every human being is the beneficiary of countless people, mostly nameless and unnamable, who delivered life, generation after generation, to the living generation and whose contribution to the powers and pleasures of life can never be told. These hidden millions and

[10] Ralph Waldo Emerson, "Experience," in *The Complete Essays and Other Writings*, ed. Brooks Atkinson (New York: Modern Library, 1950), 363.

millions cannot be requited. They can be thanked only indirectly. That happens when the living acknowledge their infinite indebtedness to the past by giving from their surplus to the least fortunate in the present. Perversions of rights-based individualism encourage fortunate people to fantasize that they are literally self-made. But the doctrine, in its pure form, as with the Levellers, Tom Paine, and Lincoln, turns against such hubris. It teaches modesty because it cultivates respect for human beings as human beings, known or unknown, near or far, dead or alive or to be born. All are equal. If, on the other hand, the theory of rights goes well enough with a sense of indebtedness to the mass of humanity as the source of one's life and its powers and pleasures, it resists, most bitterly, a sense of indebtedness to the state and to one's present and local society. The latter sense is too partial and can turn servile, as it memorably does in the Socrates of the *Crito*.

In what I have been saying there is no retreat from a commitment to the right of property or ownership. It is a true right; it is at the service of the composite right to stay alive and be unenslaved and is interwoven with a general right to as much uncoerced (putatively innocent) free agency as possible. But the right of property or ownership is not abridged when taxes are levied for a number of purposes, even beyond the relief of misery. Of course, taxation may be exorbitant or destructive, but in the democracies it tends not to be, thanks in part to self-correcting political processes. Locke, supposedly the most ardent defender of the right to property, not only makes consent to taxation procedurally equivalent merely to being able to vote for a representative, but mandates relief of misery.

The right to property is different from other rights not in being secondary but in another way. One's right to property is not a right to hold onto every bit of one's wealth and thus deny it to government. The right to own is absolute, but not the right to keep every dollar. One's personhood is not present in every dollar one presently has, or at stake whenever one is asked to part with a dollar in taxes. To be sure, having less money means having less immediate power for the individual, but often it also means, when tax money is properly spent, having more power, on balance or in the long run. Loss of a dollar is not like an innocent person's loss of a few days of freedom in jail or loss of access to a few books because of censorship. The latter losses signify reduction in the value of a right. It is well to remember that the Fifth Amendment of the U.S. Constitution allows private property to be taken for public use with just compensation, as if to indicate that property losses, unlike other ones, can be made up. Wealth is regularly spent or risked or lost; it is constantly involved in quantitative transactions of more and less. Only a miser wants it for its own sake. Nothing of value—not life itself—could go on without taxation. Giving up some of one's wealth is therefore not acquiescing in injury to one's human dignity.

Undeniably, many public regulations of property and business can also be thought to come up against the right of ownership, and courts have found ways to deal with some of the theoretical difficulties without abandoning the right. Then too, the often-unintended public consequences of private economic activity for fundamental rights are grave, and when government itself hands out abundant favors, benefits, and contracts, pervasive regulation appears necessary and natural. Regulation will seem more like keeping an artificial rule-constituted activity in good repair than like invading rightful and delimited spontaneous initiative. To a far greater extent than any other right, the right of property must adapt. Or to put the matter differently, facilitating both the creation of wealth and the remedy of misery and poverty strains the theory of rights almost too much. A complex capitalist economy requires government to be much more active or needed, makes it more resented or admired, than ideally suits rights-based individualism. The strain must be lived with.

If, all in all, the perspective of rights cannot satisfy the perspective of socioeconomic equality (or severely limited inequality), it nevertheless provides no warrant for ignoring misery or impoverishment. The one element in the theory of socioeconomic equality which must always haunt the advocate of rights is that unequal wealth usually means unequal citizenship when democracy is representative rather than Athenian. Instructive efforts have been made by such scholars as Robert Dahl and Charles Beitz to show how a representative system is, despite appearances, capable of partly getting around the influence that greater wealth or education gives, and how that capacity can be improved.[11] I would single out the crucial importance of associations: organizations of numbers of the like-minded but otherwise less powerful. Sometimes, also, the devices of initiative and referendum can substitute the direct participation of voters for the mediated politics of their representatives. But as long as rights are respected there are fairly narrow limits to the mitigation of the effects on citizenship of socioeconomic inequality. Wealth will be

[11] Robert Dahl, *Who Governs?* (New Haven: Yale University Press, 1961), and Charles R. Beitz, *Political Equality* (Princeton: Princeton University Press, 1989).

unequal, and so will other advantages, whether or not connected to wealth—though most are. The situation is not remediable within the frame of individual rights. It is probably not remediable at all, except in imaginary conditions or in desperate or unacceptably rudimentary ones.

It is right to worry about unequal citizenship. An even more important worry is about the reality of democracy for all citizens, even the rich and influential, and no matter how many benefits anyone receives. Political rights are intrinsic to the realization of human dignity. In modern times, the political rights of each can exist only in a system of constitutional representative democracy. Is, say, the American system really a democracy? Or are the American people ruled by an elite that is unelected and unaccountable for all practical purposes? If our attention were directed solely to foreign policy, I think that a strong case could be made for saying that the United States is not a democracy. What is often the most significant area of public policy is not democratically processed. I have already referred to the general phenomenon of the administrative state in its various functions, one of which is to be the warfare state. The conduct of foreign policy is only the most extreme expression of nondemocratic rule. There can be no genuine democracy so long as foreign policy figures decisively in the life of a society that aspires to be democratic.

My point is that insofar as a society is ruled, to that degree it fails of being democratic. It is ruled when important decisions are made by self-chosen or hereditary or appointed officials rather than by elected ones, or when elected officials make important decisions in secret or on their own unchecked initiative or in such a way as to evade accountability. (I exclude justices and judges from this account.) A government becomes a state (properly speaking) when either or both of these traits can be regularly attributed to it. As times goes on, democratic governing is replaced by ruling. I believe that this tendency is not solely or even substantially caused by socioeconomic inequality and hence unequal citizenship. Just as rights are to be understood primarily as rights against the government (or state), so all citizens (whatever their wealth or influence) are to be understood as subjected equally to the political power when it is a state (even if it is a state in only some areas of policy, provided these areas are significant). The two matters are connected: the erosion of rights is caused, in large part, by the intent of the government to act like a state. The perspective of rights-based individualism will always keep the political power under suspicion for that reason as much as for any other, even though a government acting openly and at the behest of popular opinion or private interests can also, of course, damage rights.

The democratic hope is to retard or reverse the tendency to substitute ruling for governing, to keep or expand the areas in which elected officials will make the important decisions and do so openly, deliberatively, and accountably. Yet, it must also be said, this hope is not for a condition in which there is popular self-government (or popular self-rule as it is commonly called) in any literal sense. Literal popular self-government can be only what Athens had, a system in which citizens not only make laws directly but also fill, by lot or rotation, all (or almost all) executive and judicial offices. Modern countries, even small ones, are too big for such practices. No, the modern hope should be that rule is avoided wherever possible, that there be no domination by unelected officials and no dictated measures in any area of public policy. Modern popular self-rule is the absence of state rule, wherever possible. That is what we must settle for, and even that minimum is hard to get and keep. I think, however, that when popular self-rule is spoken of in modern times much more than the minimum is actually meant (and earnestly desired).

What is meant is one of two things. The first is that the people are a demos, a majority class with a common socioeconomic interest which confronts a privileged minority and which should use its democratic political power to replace or curb or abolish the minority. The second is that the people's representatives should translate popular opinion into a steady stream of policies which can be interpreted as the expression of a sense of life or of the good life, or as the expression of a marked group identity, or as the deliberate shaping of the life of society. Popular self-government is thus either class struggle (on the one hand) or group self-expression or the mastery of the common fate (on the other).

I have already indicated my view that rights-based individualism is not a theory of class struggle. Class struggle, if really meant, must be careless of all rights, not only of the right of property. It is more like war, even when conducted peacefully, than peace. It is a refusal to grant legitimacy to constitutional representative democracy. The trouble with the alternative vision of democratic politics as group self-expression or group mastery is that it posits a people as a uniform collectivity, or at least that it aspires to such a condition. This assumption is no better than that of class division into a uniform majority and a uniform minority. To want to believe that there is either a fixed majority interest or a homogeneous group identity is not compatible with the premises of rights-based individualism. And to act on either view is to weaken rights. One could conclude therefore that a modern democracy that rests on respect for individual rights is not properly seen as popular self-government in any active sense. Popular self-government is a negative concept; it is the absence of rule, to an appreciable extent.

Some may think that if an advocate of rights insists on the negative or merely formal nature of modern democracy the political rights of the individual, his or her citizenship, amount to too little. (The citizenship in question is citizenship on the highest level, that which attaches a person to the most comprehensive laws and policies.) In itself voting is a meager experience. In answer I would say that the facts, however sad, must be faced. For most people, national citizenship is formal only, except in episodes, such as participation in a movement or a campaign. Otherwise the experience of (literal or modified) citizenship can be sought and may be had only outside the national arena: in institutions or workplaces or local politics and governments or juries or in everyday life. On the other hand, the experience of one's personal rights is constant, as constant, almost, as the threat to them from the state. Enjoyment of the rights of expression and privacy, safety from intrusive state action, and the absence of discrimination are the stuff of everyone's life and have a much greater felt reality than national citizenship ordinarily has. The related systemic point is that modern constitutionalism, understood as the protection of personal rights, is or can be more genuinely attained than can a true modern representative democracy. The practice of majority rule in a legislature elected by universal suffrage, indispensable as it is, is surrounded by manifold circumstances that determine the extent of political responsiveness and accountability to the people. Although both constitutionalism and democracy are rooted in concern for human dignity, their respective modes of realization and degrees of reality are (and probably must be) discrepant.

The consequence of this claim is that the best use of national citizenship for those not regularly involved as members of "the political stratum" is to become and remain especially attentive to the vicissitudes of constitutionalism, to the health of personal rights. One of the best uses—though not the only good use—of political rights is work which preserves personal rights through exploitation of all the modes of politics which democracy provides. Naturally many other concerns and interests must occupy anyone's political attention. There will always be moral or physical emergencies: wars, hard times, dangers to the environment, inadequacies of health, schooling, and infrastructure, and disturbing crises of a now-unknowable kind. Care for constitutionalism is not exhaustive of political duty, but it is a central part of it. It is an especially meaningful part because the need to keep rights in good repair arises not only in emergencies, but almost every day. Consonant with it is the project of trying to retard or reverse the tendency to substitute ruling for governing. The avoidance of rule, like the defense of rights, will often be served by resistance to the spread of state action. Both political projects serve to inhibit the state. In such inhibition, not only are personal rights enhanced, but the political rights of citizenship are also enhanced, because the main meaning of modern citizenship for ordinary persons lies in the avoidance of being ruled.

The perspective of rights-based individualism is suspicious of the political realm. Yet, as I have tried to suggest in parts of this book, the manner in which constitutional democratic government is put together and does its business radiates powerful moral and existential lessons that help to engender a distinctive culture. Constitutional democracy is in itself a great moral and existential phenomenon: it is constructed out of respect for the rights of individuals. But it also contributes profoundly to another great moral and existential phenomenon—a new way of life. It does so not primarily through its policies or through the spectacle of successfully or honestly coping with difficult problems. Indeed, if the policies of the government, or its effectiveness, were the force behind the creation or the psychological maintenance of a new way of life, we should say that the way of life is artificial and unlikely to last. The cardinal fact is that the form and routine political and legal workings of constitutional democracy give reality to personal and political rights. In doing so, the system impresses the meaning of rights on the psyche; behavior is changed because everyone's self-conception is changed.

I have pointed to such features as the tonic effects of simply being included as a citizen, when it is known that the historical norm has been exclusion of most people from any official power; the chastening effects on all authority when the principal officeholders are subjected to the discipline of elections, limited and revocable terms, and all officeholders are subjected to structural, procedural, and political restraints on their conduct; the enlivening effects of partisan dispute and alternation in power; and the concern for the human dignity of all persons which is brought home when the government respects personal rights. These are the formal attributes of constitutional democracy, and the manner of its working. In them is the source of the capacity of the political system to foster a new way of life. Compared to this indeliberate and routine achievement, many of the things that can be said on behalf of constitutional democracy's greater efficiency or good sense or adaptability or ease in gaining loyalty seem less important. Why justify constitutional democracy? The most important reason is of course that it aspires to protect rights and thus honor modest human dignity; its motive is the attempted avoidance of evil or oppression or injustice. But not too far behind in importance is the reason that constitutional democracy becomes the indispensable provocation of a new way of life. A democratic culture emerges slowly, the culture of democratic individuality.

When the theory of individual rights is embodied in the procedures and processes of constitutional democracy, attention to human dignity is established. Ordinary persons are freed of abuse and recognized as persons. It takes a while for this historically unusual or aberrant condition to be grasped. The usual fate imposed by states and the associated elites on ordinary persons has been and is to be kept down, kept in place or out of sight, to be used or exploited or ignored, to be sat on, to be thought unbeautiful. Formal membership in constitutional democracy together with the routine workings of the system tends to raise people out of inferior conditions and the internalized sense of inferiority. The coming of constitutional democracy is a liberation, a liberation of mentality and feelings.

Rights-based individualism defines the political meaning of constitutional democracy. It is an assertion against the actual government and policies, but, equally, it draws its life and nourishment from the form, the spirit, and the routine workings of that government. With time, latent or extended or metaphorical meanings in rights are found, while the continuing public embodiment of rights in the political and legal system occasions further discoveries of meanings, and magnifies old and new meanings, and makes them vivid. The combined effects, over time, of living with rights against government and also experiencing its form and routine workings are a potent force for revising human self-conception and all human relations. The meanings of rights are spread everywhere into society, in all the rest of life apart from government. As everyday life is revised, it shows more and more evidences of democratic individuality, which is a cultural, indeed a spiritual outgrowth and elaboration of rights-based individualism in a constitutional democracy. The idea of democratic individuality also re-creates public citizenship by conscientiously reindividualizing it and encouraging creative resistance in behalf of one-self or others. If made real, democratic individuality produces a culture or civilization that is the counterpart (replica and complement) of the political system of constitutional democracy. The values of each are, with allowance made for some changes, the values that inspire the other. More is involved, therefore, than the claim that the political system has some general good effects on people—say, raising their self-esteem and hence their level of energy or calling forth such virtues as good judgment, impartiality, and fair play—which are not specific to democracy. And the culmination for the democratic individual can be theorized as a state of being which rises above immersion in its culture. That psychic culmina-tion, too, has a counterpart in the anarchic qualities of the political system.

Democratic individuality can grow in a society that respects the rights of individuals. Rights-based individualism (the mentality of claiming rights) prepares the way (historically and continuously) for democratic individuality and guards the possibility of its occurrence. But, in turn, democratic individuality, when practiced, guards and fulfills rights-based individualism and signifies that the meanings of rights have been grasped and held.

In sum, the theoretical account of the individual in a constitutional democracy brings out an expansive concurrence of distant but intimately related elements. It embraces not only the basic requirements of modest human dignity but also the radical alteration of culture and, beyond that, the assertion of every individual's infinitude—and, what may come with that, an openness to sublimity.

As some chapters in this book suggest, the idea of democratic individu-ality is complex—as complex as the intelligence of its principal theorists, Emerson, Thoreau, and Whitman. Perhaps some of what follows, I am afraid, makes that idea schematic. The division of the idea into three as-pects of individuality—positive, negative, and impersonal—is not tact-ful or philosophically subtle. I may be too eager to carry literature into political theory for the sake of political theory. But I have been driven by the sense that political theorists were not paying enough attention to the work of these writers and that some schematism could be provisionally helpful. By ignoring them, for the most part, political theorists have ignored the best conception of individualism and, instead, made too

much of the effort undertaken by the late C. B. Macpherson to demonstrate that the only individualism is bourgeois individualism, which is
only "possessive individualism" and which, in turn, is only the rationalization for economic self-seeking.[12] Individualism means money; that is
all. Or, if individualism means more, other political theorists are prepared to denounce it as an advocacy of solipsism or "atomism" or self-
protective reclusiveness or aimless hedonism or amoral self-imposition.
No doubt all these tendencies, discussed by Macpherson and the others,
exist. We can find thought to the effect that oneself, or that some or all
individuals, matter only in isolation, or should exist in disregard of
others, or each of each. But there is, after all, another tendency: another
hope and another actuality. On the one hand, rights-based individualism
is a claim for a shared human dignity, simply; on the other hand, the
theory and the practice of democratic individuality are critical or hostile
toward the other kinds of individualism. It would be foolish to deny that
there are affinities and historical connections between these other kinds
and both rights-based individualism and democratic individuality. Still,
the story does not stop there. The Emersonian tradition is an attempt to
sever democratic individuality from all the other individualisms that
resemble but reject or betray it, or that developed with it but then swerve
and become narrowly extreme.

I explore the aspects of democratic individuality in some of the following chapters. I here reluctantly add, however, another schematism to
that of the three aspects: three levels of democratic individuality—the
normal level, the extraordinary level, and the transcendent level.

We find, if we look, pretty steady evidences of the normal level of
democratic individuality in everyday life. It helps, when we look, to have
read the characterization in Plato's *Republic* (Books 8 and 9) of the democratic psyche and society. Athenians did not have a theory of individual
human rights of the modern absolute and universal sort. They are not
usually thought even to have had a notion of the individual rights of
Athenians. But they certainly had guarantees for citizens. They had a
wider sense of inclusion in citizenship than was then usual. They loved
dispute; they loved exposure to difference and contrast. They, more than
anyone else in their world, tolerated philosophy. They seem to have been
free in a way that encouraged ordinary persons to take chances, to
experiment, to be mobile, and to be receptive. They gave persons and
things equal footing, an equal chance. They let roles be reversed, so that

[12] C. B. Macpherson, *The Political Theory of Possessive Individualism* (Oxford: Oxford
University Press, 1962).

slaves acted as if they were free, the young as if they could instruct the old, the guilty as if they had never broken the law, and women as if they were as good as men. They would have preferred a world in which no one ruled or was ruled.

Any halfway sympathetic observer will find these traits and comparable ones in the United States and in other established constitutional democracies. In modern times, the theory of rights against government is needed to get this culture started and keep it going, while the Athenians had some other inspiration, which was no more predictable and is no more exhaustively explainable than the birth of the theory of rights. But whatever the Athenian inspiration, one detects some version of the idea that ordinary persons (at least Greeks) have dignity and are worthy: they suffer, but should suffer less; they are capable of leading a life on their own, of living as they like, and not disgracefully; and they are capable of perceiving (some) others as themselves.

After Plato (and passages in Thucydides' *History* and Aristotle's *Politics*), we have to wait until Tocqueville visited the United States for an illumination of democratic culture.[13] The transformation of self and culture in a society governed in the manner of constitutional democracy is his great theme, concentrated especially in the second volume of *Democracy in America* (1840). His emphasis is on the many ways in which democracy changes the world over: the spirit of equality (equal human dignity) replaces the spirit of hierarchy in every sector of life. He writes about democratic manners: a more informal family life, a greater equality between the sexes, a greater mingling of people on equal terms in every circumstance of life, a greater mildness and leniency and openness, and a new sort of adventurousness.

My references to Plato and Tocqueville are meant to suggest that what I have been calling democratic individuality is not merely a theoretical construction. Great observers have claimed, at one time or another, to see a democratic culture, and their warrant was a lack of instinctive sympathy for it. Indeed, they had to overcome revulsion and did not always manage to do so. Yet they saw a phenomenon that they knew to be unusual and complex and that deserved to be looked at on its own terms. Therefore, it is not only partisans or haters of democracy who say that democracy is radically different.

The normal level of democratic culture is the culture of democratic

---

[13] There is a subtle and resourceful interpretation of the Athenian democratic mentality in Josiah Ober, *Mass and Elite in Democratic Athens* (Princeton: Princeton University Press, 1989). I mention here only works that are synoptic and theoretical.

individuality. If we revert to the schematism of facets, democratic culture shows evidences of positive, negative, and impersonal individuality. Positively, we see human beings who think of themselves as equal individuals and who therefore intermittently abandon ascribed identities and exchange roles; we see mobility and restlessness, and experimentation; we see a desire for an accumulation of experiences; we see a philosophical disposition to make feelings articulate and relationships explicit; we see a wish to escape the immemorial association of ordinariness with plainness or even ugliness; we see a passion to work on oneself; we see a powerful urge to pick and choose the people in one's life and to initiate enterprises with them. All these are the normal or common manifestations of positive democratic individuality, and all flow from an initial commitment to personal and private rights against government and their embodiment in the structure and routine workings of constitutional democracy.

As for the negative facet, we see marginal, stigmatized, or victimized groups who say No to their condition and insist that each member of any group is an individual and not a mere member of a category. (Claims for the intrinsic group worth of the despised group are understandable as compensatory but not permanently commendable from the perspective of democratic individuality.) Such resistance is undertaken not only for recognition of rights by government but also in behalf of a reconstruction of everyday life. The latter project searches for everyday equivalents of equal rights against those who have more power and status, for private and institutional versions of equal citizenship. Full acceptance is the goal. Participants may find the resistance itself to be pleasurable, unguilty. Even more, when a group nonviolently resists denial of its rights by the state or in society, when it allows both conscience and serious playfulness to shape its tactics, it can become creative and transform a self-concerned struggle that needs no apology into something more: a process that by being self-denying is individually self-defining and also exemplary and noble. The great contemporary American instance is the movement led by Martin Luther King, Jr.

The impersonal facet is shown in a widespread and almost promiscuous acceptance of one thing after another, almost no matter what. An all-forgiving tolerance can appear; it is a perpetual possibility. It can also turn into a recognition of equality, in spite of reluctance. What makes such tolerance and recognition impersonal is a degree of play in oneself, a certain detachment in the midst of involvements that permits unanxious observation.

It would be foolish to say either that any actual democratic culture is purely democratic or that the more democratic it is, the necessarily better it is. Nevertheless, such a culture is distinctive. Not all values, principles, virtues, experiences, or achievements will find theoretical accommodation in a democratic society. It may in fact, shelter more human diversity than any other society; it even gives a chance to what is different from or antagonistic to democratic individuality. But I would hesitate to include within the theory of democratic individuality principled allowance for any cultural condition that seems to violate democratic individuality.

Plato says in *The Republic* (557) that in a democracy there will be the greatest variety of human natures and that "they have a complete assortment of constitutions." Liberty produces diversity. But I think that the diversity suitable to a modern democracy cannot be unlimited. Respect for equal human dignity, which is the *inspiration* of everyone's rights-based individualism, is also the *restraint* on anyone's (positive) democratic individuality. (It is also much of the inspiration for the other facets of anyone's democratic individuality.) Democratic individuality is not boundless subjectivist or self-seeking individualism. Though democratic surfaces change with extreme quickness, individual expression may take place, to a great extent, within a range of small differences. (This smallness was one of Tocqueville's complaints.) An observer needs a sympathetic eye to notice many of the differences. The most desirable democratic diversity is that shown by each person in relation to himself or herself in the instant or over time, a self-overcoming driven as much by self-displeased honesty as by a taste for adventure.

The theory of democratic individuality rejects or attenuates or does no more than flirt with such individualist self-conceptions as the Byronic (to be at total war with one's society in behalf of one's transgressive uniqueness), the vulgar Nietzschean (to define oneself by reference to one's ability to look down on others or impose oneself on them), the Napoleonic (to use people as one's artistic medium), and the idealist (to imagine that oneself is alone real and the world is either one's effluence or only shadows and images). (I simplify.) None of these self-conceptions suits the theory of a democratic society of individuality: each is built on unending antagonism or a refusal of moral or existential equality.

Further, the diversity favored by the spirit of democratic individuality is the diversity of individuals, not of groups. Any individual can learn lessons from the spectacle of diverse groups or find it aesthetically refreshing. But this attitude easily becomes instrumental or condescending. The very idea of a colorful and stable group scene stocked with representative types is not democratic. Diverse groups can exist only when a universal disposition to conformity makes each group internally uniform or at least confines individual differences to those of temperament or eccentricity. Group diversity is all the more democratically unacceptable when it takes the form of caste or permanent cultural classes.

Democratic diversity is therefore not, in principle, infinitely permissive; nor is it in practice. The democratic culture is too fluid and uncertain to be a shapely stylization, but it is not incoherent. The point of special relevance is that if ever greater numbers of individuals stop thinking of themselves as individuals and, instead, retribalize in ethnic or other sorts of fixed-identity groups, the normal level of democratic individuality would grow weaker. The heart of rights-based individualism would also sicken. Fixed pluralism, rather than limited and temporary associations, is foreign to the culture of democracy. If, also, fixed-identity groups, new to a democratic society, pondered the spirit that gives them protection, they would perhaps come to dissolve or individualistically reform themselves. They receive the tolerance they would never give. They are given the recognition they deny others: recognition of equal worth and dignity. They have been received as individuals but think and feel as an exclusive herd.

Plato and Tocqueville can help us see much, and they also lead us to trust our own feeling for the distinctiveness of democratic culture. I think, however, that their superb powers of perception do not exhaust the subject. Their analysis pertains, for the most part, to the normal level of democratic individuality. There are, however, other levels, higher levels. I mean, first, that democratic society shows moments, moods, and episodes of extraordinary democratic individuality. And, next, there are moments, moods, and episodes in which one experiences a democratized understanding of all reality, an understanding which goes beyond self and society but does not (necessarily) aspire to the supernatural or the more-than-human. This is democratic transcendence.

The invaluable work of glimpsing evidences of democratic extraordinariness and democratic transcendence in the United States (then the only modern democracy), and of proceeding to theorize them in order to encourage them was done by Emerson, Thoreau, and Whitman. They theorize the movement of democratic individuality to its higher levels.

Do they work alone? I am inclined to think so, but I am not able to say for sure. It would be better, therefore, just to say that their contribution is the best and that hence it has not been superseded. My conviction is that it is also not obsolete, for all the tremendous changes that have come over American and Western life since they wrote.

The work of these three is an emanation and expression of democratic culture. It is also an exploration of it in every direction. They aspire to raise the level of the culture; the quality of their work signifies that it is raised, that they have raised it. They encourage the consolidation of the normal level of democratic culture and then urge moving that culture further in its own direction toward more of the extraordinary and the transcendent. Their work thus illustrates and embodies what they advocate. They exceed any doctrine, even the most elevated; they try to escape containment. But, finally, they are the greatest teachers of democratic individuality because they are its greatest students.

How do the moments, moods, and episodes of democratic extraordinariness show themselves? Positively, in bursts of what Emerson calls self-reliance. These are occasions of independent thinking, newly innocent perception, self-expressive activity, unexpected creativity—occurrences possible in any individual's life. Release from convention is the key; all the conventions of democracy exist for such release: they sponsor their own abandonment, fleeting and incomplete as such abandonment must (and should) be.

Negatively, extraordinary democratic individuality manifests itself in episodes of public citizenship in which some people whose rights are protected initiate resistance in behalf of others who are denied their rights, or join them in a common struggle. What makes this politics of resistance individualist is the presence of conscience, which means, in this context, the courage to stand for what all the advantaged profess but many do not follow. Thoreau, more than any other, has crystallized the sentiments of resistance for the sake of others. Certainly his conscientious refusals are a powerful example, but it is not the only one. Extraordinary individuality can also be displayed in acts of resistance that are not solitary or uncoordinated but rather associative and organized. The provision for extraordinariness is that each person enters the fight after self-examination and persists, as a fighter, in the effort to avoid the political vices of partiality, self-deception, and insensitivity to the claims of the other side.

Democratic individuality becomes extraordinary in the impersonal sense when one labors to bestow sympathy abundantly, especially on what seems most to discourage or repel it. The underlying mental effort is to see beauty in everyone, in everything. This determination is a belief in radical equality made aesthetic. Giving is receiving: generosity is shown in receptivity. Each particular person or creature or thing is beheld, one at a time, one after another, and taken on its own terms or on better terms than it is able to assert for itself. One must be a democratic individual to individuate one's sympathy and perception, to feel and see for oneself and to feel and see what is there as itself. One becomes an individual above one's normal level by breaking up the world into individuals equally worthy of attention and response.

I find that the theory of democratic individuality, like some other individualisms, cultivates a sense of individual infinitude; that is, a sense of one's inner ocean, of everybody's inexhaustible internal turbulent richness and unused powers. What helps to separate democratic individuality from other individualisms, however, is the conviction that one can make the sense of one's infinitude a bridge to other human beings and perhaps to the rest of nature. The world is aspects of oneself, of anyone, made actual. One has some affinity to every particular. On the other hand, Thoreau is riskily intent on intensifying the feeling of wonder one can have before any particular just because one may have no affinity to it. Both strategies catch a truth and both can yield amazed acceptance and serve the impersonal (self-forsaking) receptive capacities of democratic individuals. One needs both strategies; mood will decide which to adopt at a given moment. Either way, one is trying to dispel the trance of conventional definitions, categories, and preconceptions. One is straining to make individual what often is content to be indistinguishable but that is—as Emerson often suggests—better than it knows.

Beyond the experience at even the extraordinary level lies a rare moment, mood, or episode of transcendence. This highest level is contemplative and consequently only impersonal: an evanescent loss of the sense of one's unique self in favor of everything outside it. I think that on all its levels democratic individuality is not egocentric, that the democratic ego is not sharply defined, grasping for more than its share, sure of its identity and therefore sure of its wants and desires. Plato's democratic soul and Tocqueville's individual are moody, dreamy, rather dispersed or fragmented or unconsecutive. The democratic energies and concentrations come out of uncertain soil. Democratic reality validates their observations enough of the time. But democratic transcendence makes this tendency to free self-loss qualitatively different. Emerson, Thoreau, and Whitman all give voice to the need to bless existence in its entirety, not only to bless particulars as they come along. In part of this book I try to understand this need and to connect it to the will to take the moral and existential meanings of democracy seriously. But that will is too religiously dependent.

All these writers are given to religiousness, unorthodox as it is, for they do not appear to take the last step and renounce the will to have supernatural sponsorship and authentication. Someone can say that the last step—to decide to be without religiousness and without religion—leaves one too lonely, and all the more so because one is trying resolutely to be an individual and not merely a social being. One becomes a ghost haunting one's life, rather than a person living it. The world itself becomes unreal. Is it any accident that democratic life in the United States strikes many who lead it or watch it as unreal precisely because it is such a willed, contracted, chosen life, or such an improvised, unprescribed, made-up life?

Well, religions do nothing honestly to make the world more real (rooted, stable, solid). Neither does Emersonian religiousness. The burden of unreality is democracy's heroism. There is no lasting way of evading it, except to destroy democracy. For me, Emersonian religiousness cannot be allowed to spoil a transcendence that the Emersonians inspire and that requires no more-than-human agency above or behind the world as it is. That humanity could not have made the world does not mean that some more-than-human agency did make it. For us to regard the world as worthy of wonder does not require that it be a designed whole. These three writers deliver formulations that can be severed from their religiousness and set up as the consummation of democratic individuality. Are there evidences for it outside the pages of these writers? Or are their greatest pages the evidence itself that democratic individuality is capable of sublimity?

CHAPTER ONE

The Moral Distinctiveness
of Representative Democracy

In representative democracy the source of laws and public policies is a collection of officeholders who have attained office by winning contested elections. The contested elections, by their very nature, provide some general guidance to the winners concerning public opinion and preferences on laws and public policies that have been and are to be made. The offices are specified by a constitution originally ratified by the people and subject always to their amendment, or by a basic common understanding. Thus, the fundamental institution of representative democracy is the electoral system.

All the foregoing is a repetition of truths too obvious to need repetition. Yet to say these banalities is only preliminary to restating their sense in a perhaps slightly less banal way, and therefore in a way that might rescue them from banality. Let us say that in a representative democracy political authority is held by a collection of officeholders who have attained office by winning contested elections. The right to make laws and public policies is granted by those who are to obey the laws and endure and experience the policies. The exercise of political authority is not only enabled but guided, in some general way, by those who are to obey the laws and endure and experience the policies. The ultimate authority is not the people *tout court* but the expressed will-to-political-right of the people aware of itself as a people, whether that expression is contained in a written document or not.

Perhaps this alternative way is also banal, no better than banal. Be that as it may, it is meant to recall us to what was once not banal at all: the fact that authority—political authority, in the first instance—undergoes a change when its fate is joined to the workings of the electoral system. Political authority is demystified or desacralized (clumsy words for an enormous alteration) when it is regularly recreated. The artificial nature of political authority is continuously being asserted, and to a degree that some of the main seventeenth-century theories of social contract, government contract, and voluntary civil society do not match because of the absence in them of provision for the electoral system. Or, where there is provision, the system is restricted in popular basis or in the real daily work entrusted to it. The very notion of ruling and being ruled is alien to the spirit of representative democracy, and so are the related notions of the state and of sovereignty residing in the state rather than in the constitutionally organized people. Perhaps even the idea of a sovereign people is democratically inappropriate because it suggests that a group is free to become unfree or allow some systemic wrong to be inflicted on a sector of the population.

When people acknowledge, as they must, that some political authority (some government) is necessary—that life or social life or civilization would not be possible without it—the fact that it is regularly recreated invests the feeling of necessity with some mitigation and removes gratitude from the picture altogether. Although people cannot but choose to have political authority, they nevertheless choose those who wield it. Just by doing that they loosen authority's hold: not, here, in the sense that the electoral system provides some general guidance on laws and public policies, but in the sense that there would be no political authority at all without the willing participation of the people in the electoral system. There would be no person or group who could properly claim it or confer it or validate it if the people did not take part. Imprecisely put, but not metaphorically, the electoral system is a form of people's self-rule. If that is the case, the very nature of rule, of authority, is qualitatively different in representative democracies.

When, therefore, we try to determine the moral distinctiveness of representative democracy, we must begin by taking note of the most banal considerations. In contrast to dictatorship, oligarchy, actual monarchy or chieftainship, or other forms, representative democracy signifies a radical chastening of political authority. When political authority is, at every moment, a temporary and conditional grant, regularly revocable; when suffrage establishes the sufferance, so to speak, in which the people hold political authority, a major moral distinctiveness enters the life of society. Society is taught—society teaches itself—a fundamental lesson about the nature of all authority by handling the problem of political authority as it does. The overall lesson can be expressed in a number of ways. Most commonly, we speak of a pervasive skepticism toward authority, a reluctance to defer, a conviction that those who wield authority must themselves be skeptical toward their roles and themselves and that necessary authority must be wielded in a way that inflicts minimum damage on the moral equality of all people. Furthermore, there is a tendency to try to do without authority wherever possible or to disperse or disguise it, and thus to soften it.

From the perspective of societies that do not constitute political authority by means of the electoral system, it might seem that political authority does not exist in representative democracies. Or, at the least, that political authority is in a constant state of crisis or always on the verge of dissolution. On the other hand, within representative democracies there are many who, in the thrall of sociological or anthropological habits of mind, fail to see any difference between a people's self-rule and all other forms of rule. These habits issue in the effort to show that despite appearances all governments must do the same work and secure the same ends, that the form of government has no consequences for the work and the ends, and that there is no inevitable transformation of the very nature of governmental and political action. It is as if efficiency were the sole political reality and that, therefore, representative democracy is at best circumstantially usable.

I will not now offer a more detailed resistance either to those who find no authority but only near-anarchy in representative democracy or to those who see nothing distinctive in the authority present in representative democracy. It must be sufficient to refer to the banalities we have mentioned. The aim of this chapter is to suggest that certain moral phenomena that appear prominently in societies with representative democratic governments are traceable to the existence of that form of government. That is, the fate undergone by political authority helps to account for these phenomena. Now, I am not saying anything that empirical research into public opinion could verify to the satisfaction of all observers. Even discursive conversations with patient and subtle researchers—as patient and subtle as Sennett and Cobb[1]—need not yield abundant confirmation, though some degree of confirmation is not impossible. People may not be totally aware of the sources of encouragement to their conduct, for some of these sources may be "in the air." I wish only to propose a reasonable imputation: these phenomena are perfectly intelligible in light of the fact that political authority is pro-

---

[1] See Richard Sennett and Jonathan Cobb, *The Hidden Injuries of Class* (New York: Knopf, 1972).

foundly chastened by the electoral system. It makes sense to think that these phenomena would not occur, or would occur less frequently, if the electoral system did not as it were sponsor them. The psychological effect of that system permeates the whole society and helps to liberate those energies and that self-conception that manifest themselves in these phenomena. The spirit of the electoral system fits or suits or is consonant with the feeling for how to live that is surely at work—in play—when people act in certain characteristic ways. The moral distinctiveness of the arrangements of representative democracy sponsors distinctive moral phenomena in the life of society.

What, then, are these moral phenomena? They are all familiar from the theory and practice of representative democracy. I would bring them together only in order to posit their special affinity to the spirit of the electoral system. First of all, there is independence of spirit. I do not refer to scholars, intellectuals, and artists and the extraordinary independence they should show, given the very nature of their vocation. Instead, I wish to point to the independence that ordinary people show in their extraordinary moments—moments that help to give a larger sense to their whole lives. The chastening of political authority encourages individuals to be less fearful of all authority, whether concentrated in particular figures of authority or impersonally present in given rules and conventions. The positive expression of independence in the face of personal and impersonal authority can be called *autonomy*. Just as in claiming autonomy one does not want to be legislated for, so one cannot express autonomy by legislating for others, even when all comprise the legislative power. The Kantian notion of autonomy as legislation cannot be extended into the political sphere: the acknowledgment of the basic moral principle and a few incontestable derivations help to frame legislation in our usual sense, but are not its stuff. The Rousseauist political equivalent of autonomy rests on a homogeneity of citizenry and on an infrequency and simplicity of legislation which are scarcely political. Autonomy is not implicated in our usual sense of legislation. Autonomy does not exist when all are bound to act in the same way; it cannot be, therefore, a politically relevant value, except in the negative way, of supporting a claim to limited government, and in the formal way of requiring inclusion as a citizen with full political rights. On the other hand, the Kantian notion is not relevant, except as part of the frame, to nonpublic life. Autonomy is acting on one's own, making one's life one's own, freely making commitments, accepting conventions known to be conventions, and straining to construct the architecture of one's soul. Emerson's self-reliance, Thoreau's doubleness, Whitman's Myself, Mill's individuality are all approaches to a conception of autonomy. Autonomy consists in significant differentiation achieved through some distance between one and the world, and between one and oneself. (Of course it does not exclude politics as a career, a "vocation.")

The negative expression of independence is the disposition to say no, to dissent, to engage in acts of principled or conscientious disobedience or resistance or rebelliousness, whether in acts of citizenship or in the rest of life.

Second, the mere status of citizen which enables one to run for office and to vote in the contested elections for office is a continuous incitement to claim the status of citizen—or something analogous—in all nonpolitical relations of life. Indeed, the incitement is to politicize the nonpolitical relations of life and thus to democratize them. As we know, this politicization may invade the most intimate and domestic relations of life as well as the more formal relations inherent in institutions, organizations, and associations of every sort.

The third moral phenomenon follows from the electoral system's partisan or factional basis. In a representative democracy, political authority is in essence partial (to leave aside the judiciary). A part—a party or faction or coalition—is temporarily allowed to stand for the whole. Parts take turns standing for the whole and giving it a temporary moral emphasis or coloration. The very association of authority and partisanship promotes a sense of moral indeterminacy. This should not be confused with skepticism or relativism. It is rather the belief that within a frame of settled commitments, a number of contrasting and competing responses or answers to morally tinged questions are to be expected and welcomed. (The judicial equivalent is dispute over constitutional interpretation.) A struggle against those in authority understood as defenders of one possible right answer rather than the only possible right answer is thus encouraged. Disseminated into society, this notion not only intensifies the demand to democratize all relations but cultivates a general tolerance of, and even affection for, diversity: diversity in itself, and diversity as the source of regulated contest and competition.

There are other moral phenomena that suit the spirit of the electoral system, but I think that these three are the principal ones. In brief, the existence of a method of filling the major political offices—the major loci of political authority—by contested elections (regularly held) that are specified by a written constitution or by unwritten constitutional understanding so affects the sense of all authority in society at large that we may reasonably posit these moral phenomena as consequences. Reciprocally, of course, these phenomena indicate the presence of feelings, attitudes, and ideas that work to sustain the functioning of the electoral system. The main point here is that the existence of an electoral system—rather than all other kinds of gaining office or position—supplies a vivid, public, and continuous imparting of the moral lesson that the only tolerable authority is a deliberately chastened authority and that every effort must be made to have authority offend against moral equality as little as possible. Without such an imparting, the meaning of the lesson would be much more alien and artificial. We can expect that in societies without the electoral system for filling major offices there would be much less popular independence of mind in the forms of autonomy and the disposition to say no, less democratization of nonpolitical relations, and a much greater hostility to any diversity that was not sanctioned by a hereditary principle of class or caste or by a dictatorial directive.

But the electoral system usually does not exist without some kind of constitutional accompaniment. The root value of constitutionalism is restraint on political authority. If filling political offices by means of the electoral system is in itself a chastening of authority, the devices of constitutionalism are a further chastening.

It is not possible for me to estimate the comparative force for chastisement of the electoral system and of constitutionalism. Needless to say, some part of constitutionalism can exist without the copresence of the electoral system. But though constitutionalism is meant to restrain all political authority, even that created by the electoral system, and though in democratic societies the most familiar political dualism is "majority rule versus minority rights," the moral fact is that, at bottom, the electoral system and constitutional restraint serve the same value or cluster of values. Each needs the other not only for practical durability and efficacy but also to fill out the other's moral meaning. The strain between them is an indication of their affinity.

In any case, American political ideas and experience offer the most theoretically developed instance of constitutionalism. At base there is the rule of law: that government shall work by the rules it makes and that these rules shall adhere to certain conditions.[2] But constitutionalism is not exhausted by this minimum. There are the restraints on political authority of an absolute or near-absolute kind—the circumscriptions and

---

[2] For a specification of these conditions, see Lon L. Fuller, *The Morality of Law*, rev. ed. (New Haven: Yale University Press, 1969), chap. 2.

prohibitions of the Bill of Rights. The Bill of Rights says to political authority, You cannot do certain things at all, and in doing other things you must do them in one way and not in any other. You cannot abridge the exercise of religion or speech; you can search, arrest, try, and punish only if you deny yourself certain tempting methods used freely in other societies.

In addition to the Bill of Rights, such features as the separation of powers, checks and balances, and federation all conduce to the values of constitutionalism. It is very difficult to restore the moral sense of these features, obscured as they are by piety, cynicism, boredom, and familiarity (as, indeed, the whole subject of representative democracy is). Yet their sense is there to be seen by the moral eye. The sense, cumulatively, is that political authority is suspect when undivided and thus untroubled by antithetical voices. Political authority is suspect when it moves too easily or takes shortcuts to accomplish its ends, or when it prevents appeals and second thoughts, or when it closes itself off in secrecy or unapproachability.

What moral phenomena in the larger society do the practices of constitutionalism inspire or enlarge or ratify? One of them stands out: a certain delicacy of conduct often called fairness. But the word "fairness" ordinarily lacks all the connotations of that delicacy which constitutionalism teaches. Constitutional delicacy consists in scruples, self-doubt, self-criticism, self-correction, as well as the disposition toward an engaged detachment that most resembles a serious playfulness, a playfulness that wants to win but only in accordance with rules, only after a fight, only after, perhaps, aiding the antagonist to become equal. By following the rules enjoined on them by a Bill of Rights, those in authority act delicately (whatever their inner resistance or actual efforts to evade or distort the inhibitions placed on them). They are chastened into delicacy. (This delicacy is related to that shown in accepting the constraints of the electoral system—accepting loss, especially.) This delicacy can then pervade all life in society so that an analogous or approximate or transmuted constitutionalism might be found in all relations, formal and informal—just as the electoral system may influence people to seek democracy in all relations.

If to the chastening effects of the electoral system and constitutional discipline are added a continuous effort to restrict the scope of authority's action and a continuous effort to avoid paternalist action within the properly restricted scope, one further moral consequence ensues. Actually, it is the intensification of one of the moral phenomena already mentioned: the positive expression of independence of spirit, autonomy. The smaller the amount of explicit regulation meant to bind all, the more room there is left for individuals and groups to regulate themselves, to achieve a lawful autonomy. The less discretionary authority exercised, the less awesome is political authority and, with that, the weaker the inhibitions in regard to independent action in the face of all kinds of authority. The less paternalism there is, the stronger grows the readiness to reject paternalism in all the relations of life. It seems to me that necessary to the completion of constitutional representative democracy as a morally distinctive polity is limited, nonpaternalist government, for the reason that the morally distinctive phenomena it sponsors are more fully realized in that case.

The overall chastening that political authority receives at the hands of constitutional representative democracy (limited and nonpaternalist in its scope of action) is a chastening of all authority. At the same time, the chastening is not only a diminution but also an inducement to act in ways and by procedures that carry great moral significance, that teach specific moral lessons. On the one hand, the chastening of political authority liberates citizens. On the other hand, the particular modes of chastening may suggest an ethic of action and forbearance from action for citizens in all the relations of life. Thus, the chastening of public authority not only liberates citizens by liberating them from certain attitudes to all authority, it also teaches them how to wield authority in the nonpolitical relations of life (nonpolitical in the sense of nonpublic). In its distinctive way of forming political authority, representative democracy cultivates distinctive ways of acting in nonpolitical life—of seeking and giving, of making claims for oneself and one's group and acknowledging the claims of others. The actual public citizenship of those who do not hold or run for office is, in turn, affected by the transformation of nonpolitical life which the political system facilitates—especially the acts of episodic, morally heroic citizenship.

We may say then that constitutional representative democracy helps to foster certain traits of character and hence certain ways of being in the world that no other form of government does. Naturally these traits and ways may appear almost anywhere and at almost any time. But it surely matters that the fate endured by political authority in nondemocratic societies has played no role in sponsoring them. Nondemocratic authority, furthermore, does not use the (relevant) traits and ways: there is neither public enlistment nor public acknowledgment or reward for them. The moral give-and-take between the political and nonpolitical spheres is absent. There is, instead, either a regimented harmony or an imposed discontinuity between them.

There is, of course, no one type of self, of personal character, which is unique to representative democracy and wholly unlike all those types found in other systems of government. Rather, it is a matter of the emphatic presence of the traits and ways I have mentioned: such is the moral distinctiveness. And though the presence is emphatic in comparison to other kinds of society, it is still episodic and dispersed. It is a rare self that shows all the traits and ways or that shows any of them over a whole lifetime. Even autonomy is a temporary conquest constantly tending to forfeiture through forgetfulness or thoughtlessness. There are some people who—at least to the impatient eye—never show any of the traits and ways. One must not exaggerate the teacherly or educative power of the procedures and arrangements of representative democracy. Nevertheless, its existence makes a difference: it adds chapters to the record of human moral achievement which otherwise would be missing. A large difference must, in the nature of things, be made when vividly present in a society are such constant dispositions as those toward independence of spirit, the search for democracy in all the relations of life, the acceptance of moral indeterminacy, and the expectation of constitutional delicacy in all the relations of life. A culture attains some part of its distinctiveness, receives some part of its tonality, from such dispositions.

In passing it should be noted that there are alternative descriptions for the moral phenomena I have touched on and, therefore, for the type of self at home in representative democracy. More familiar perhaps (but not, for that reason, less important or eligible) are descriptions that employ the conceptions of the individual as the bearer of unearned rights and self-imposed duties, the claimant individual, the individual as owner of his or her self, the freely contracting individual, the freely associative individual, the emulative or competitive or agonistic individual, the self-made individual, the all-embracing I. These conceptions are not exactly synonymous, though they have, in various couplings and groupings, common aspects. Each catches something that the others fail to catch, or catch less effectively. Some are the precondition of others; some are richer than others; some may be the fulfillment or perfection of others. We are dealing with the complexities and numerous variations of the modern self, most abstractly considered. Which is to say that the moral distinctiveness of representative democracy finally lies in the contribution its procedures and arrangements have made and do make to the emergence and repeated redefinition of the modern self. The modern self is a partly novel self. More precisely, the procedures and arrangements of representative democracy have facilitated certain partly novel human aspirations and experiences. And because these aspirations and experiences are morally commendable, it may be that the grandeur of representative democracy lies as much in its facilitation of aspirations and experiences as in anything else that may be true of it. More than that, its characteristic failures may be outweighed, though not completely forgiven, when the contribution it thus makes to the record of human moral achievement is remembered or seen afresh.

I have so far argued in a way that seems to suggest that representative government suddenly appeared on the scene and that subsequent to its (unexplained) appearance, and because of it, a number of beneficial moral phenomena also appeared. I wish to rectify that possible impression by acknowledging two considerations. The first is that representative government has a history, often a tortured and bloody history and, when not tortured or bloody, often unself-aware or confused or groping. For all the force of these elements, however, the process of creation has had its great self-conscious, deliberate, articulated moments. Even a cursory look at the speech and writing in these moments shows that some of the moral energy behind the push for representative democracy has come from people (learned or not) who sought to hold political authority to standards that to some degree had their original home in nonpolitical life, private and social. The modern birth of representative democracy, in England, North America, and France, was itself facilitated by the urgencies of the private or domestic or neighborly voice, or the voice of friendship or brotherhood or religious devotion. There was a passion to repudiate the claimed immunity of the political sphere from the exacting requirements of the best morality of everyday life. The best moral claim of the old order—paternal benevolence—was simply not good enough; indeed was not good at all, as Tom Paine, for one, made brilliantly clear. Thus, if a more mature representative democracy facilitates certain commendable moral phenomena, it is, in effect, repaying a debt to its sources. This is not to deny the fundamental significance of more purely political or impersonal arguments made in behalf of representative democracy: arguments of security, welfare, liberty, justice. Yet even these sometimes showed evidence of translation from something personal or intimate (as distinguished from selfish or self-concerned).

The second consideration is that even in a more mature representative democracy the commendable moral phenomena rest on certain sentiments and attitudes that are naturally (so to speak) suited to nonpolitical relations of life and continue their existence in partial independence of the educative influence of the political sphere. As always, there are numerous nonpolitical sources for such sentiments and attitudes as decency, fairness, detachment, delicacy, self-doubt, tentativeness, tolerance, playfulness.

All I wish to claim is that the workings of representative democracy magnify certain sentiments and attitudes and thereby strengthen and enrich them. One major result is the cluster of moral phenomena that I have mentioned. They are crystallizations or concentrations of sentiments and attitudes that may exist in any society in a weaker form, but so weak, it may be, as to leave everyday life untouched by them. At the same time, the absence of representative democracy forecloses those acts of citizenship that are linked to them.

It would be foolish to ignore the dislike or even strong aversion that many feel toward these moral phenomena. Such sentiments need not reach to representative democracy itself, the sponsor and facilitator, though sometimes they do. Rather, the feeling is that it is unfortunate that the chastening of political authority emerges with such power as a great moral instigation to the alteration of the rest of life in a consonant manner (as well as to a spasmodic citizenly adventurism). Could not a chastened political authority coexist with nonpolitical practices and relations that retained the kind of authority found elsewhere in the civilized world? Or, at least, if representative democracy must have some effect, could not that effect be slighter than it is in fact, especially (but not only) in the United States?

In the 1960s and early 1970s, the moral phenomena associated with a (systematically) chastened political authority were manifested with a heightened intensity. Long-standing tendencies in American history once again displayed themselves dramatically. The reaction has set in, as it always had in the past. From this reaction, and from some less passionate cogitations of one's own, a number of responses can be distilled. Not even a brief treatment of the moral distinctiveness of representative democracy, such as this one, can be minimally scrupulous without paying some attention to those who find the moral phenomena I have singled out to be less than commendable—in some cases, far less.

The moral phenomena require a full consideration; they should also be discussed separately and in themselves, not only as a cluster. I am not able here and now, however, to do more than make up some general points. I am guided by the sense that after all is said the phenomena are commendable, yet in some instances, barely so or ambiguously so. The political system may teach bad lessons, or good lessons badly, or lessons too advanced for its teachers and students, the people.

What I offer here is a scheme for discussion rather than a discussion itself.

Each disposition may sometimes or always be out of place, inappropriate, or destructive. For example, the quest for autonomy may be destructive of the self engaged in the quest: taking upon oneself an unusual amount of the burden of being the architect of one's soul and life may damage sanity or poise. The readiness to say no may poison that amiable fellow feeling that many kinds of personal and institutional relations need for their most productive or rewarding functioning. The democratization of all the relations of life (or as many as possible, as extensively as possible) may impair the quality of the work or effort served by the given relation or ruin the trust or affection or love that defines its very essence. A sense of moral indeterminacy may deprive a given relation of the definiteness of shape or clarity of aim it must have if it is to survive and prosper. The insistence on constitutional delicacy may paralyze a relation or convert it into a litigious one.

Each disposition may too often issue in a thin or hollow or merely ritualized effect. The quest for autonomy may lead to little more than a silly eccentricity or an unconscious conformity or a compulsive faddishness or a mere "life-style." The readiness to say no may turn into a mindless obstinacy. The democratization of the relations of life may yield only manipulation or a democratization of small matters which is subtly made into a substitution for real democracy, with honesty the greatest loser. A sense of moral indeterminacy may turn into a mindless skepticism or relativism. The insistence on constitutional delicacy may degenerate into a mechanical formalism.

Each disposition may be twinned with a pathology or an excess. The quest for autonomy, if encouraged (what an enormous paradox that is, in itself!), may tempt the base or reckless into such excesses as sensation seeking, "scoring," unending and purposeless experimentation, a practiced insincerity, an inability to maintain commitments, a refusal of the necessary limitations that performing a social role necessitates, suicidal overextension, cold indifference to the rights or needs of others, an unembarrassed immoralism. The readiness to say no, if encouraged, may inspire the already misanthropic to a life-denying reclusiveness, or to a perpetually unappeased Bartleby-like state that knows only what it does not want: what it does not want is precisely what is offered. The democratization of the relations of life, if encouraged, can easily become a sanctification of selfishness or, worse, self-indulgent indiscipline: the source of an adult inability to be anything but a child. A sense of moral indeterminacy, if encouraged, can oppress those who need surety and turn them toward nihilism or, relatedly, validate the cynic's flight from personal responsibility. The insistence on constitutional delicacy may become an excuse for obstruction or a mask for indecisiveness.

To leave aside the possibility that there may be warfare among these dispositions and that they may, therefore, create appalling contradictions for the soul that tries to embrace them all (Do I contradict myself?) the more stark possibility is that they may be at war with the continuance of the very form of government that sponsors and ratifies them. In a word, the demands on life (including the demands on the political system) which grow out of these dispositions may be too great for life (and the political system). Or, the dispositions that citizenship in a representative democracy depends on may be largely incompatible with those that representative democracy sponsors and ratifies. There may be some lethal—or at least quite dangerous—contradiction or tension between what the political system requires and what it as it were helplessly and ineluctably engenders. It is as if a system of chastened authority could endure only if the people did not take its basic moral teaching too seriously: if they did not see in the political system a metaphor of immense suggestiveness. In particular, the dispositions toward modesty, denial of gratification, obedience to legally constituted authority and its enactments, self-control, a regard for the common as opposed to the individual good, and a decent propriety—all necessary for "republican" citizenship—are gravely weakened by the so-called morally commendable dispositions I have singled out.

To ignore the foregoing contentions would be folly. Yet to conclude that all together or in some plausible selection they outweigh the worth of the dispositions fostered by representative democracy is to forsake representative democracy. It is to commit oneself to the view that a form of government is only a form of government and may operate without the sentiments and attitudes of the people as its foundation and without affecting those sentiments and attitudes in turn, and not merely affecting them in the sense of strengthening them but also in the sense of spreading them to hitherto untouched relations of life. To say it again, the workings of representative democracy, its procedures and arrangements, will inevitably impart or reinforce moral lessons, will be indefinitely expressive, will engender moral phenomena. Commendable or not, these phenomena are the true exfoliation of representative democracy, the truly distinctive consummation of distinctive procedures and arrangements. These phenomena are consonant with the procedures and arrangements of representative democracy: the nonpublic manifestation of the "spirit" of the public sphere. Certainly there are both ugliness and danger in each of these phenomena; but to see only or mostly ugliness and danger is to fail to see the meaning of representative democracy as, more than anything else, a method for chastening political authority and hence all authority. The paradox is that representative democracy may help, by its insidious educative power, to sustain and promote a culture that is, in sectors and particulars, more directly democratic, more constitutionally delicate, and more beautifully illustrative of moral indeterminacy than the political system itself; while in the encouragement given to independence of spirit in the twofold sense, it may attain its most splendid result.

Could it be, then, that a more important justification for this form of government is found in the qualities of the vast life lived apart from government (and in the qualities shown in occasional acts of citizenship) than in the general substantive tendencies of public policy which we expect from it, even at their best? To be sure, the dire possibility that representative democracy is inherently suicidal, that its virtues prepare the way for its demise, that it can survive only if it is not truly realized in the life outside the workings of government, is not just another danger like other dangers. This danger is the risk of extinction: killing the goose that lays the golden eggs. To the prophets of that doom one can answer only with a hope, supported, in the American case, by American history. The hope is that the tendency to anarchy (or seeming anarchy), the tendency to the effacement of restraint and moderation, always checks itself, even though there is never a simple restoration of the general moral condition that existed before the latest surge. But that is only a hope: no guarantees can be given. Furthermore, changed political and economic circumstances can also change the perspective from which the question of the durability of representative democracy and its morally distinctive phenomena is examined.

Some may think that the foregoing examination of the moral distinctiveness of representative democracy suffers from many blindnesses and omissions. I have paid no attention to so weighty a matter as the social and economic context, especially to the decisive fact of social and economic and hence political inequality. I have paid no attention to the quality of normal involvement—such as it is—of citizens in the political process. I have paid no attention to the daily accountability and responsiveness of representative government or to the related problems of secrecy, official lawlessness, bureaucratic independence, covert and disproportionate influence, bribery and the dependence of officeholders on the few, and the necessary and unnecessary withdrawal of large areas of public policy from the grip of the electoral system. Is it not cavalier to rest the moral distinctiveness of representative democracy on, above everything, the moral phenomena it allegedly sponsors in everyday life and in occasional or episodic acts of what must be irregular or civilly disobedient citizenship (the kind of citizenship most consonant with the dispositions I have singled out)? Have I not illicitly transferred the field of attention from the really political to the tangentially political? It may be that representative democracy can stand up to certain kinds of scrutiny in comparison with, say, party and military dictatorships of the right and left. But that may be a small achievement, even if successful withstanding of such scrutiny is granted. Is there not some tremendous cause for disappointment in the actuality of representative democracy, whether in the United States or elsewhere? Should we not—perforce only in theory—affirm the moral superiority of direct democracy: that is, affirm its superior moral distinctiveness? Would not a direct democracy—if only it were possible to have one—achieve moral effects superior to representative democracy?

My belief is that representative democracy is morally superior to direct democracy because of the dispositions I singled out. To sustain this view, I should have to be able to show the following things: (1) The peculiar moral phenomena that a direct democracy embodies in its procedures and arrangements and sponsors in the society at large are not as morally commendable as those of representative democracy. (2) No important model of direct democracy can achieve, and no actual direct democracy from the past did achieve, the moral phenomena I have singled out to nearly the same degree that I have alleged representative democracy (say, the United States) does. (3) The enormous social and economic and hence political inequalities of modern democratic society, together with the numerous enfeeblements of accountability, responsiveness, and citizenly involvement, do not threaten to overwhelm the capacity of the procedures and arrangements of representative democracy to sponsor great moral phenomena.

To take up the third point first: no one can say whether or when the fact that modern representative democracy is, in some measure, only formalistically a democracy will bring down vengeance on it. All one can say is that so far the capacity to sponsor great moral phenomena is intact. Indeed, some of the acts of episodic citizenship—say, civil disobedience in the 1960s—derived in part from the spirit of representative democracy and in part from its failures. Civil disobedience is the child of representative democracy: faithful in rebellion, faithful because rebellious. The other moral phenomena, as I maintain, are also faithful to the spirit of representative democracy: they are conceived in some kind of awareness of and pleasure in the chastening of political authority. Of course, if large numbers of people conclude that the procedures and arrangements do not work, even in some measure, as they are supposed to, then their educative power will be nullified. If any view like that of, say, Herbert Marcuse in *One-Dimensional Man*[3] becomes widespread, the game is up. Will this happen? Who can say? If it happens, will it be because the political system has become even more only formalistically a democracy? Not necessarily. One can only speculate and have one's fears (or hopes). Should the game have been up a long time ago? Should the formalism have been seen through a long time ago? No—if for no other reason than the commendable moral phenomena the political system has sponsored, while doing so in spite of all its imperfections.

The first two points are far more difficult to treat. The discussion pits actual societies against extinct societies or theoretical models. Anything said must be either vague or far too abstract. Yet there may be some point in persisting, if for no other reason than the prestige the idea of direct democracy has: the prestige of a high ideal indistinguishable from a keen longing.

We have before us as direct democracies the Greek city-states and the major theoretical contributions of Aristotle, Machiavelli, Rousseau, and Arendt. No generalization covers the disparate moral claims made by the theorists in behalf of direct democracy.[4] The sort of claim perhaps most

---

[3] Herbert Marcuse, *One-Dimensional Man* (Boston: Beacon Press, 1964).

[4] I use the word "democracy" loosely. Aristotle does not refer to the city of virtue as a democracy despite the egalitarian life of its citizens; Machiavelli advocates a direct role for the people, but in a mixed republic; and Rousseau uses "democracy" to refer only to a form of executive power, a form he rejected.

relevant to our discussion is one that holds that direct democracy (or extensive participatory politics) does truly or fully or better what representative democracy aspires to do, that representative democracy is only an approximation, if not a caricature, of direct democracy. Thus, Rousseau's theory provides the suitable starting point.

I do not mean to restate Rousseau's theory, but rather to name him as the one who memorably associated political legitimacy with direct democracy and to present a very coarse rendering of a position that is Rousseauist, at least faintly. (Obviously, the theory of direct democracy cannot stand or fall with the validity of any single philosopher's work.) I would say right off that direct democracy is the only form of politics in which a direct obligation to obey the law can be theoretically maintained. The basis is in Rousseau's mode of thinking if not in the explicit arguments. Only in direct democracy do the people literally rule themselves: there is an unambiguous because unmediated realization of the continuous consent of the governed. The governed directly impose the needed laws and public policies on themselves. Political authority is transformed beyond the chastened character it possesses in representative democracy; it is no longer remote from the people and a perpetual reminder of their alienation from power. At the same time, in the making of law and public policy there is an equality of citizenly power—one person, one vote— that no known system of representative democracy (not even in the northern states in early America) has ever achieved. The result is that law and public policy become, ideally, the considered (in some sense constitutional) judgment of one's equals. If I chance to be in a minority, I cannot morally claim to prefer my own judgment to that of my equals; nor can a minority make an analogous claim.

Less legalistically, we may say that in a system of direct democracy the people directly decide what they shall do and in what conditions they shall subsist, and do so in a way in which each counts equally. The system of representation does not provide opportunities for social and economic inequality to turn into political inequality: the politics of direct democracy is pure numbers.

In the face of the (imputed) reality of self-rule by the people and a genuinely equal citizenship within the people, what could possibly count for more? What could possibly count for more than the solution of the problem of legitimacy? Are not the moral phenomena embodied in the procedures and arrangements of direct democracy superior to those embodied in representative democracy? I would answer yes. But then I would try to unsay that yes by pointing to the moral costs of direct

democracy. I would try to show that the moral costs of political legitimacy are too great, and that, therefore, on balance, representative democracy is superior, even though it cannot offer a solution to the problem
of legitimacy that is unambiguous and unmediated. Its solution is indirect or derivative: ambiguous and mediated.

If it were just a matter of procedures and arrangements by themselves
direct democracy would be more morally commendable. (Here I revert
to the formulation in point 1 above.) If we "extend the sphere" of
considerations, however, the picture changes. If we look to the moral
phenomena that are sponsored and fail to be sponsored, the picture must
change. (Here I must combine point 2 and the second part of point 1.)
The moral costs of direct democracy (most abstractly considered) are
prohibitive, involving as they do the attenuation or loss of the commendable phenomena sponsored by representative democracy and the presence of other phenomena that are not commendable.

The source of the radical moral deficiency of direct democracy is its
social context—community. The existence of community spells the absence of certain commendable moral phenomena and the presence of
noxious ones. Some of the noxious ones follow automatically from the
absence of the commendable ones; other noxious ones grow out of the
very nature of community.

Community, in its Rousseauist understanding, must be small, simple,
and static. Every effort is made to achieve a uniformity of interests and
mentality. The people are one enlarged person; or the people are interchangeable, each with any other. When we decide I decide; when I
decide we decide. "We obey ourselves" equals "I obey myself." We move
together in the same dance: if we can be said to move at all. Our
movement is the ritual of justice.

For justice to be secured in a way that is compatible with the moral
freedom of each, there can be no individuality. That is the meaning of
community, of a uniformity of interests and mentality. Individuality
would indicate differences, divergences, contrasts, disagreements, deviations. Rousseau is not a lover of "totalitarianism": he is simply sure-
sighted about the nature of the community that realizes justice by means
of moral freedom—by means, that is, of the direct and explicit acknowledgment that each is procedurally enabled to give to the requirements of
justice. Justice is the preservation of each in his own: if the law preserves
radical inequality, how can that be justice? If there is radical inequality,
how can there fail to be arrogance and envy, exploitation and slavishness?
Community means social and economic equality (or severely limited

inequality) and hence a condition in which all are affected in the same way by laws and public policies.

This is a great moral vision; but the loss to humanity, the loss in humanity, is unspeakably great. The raw materials of the modern self are removed from community. Not enough of its necessities are accommodated: distance between people, more people than can be known or recognized, the stimulation of passion and knowledge, the sense that the world is a strange place. Moderate alienation and moderate anomie are extinguished. The preconditions of the dispositions sponsored by representative democracy are absent or enfeebled. The Rousseauist community discourages independence of spirit (in its twofold meaning) and the sense of moral indeterminacy. As for the democratization of the relations of life and the dissemination of constitutional delicacy, Rousseau is hardly famous for espousing, for example, equal relations between the sexes; and his stress on transparence and directness of expression in human relations is not conducive to constitutional delicacy, or indeed to any kind of delicacy. He is perfectly consistent: the latter two phenomena would threaten community in its solidary nature.

Thus, the political procedures and arrangements of direct democracy in its most modern form, the Rousseauist, require a social and economic context that wars on psychological and spiritual complexity, on the extensions and display of human faculties, on the illimitable annexations of human experience. On the other hand, some of the positive qualities that suit direct democracy, some of those that are not simply the reverse of the dispositions sponsored by representative democracy, are not commendable. The insularity, literal-mindedness, complacency, inexperience, crudeness, chauvinism, perhaps bellicosity, are all unattractive. The political procedures and arrangements depend on and sponsor such dispositions. If the expectation is that people who come together to decide will agree, and will agree because they are much alike and the matters they have to decide are straightforward, and if, concurrently, a feeling of uniqueness or precariousness pervades the community, what room could possibly be left for the dispositions sponsored by representative democracy? (We shall leave aside the enormous powers Rousseau grants the executive, the "brain" of the community.) Positively, how could a confident sense of superiority to the outside fail to occur? At the basis of the educative power of the procedures and arrangements of direct democracy, then, is being at one with the world, and the world understood as one's world, and one's world understood as our world. The distilled sense of such a relation to the world is that there is one and only one right way of living, of doing things, of thinking about the world, and that there is one and only one right answer for every problem or question that arises, in private life or public.

The lack of distance between citizens and political authority may also render authority much more psychologically oppressive by making any impulse to dissent into an act of shameful rebellion against oneself, of shameful inconsistency. A chastened but separate authority may be more morally advantageous than one that nobody can sever his identity from.

The life of direct democracy is the life of citizenship, public and continuous and all absorbing, and laid as an obligation on all, not freely chosen by a random few. But the life of citizenship is procrustean. Of course any life must be; at least in the absence of community, however, there can be a diversity of narrownesses, while all are encouraged to change now and then, change a bit or a lot, acquire a new narrowness, reassert autonomy. So far from being the "politics of autonomy"—there is no politics of autonomy except for group autonomy[5]—the politics of direct democracy and its social preconditions and consequences are the death of autonomy. That, perhaps, is the greatest moral cost.

In general, representative democracy is committed to respecting the boundaries of the individual and the related separation of society and state; yet it establishes a mutual moral permeability between public and nonpublic. In contrast, direct democracy effaces boundaries and separations, while subjecting everything to the publicly political imperative. This imperative repels the exploration of possibilities in nonpublic life which the spirit of representative democracy fosters. Indeed, one such possibility is community, but the voluntary and temporary community: playing seriously at community. This kind of community is conceptually related to, and often practically the same thing as, the episodic and irregular citizenship of representative democracy.

Could there not be some plausible vision of direct democracy that escapes Rousseau's constrictions of humanity? I know of none that does not disparage nonpublic life (with the possible exception of the life of contemplation). Everything is seen as intrinsically inferior to, or as an unfortunate distraction from, the life of citizenship. There is no doubt that citizenship may be valued for reasons significantly different from those of Rousseau and any similar theory of political legitimacy. Then,

---

[5] As I have tried to suggest, the use of autonomy as a political standard is misconceived. The most prominent recent effort to argue its relevance is made by Robert Paul Wolff in his *In Defense of Anarchism* (New York: Harper Torchbooks, 1970).

too, the utter simplification of society may be avoided or diminished. Nevertheless, all visions of direct democracy as a polity (rather than as a local enclave or as a voluntary and limited institution) subject life to the demands of citizenship. In doing that, all sacrifice the dispositions that the procedures and arrangements of representative democracy sponsor. No writer, it seems to me, not Aristotle or Machiavelli or Arendt, manages to show that the values embodied in the workings of direct democracy, in the activities and relations of public citizenship, equal in worth those they abandon—in particular, the dispositions I have singled out or something like them. The modern self is larger and therefore better than the classical self.

But what about Athens? In answer, one could follow Hegel's steps in *The Philosophy of History.* Or one could say that Athens was too blessed and too good to serve as a model for anyone else. Or that its nonpublic greatness depended on slavery and imperial theft. Or that it was, and necessarily, short-lived. Or that its nonpublic greatness flourished because many escaped the demands of an all-absorbing public citizenship. Or that many performed the duties of public citizenship routinely or not at all, thanks to the size of Athens. Or that though the democratization of all relations was attempted (if Plato's satire is to be believed), the other dispositions I have singled out did not: they never emerged or were repressed. The best answer is that if the adherents of direct democracy could guarantee that Athens would somewhere be reproduced on condition that the existent representative democracies gave way to numerous direct democracies, then maybe one would reconsider. In any case, Athens is exceptional. Sparta is the horror: direct democracy at its most consistent, politically segmented though it was.

The latter part of this chapter offers a sketch of a non-Madisonian way of preferring representative democracy to direct democracy. The time may come when the nostalgia for representative democracy will replace the nostalgia for direct democracy.

CHAPTER TWO

Remarks on the Procedures
of Constitutional Democracy

Here I explore tentatively the view that certain political and legal procedures, those of constitutional democracy, have intrinsic moral value. This contention is hardly novel;[1] it is also full of difficulties. I would be satisfied if I could make a few distinctions and perhaps add a bit to the labors of others.[2]

1. Undoubtedly, it is extremely tempting to think of procedures as neutral. On many occasions in the life of any institution, as well as in talk

---

I thank Professors L. A. Babb, the late E. Bruss, J. Dizard, T. Kearns, B. O'Connell, and A. Sarat, my colleagues in the Kenan Colloquium at Amherst, for all that I learned from them on the general subject of constitutional democracy, as a political form and as a culture or civilization. I also acknowledge the stimulation given to thought about procedure by John Rawls in *A Theory of Justice* (Cambridge: Harvard University Press, 1971). This chapter is a continuation of an argument made in an earlier article, "Imperfect Legitimacy," presented in 1972, and printed in Dante Germino and Klaus von Beyme, eds., *The Open Society in Theory and Practice* (The Hague: Martinus Nijhoff, 1974), 164–87.

[1] For the intrinsic moral value of the political procedures of constitutional democracies, see, among other works, Henry B. Mayo, *An Introduction to Democratic Theory* (New York: Oxford University Press, 1960); Henry S. Kariel, *The Decline of American Pluralism* (Stanford: Stanford University Press, 1961); and Carl Cohen, *Democracy* (Athens: University of Georgia Press, 1971). For the intrinsic value of the legal procedures, see Sanford H. Kadish, "Methodology and Criteria in Due Process Adjudication—A Survey and Criticism," *Yale Law Journal* 66 (January 1957), 319–63; Charles Fried, *An Anatomy of Values* (Cambridge: Harvard University Press, 1970), esp. chap. 8; and Robert S. Summers, "Evaluating and Improving Legal Processes—A Plea for 'Process Values,'" *Cornell Law Review* 60 (November 1974), 1–52.

[2] My position is closest to that of David Resnick, "Due Process and Procedural Justice," in J. Roland Pennock and John W. Chapman, eds., *Nomos XVIII: Due Process* (New York: New York University Press, 1977), 206–28, but that whole volume is rich in relevance to my theme.

about public matters, one hears that disagreement over ends or values, over policy and choices, is endless and would be fatal in the absence of a procedure to work things out. The assumption is that the essence of any procedure is regularity; that regularity is both the antithesis to strife and the guarantor of its absence; that regularity is a matter of efficient functioning; that inefficiencies are corrected by technical improvements; and that though the results of a procedure, the decisions or "outcomes" are ends or values, the procedure itself has worked neutrally to attain them.

Why is it tempting to think of procedures in this way? One main reason is to seek relief from moral perplexity. A procedure in its seeming automatism may appear to be an impersonal agent—some great machine which, once activated, accomplishes its task without the intervention of personality and all its deviations, all its deviance.[3] It seems to be a way of choosing in which no one chooses, like throwing dice or picking the short straw. Human agents are involved, but not as real agents—only as the vehicles of something not human, something outside themselves. Those unhappy with the decision may be told that they have no reason to complain: they had their chance, and no one can be blamed. The procedure was neutral and its decision must be accepted. To refuse to accept it is to try to replace neutrality by partisan or willful imposition, to reintroduce the moral confusion that the procedure was meant to dissipate.

This way of thinking need not be malign. Yet insofar as it is in the service of exonerating an established arrangement it can operate to discredit a proper sense of grievance, to silence complaint by a counterclaim of helplessness. But whatever the conservative uses of the view of procedures as neutral, the view itself is inadequate, as I hope to indicate. If we seek relief from moral perplexity in procedures, we seek it in the wrong place. If failure to agree on ends is felt as intolerable, we would inevitably have the same feeling when we looked again at the nature of procedures. Procedures are not "value-free" devices of deliverance but morally charged and therefore morally problematic modes of activity.

Alternatively, one may believe that procedures are merely neutral means to a clearly specifiable end, a serviceable technique that has been discovered under the stimulus of a commonly experienced lack. A job has to be done; everybody knows that a job has to be done. The people need a government, or there has to be a system in which a person will be tried for an alleged crime. If, in the first account, all ends but peace appear as hopelessly contestable on any given occasion, here, in the

---

[3] See Duncan Kennedy, "Legal Formality," *Journal of Legal Studies* 2 (1973), 357.

second account, ends appear as obvious: they pertain to the most basic and general human needs. Circumstances will dictate which government or which legal system (or which particular procedures) will be the best. The ends are fixed and not affected by the means used to attain them; the means have no separate moral identity and may be picked up and dropped without moral compunction. Nothing is morally at stake in the choice of procedures.

From this practical-minded or pragmatic outlook, political and legal procedures appear, then, as without intrinsic moral meaning. In response, one must acknowledge that procedures are means, are methods of getting a job done; that they would not exist without some initial need, some end in view; and that unless they are seen to get the job done, they will be distorted and perhaps discarded. Such acknowledgment, however, is compatible with further assertions that this practical outlook ignores. The great political and legal procedures of constitutional democracy are means, but not merely means; and they partly redefine the ends they serve, as they are changed by their own consequences and the emergence of new ends for them to attain. Called into being by some necessity, they convert that necessity into a positive moral opportunity, while altering the very understanding of necessity. Procedures may transcend their own root nature and become the real ends (though not statically), the real raison d'être, of the society in which they exist. Certain procedures are the soul of constitutional democracy, precisely because of their intrinsic value. I hope to indicate how the pragmatic view, like the morally skeptical view, is seriously deficient.

Other reasons for finding tempting the idea of procedures as neutral may be given. And of any given procedure one can rightly say that it shows neutrality in the sense, for example, of impartial maintenance or enforcement of the rules in all cases. I do not mean to say that this idea as a whole is either implausible or without the power to instruct. I want, rather, to resist it, certain that it is immune to annihilation: the temptations to espouse it are strong.

2. We usually say that restriction or limitation on the power of the government is the soul of constitutional democracy and that the political and legal procedures are modes of restriction (or limitation). Specifically, the political procedure (the filling of offices through contested elections held at suitably frequent intervals, decided by the majority, on the basis of universal adult suffrage) and the procedure of criminal law (due process) are modes of restriction. These two procedures would seem to be the most important procedures of constitutional democracy. We go on to

say that one other mode of restriction is characteristic of constitutional democracy: absolute prohibition of governmental intervention in certain areas of life, such as religion, speech, press, and assembly. Taken together, all these restrictions are preliminarily justified in the name of avoiding gross oppression (in the most general sense). Submission to the electorate is meant to keep officeholders on their best behavior; acceptance by the government of rules guiding it in its dealing with suspected or actual violaters of the law is meant to prevent arbitrary action; total abstention by the government in regard to many of the most sensitive areas of life is meant to leave them strong and spontaneous. Putting aside the absolute prohibitions of the First Amendment, we may say that, at its simplest level, the defense of the procedures of constitutional democracy is oriented toward an outcome or result, even if "negative" in nature— the avoidance of gross oppression. The pragmatic outlook on procedures in general (to which I have referred above) is thus brought to bear on the political and legal procedures of constitutional democracy. The end is defined in a fairly clear way: the avoidance of gross oppression; and the appropriate means, if not forever, then in the modern age, is some version or other of the electoral system and some version or other of due process of law. The means have enormous importance, but only as instruments; they are not considered to possess intrinsic value.

At the same time, the morally skeptical outlook may furnish another initial justification of the procedures of constitutional democracy. They may be seen as peculiarly likely to elicit popular acceptance because of the overall indulgence the people receive by means of them. Elected government gives the people what they want; due process of law makes it comparatively easy on them in their waywardness. With such complaisance, with this congruence of what the people want and what officeholders do, the question of values subsides. Consequently, complaint should be severely limited: it should not touch the procedures themselves, while complaint about any outcome is tolerated but seen only as a subjective expression. The political or legal procedure has spoken: the vote or verdict must be accepted. To say it again, those unhappy with the result had their chance; no one can be blamed. Hence the procedures, if understood by society in this way, attain the valuable outcome of stability but have no intrinsic value.

3. But the procedures of constitutional democracy deserve a richer defense. This is not to disparage either the avoidance of gross oppression or the stability of popular acceptance. It is only to say that valuable outcomes are not the only matter of value attached to the political and

legal procedures of constitutional democracy. These procedures are not neutral or value-free in themselves. They attain values but are also themselves valuable. Even when we take the broadest possible view of the valuable outcomes (besides the avoidance of gross oppression and the stability of popular acceptance) which the procedures attain,[4] we have not reached the essential matter. Even when we say—on the assumption that our reality permits us to—that the electoral procedure conduces to the attainment of sensible and equitable social policy, and the due process procedure conduces to the attainment of correct verdicts and punishments, and each procedure is more likely to attain these things than other procedures, we have still not reached the essential matter. We still have not given constitutional democracy the defense it deserves—or that it would deserve if social conditions were different and better.

We may say that the procedures of constitutional democracy not only *attain* valuable outcomes (attain values); they also *accommodate, embody*, and *express* values. The meaning of saying that these procedures have *intrinsic value* or that they *contain values* is that they accommodate, embody, and express (or sponsor) values. (We cannot discuss here the question of the intrinsic value, if any, of other political and legal procedures, or of other kinds of procedure. The unelaborated intuition is that the political and legal procedures of constitutional democracy are the most intrinsically valuable of all political and legal procedures.)

Let us take up the three terms and suggest briefly what they mean and how they are illustrated.

The electoral system[5] accommodates values by giving citizens—both episodic citizens, and "the political stratum" (including officeseekers)[6]— the opportunity to have morally valuable experience, and also experience

[4] See, for example, Mayo, chap. 9; and Cohen, chap. 14.

[5] I speak throughout of the electoral system. Obviously, the filling of offices is instrumental to the continuous making of policy in the largest sense. In turn, the making of policy involves other procedures, formal and informal, which may be intrinsically valuable, but which I do not specifically discuss here. All this is in addition to the value of the experience of holding office, though, of course, democratically filled offices are hardly the only ones that afford this opportunity. And there are the varieties of valuable experience one gains from regular or episodic involvements in helping to make policy, without holding formal office. Democratic political life as a whole is full of accommodation for extensive valuable experience. But my stress here is on the electoral system, which is the basic frame and hence the decisive procedure.

[6] For the concept of the political stratum, see Robert A. Dahl, *Who Governs?* (New Haven: Yale University Press, 1961), 90–94 and throughout. Dahl also throws light on the notion of episodic citizenship, though the book was published before the New Left gave its version of such participation.

that is aesthetically, spiritually, or existentially valuable. The experience is enriching, even transforming. Within the basic ground rules covering elections, such forms as the campaign, party caucuses, public opinion groups, pressure groups, protest groups, and other politically connected voluntary associations provide the occasions for regulated contest, "serious play," the democratic agon. The electoral system (and all that supports and sustains it) withdraws quantities of possible experience from the rigidities or quirks of such nonelectoral strategies as inheritance of office, personal favoritism, meritocratic promotion, or the lottery. By these withdrawals, the electoral system elicits, shapes, restrains, intensifies, civilizes, makes intelligible, and beautifies energy, courage, alertness, conflict, and aspiration; and it does so noninjuriously. Or, if it does so not entirely noninjuriously, then at least the right-minded will see that the injuries are mostly to the vanity: injuries that must hurt but should not count.

The electoral system embodies values by establishing formal relationships (first) between the government and all citizens, and (second) among all citizens. These relationships reach directly to many aspects of personal identity. The first relationship is a crystallization of the idea that superiors (officials who make and enforce the law and policies) are inferior to those whom they govern, because their authority is merely temporary and revocable, and they must ask for it and win it and yet not think of themselves as deserving or meriting it. Authority is a beggar. The people's obedience is not to natural persons, inspired understandings, or naked wills, but to officeholders using their authority by means of rules and manifesting it in rules. The electoral system is not really consonant with the idea of governmental sovereignty. The second relationship is a crystallization of the idea that though I am only a voter, and only then when I choose to be, I may nevertheless find in that status—as all the rest may find in it—a series of attributions to me as a citizen affirmed and acknowledged by my fellows, as theirs are by me. These attributions include: I count; I count only as one; I am owed an account; I take part guiltlessly; I help to determine; I press myself forward without feeling shame; I can talk back; I have a right to be talked to; I am part of the ultimate constitution of the body politic; I take sides without wickedness; I should have access; I judge and accept judgment without the odium of presumptuousness; I win even when I lose. (In passing, I would say that certain values some theorists have found embodied in the electoral system, such as individual self-determination or autonomy, and *individual* consent [as opposed to the consent of the people], seem to me not present, or present in an extremely attenuated, not to say spectral, form. Thus, the present theory of the intrinsic value of the procedures of constitutional democracy itself needs revision, when the matter at issue is the values embodied in the two relationships I have just taken up. The work of enlarging our sense of the worth of our procedures must also incorporate some important deflation.)

The electoral system expresses values by teaching valuable lessons— again, lessons that are not only morally valuable but also aesthetically, spiritually, or existentially valuable. Those who are willing to contemplate the electoral system as a whole may find in its opportunity for experience, and in its relationships, models for all sorts of institutions and for all sorts of informal, even intimate relationships as well and, besides, a sense of self, of identity characteristically democratic. The values accommodated and embodied in the political procedure may be transferred out of public life and put into social and domestic and personal life. The electoral system may be reproduced, say, in some organization; or people in an organization or institution may demand not only representation but actual direct, democratic participation; or daily life, family life, relations between men and women may all be democratized or politicized, changed into something more citizenly or egalitarian. The spectacle of the electoral system may radiate a large number of influences; it may indeed help to form or maintain a culture that thus reflects it, though sometimes distortedly or only superficially, and, of course, for good and bad. Good and bad: in reference to the health of the electoral system itself, and the health of all the electorally influenced nonpublic institutions and relations, too. What is involved is the capacity of the electoral system to work on the imagination of the beholders and lead them to see in that system illustrations of truths that spill over all confines. It operates as a continuously potent force of suggestiveness. The electoral system exemplifies or may be thought to exemplify, or may only appear to exemplify permanently valuable qualities. All of these may exist first in nonpublic life. But they are vivified and strengthened in nonpublic life when seen in the public realm. And as the public realm may alter them in absorbing them into itself, so it may alter them, by expressing them, outside itself. The spectacle is brought home.

The continuities between public and nonpublic life are complex, sometimes hidden, sometimes only incipient. Then, too, there are perhaps ineffaceable discontinuities and peculiarities; and they are probably desirable, from the point of view of both public and nonpublic life. Where, however, significant continuities appear, there we may speak of at least a partly integrated culture. To put it briefly: the electoral system helps to promote a culture of energy and dignity. Energy names the main value accommodated; dignity names the compound value embodied. Because of the public way in which the electoral system accommodates and embodies its values, it may be said to express values that are the colloquial translations (so to speak) of those accommodated and embodied; and thereby to invite their extension, in variously "translated" or adapted forms throughout society.

Of the three aspects of intrinsic value, which is the most important? I cannot answer with any confidence, except to speak quantitatively. The quantity of voters and observers is much larger than that of the more active citizens, even though almost anyone can become active. That would lead to supposing that the embodied and expressed values are more important than the accommodated values. Furthermore, embodied and expressed values seem to me to be seamless: the mere voter, influenced if only half-consciously by his or her status as voter, may be the very person who demands greater democracy in the immediate surroundings. What is more important: public status or private and social relations? To assess their relative importance is artificial. What prevents this effort from being totally unprofitable is that even if leftist criticism of the authenticity of the embodied values were true, the electoral system might still manage to express values transferrable to nonpublic life. Inauthentically democratic as a political procedure, it may still work to democratize the rest of life. The greatest kind of intrinsic value in the electoral system would then turn out to be the expressive value. The power to teach valuable lessons, however, would end if most people thought that the leftist critique was correct, that the embodied values were only deceptively present.

Let us turn now to the other great procedure of constitutional democracy: due process of law.

I realize that in speaking of due process of law one is using a term that is restricted to English-speaking jurisdictions (and other jurisdictions that have come under their influence). That means, quite baldly, that it will turn out that the English-speaking constitutional democracies contain a legal procedure—one of the two most important procedures in any constitutional democracy—that is intrinsically more valuable than the corresponding legal procedure (usually that of the civil-law tradition) in non-English-speaking constitutional democracies. Due process of law is intrinsically more valuable than the civil-law tradition of dispensing criminal justice—if we may associate justice with the deliberate infliction of pain and death.

I also realize that the term "due process" has a long history. It has been given competing interpretations. In American jurisprudence, as we know, these questions have been raised: What does the phrase mean? What is the relation between due process and the rights and entitlements specified in amendments four to eight in the Bill of Rights? If it is assumed that most or all of the specified rights and entitlements are part of the meaning of due process, how should each of them be interpreted? Are the states of the union bound by the prevailing federal interpretation of due process?

When I speak of the intrinsic superiority of due process to the civil-law tradition, I mean due process in the conceptualization made of it by Herbert L. Packer in *The Limits of the Criminal Sanction* under the name of the "Due Process Model."[7] I suppose another name for it could be "enlarged due process." Packer's contrasting term is the "Crime Control Model," which names that tendency in American jurisprudence and legal practice to narrow due process as much as possible, while still retaining a process recognizably Anglo-American. This latter tendency either excludes most or all of the specified rights and entitlements from the meaning of due process, and thus frees the states from them (where the state constitution permits); or includes them in a narrowly interpreted form, asking even less procedurally of the states than of the federal government. (Needless to say, when exponents of this tendency are faced with the clear necessity of holding the federal government to amendments four to eight, they provide narrow interpretations.)

For our purposes it does not especially matter whether or not due process includes amendments four to eight as part of its very meaning, as long as it is understood that, in this context, I do use due process to mean just that, to mean enlarged due process. It stands not only for the minimal requirements of nonarbitrary rule of law (as formulated by Lon Fuller in *The Morality of Law*[8]) but also for the adversarial system and the rights and entitlements specified in amendments four to eight, generously interpreted and read to include the exclusionary rule. (I would, however, like to think that the moral reasons given for having due process

[7] See Herbert L. Packer, *The Limits of the Criminal Sanction* (Stanford: Stanford University Press, 1968), chaps. 8–12 and throughout.

[8] See Lon L. Fuller, *The Morality of Law*, rev. ed. (New Haven: Yale University Press, 1969), chap. 2.

in the narrowest sense are sufficient to necessitate enlarged due process.) Let us put these complications to one side and consider our notion of due process.

The citizen—voter, episodic citizen, or officeseeker—is the basic unit in the electoral system, the agent who finds in it an opportunity for experience and who is implicated by it in significant and suggestive relationships. The experiencer of the intrinsic value of the political procedure is the citizen (as he or she is also the presumed beneficiary of its valuable outcomes). What do we say about due process? The government is the agent. It creates and administers a system that tries to attain the valuable outcome of legal justice. In that system, due process asserts itself by forcing abstentions and inhibitions on the government. From the perspective of intrinsic value, the government is the principal agent or actor in due process, and its intrinsically valuable actions are abstentions and inhibitions. It is restrained from doing (it restrains itself, ideally, from doing) what it would like to do, what it may think it must or should do, what other governments do as it were without thinking. (More properly, officeholders connected with the administration of criminal justice are so restrained, or restrain themselves. They are as a group the principal actor.)

But to say that is not to say that the principal agent is the principal experiencer of intrinsic value. The person who is, so to speak, the target of the abstentions and inhibitions, the one whose due process rights are recognized, is the principal experiencer of the embodied values. On the other hand, the people at large, if they are receptive, stand to learn the great lessons taught by due process, to be the principal experiencers of the expressed values.

I will now take up the aspects of intrinsic value in due process, in order.

Due process accommodates values by giving various individuals the opportunity for certain kinds of valuable experience. It gives the relevant officeholders the experience of restraint; judges, the experience of impartiality; juries, the experience of deliberation; and lawyers, the experience of serious play. But, above all, it gives suspects, defendants, and prisoners the experience of having their dignity respected when they seem, in the eyes of others and often in their own, to have lost their dignity because they failed to respect that of others. In that sense, they are the principal experiencers of the intrinsic value of due process.

But I do not think that the values accommodated by due process are nearly as important as the values it embodies and expresses. Where I find it dubious and difficult to estimate the comparative moral importance of the various aspects of the intrinsic value of the electoral system, I think we should do so when considering due process. I will only mention here this asymmetry between the political procedure and the legal procedure.

Due process embodies values by establishing formal relationships between the government and certain persons, those caught in the toils of the criminal law. In defending the extension of the particular privilege against self-incrimination to pretrial interrogation, the late Chief Justice Earl Warren succinctly stated the values which, in effect, due process as a whole embodies. In a key sentence, he wrote:

> To maintain a "fair state-individual balance," to require the government "to shoulder the entire load," . . . to respect the inviolability of the human personality, our accusatory system of criminal justice demands that the government seeking to punish an individual produce the evidence against him by its own independent labors, rather than by the cruel, simple expedient of compelling it from his own mouth.[9]

By recognizing the great rights in amendments four to eight, the government creates relationships that have moral meanings of immeasurable worth. To expand Warren's passage: no matter what you do, you can never be thought of or treated as having forfeited certain rights; vice and error have their rights; your status as person before the law is not diminished by the evil you may have done; the government may not use any means, even if efficacious, but only some means, even if seemingly inefficacious, to attain indisputably valuable outcomes; the benefit of every doubt is given to the person who is now at the mercy of the government; government will strengthen its adversary so that the contest be a good one; "inferiors" are to be treated equally; the government cannot profit from its wrongdoing; the government takes no pleasure in punishing; there is only false majesty in condemning and punishing; leniency is part of strict morality; appealing a verdict is normal; it is indecent to force a person to cooperate in his own hurt; strife is justice; and so on. Customarily, the words "fairness" and "justice" are used to name the totality of due process restraints and inhibitions. We may therefore say that due process embodies the values of fairness and justice, provided we see that both are embodied in a fully developed way. Due process seeks to do legal justice within the constraints of fairness and

[9] *Miranda v. Arizona*, 384 U.S. 436, 460 (1966).

justice. Crudely: justice is done justly. There is a unity of means and ends, not only some vague consonance. Due process is no mere luxury or trifle.

Due process expresses values by teaching valuable lessons. The way the government restrains itself and yet seems to get the job done composes a pattern that we, if prepared, may revolve in our minds and from which we may derive attitudes and motivations for our whole lives. What is at stake is more than fairness in the narrow though perfectly estimable sense: the right to notice and a hearing, and the right to know what is expected of one. What is at stake is also more than rationality, estimable as that, too, is: to let everyone have a say, to consult, to lay down clear rules and stick by them, and so on. Due process is somewhat reduced when it is equated with fairness and rationality in these senses. It is good, but not the greatest good, when the government's employment of due process in criminal law, thus reduced and adapted, serves as a model for the internal workings of all types of organizations and institutions, or at least encourages preexistent tendencies. It is, in truth, a great good to have "fundamental fairness" and decent sense spread throughout the culture.

Beyond these expressed values lie those which any individual may internalize as one goes about one's life. A person may imitate the government in its dealings with those caught in the toils of the law by practicing the everyday equivalents of the restraints and inhibitions of due process. Whereas the electoral system promotes energy (though disciplined by the rules of contest), due process promotes restraint (though not paralysis). It teaches the transcendent importance of scruples, while, to be sure, tending to inculcate some readiness to forbear altogether from some actions and to expect to feel remorse after many actions. Packer speaks of the self-doubt and self-correction that are inherent in due process.[10] We see these qualities as the essence of the values expressed, the values radiated through the society, by due process.

It may be that as a moral phenomenon constitutional democracy is most interesting when the tensions and resemblances between the electoral system and due process are studied.[11] The two major procedures absolutely belong together. But it would be wrong to say that a fine

[10] See Packer, 167–77.

[11] See, for example, Edmond Cahn, *The Predicament of Democratic Man* (New York: Macmillan, 1961); and Herbert J. Spiro, "Privacy in Comparative Perspective," in J. Roland Pennock and John W. Chapman, eds., *Nomos XIII: Privacy* (New York: Atherton, 1971), 121–48.

harmony prevails between them. Nor are they constantly at odds. In the values they attain as well as those they accommodate, embody, and express, they have in common a devotion to the idea that the individual is the moral center of society. Both are committed to the principle of dignity or "respect for persons." But they give different emphases to that principle.

The electoral system, like due process, respects the person in the capacity to suffer. They both try to reduce suffering. But in regard to the two other capacities that fill out the notion of that which in any person deserves respect—the capacity to be a free agent and the capacity to be a moral agent—the two procedures diverge. As we have said, the electoral system is actually and symbolically a procedure of energy. Its workings demand energy; its relationships create energy by creating self-respect. For that reason it pays enormous homage to the person as free agent and as moral agent, more, by far, than any modern alternative. It liberates.

What of due process? It begins and ends by trying to reduce suffering, to reduce the suffering of those who may have caused others to suffer. The kinds of energy it liberates in judges, juries, lawyers, and even in shrewd and alert suspects and defendants are commendable for the most part, but not large. They are anyway found in many sectors of the culture and do not need their presence in due process to survive and flourish outside it. In fact, they are all found—even judiciousness—in the electoral system. The frame that due process provides for the free agency of these participants cannot finally count hugely. What does count hugely is that due process (in the values it embodies and expresses) tends toward the absolutist end of the moral scale. Not that in its treatment of suspects and defendants (to leave aside prisoners) it exemplifies the morality of altruism; or of resist not evil, or never inflict pain; or always be merciful or charitable or loving or caring. It is not a system that holds it is better for oneself to suffer than to inflict suffering. Nor does it show forth only leniency (though, in some secondary respects, it does). Rather, it redefines the concept of justice to embrace such qualities as generosity, detachment, and honor—the honor that consists of being willing to win only on certain terms and to lose because of a little lapse of form. If we take due process seriously, we say that we owe each other, all through life, generous, detached, and honorable conduct. The values embodied and expressed in due process comprise one of the ultimate refinements of secular morality—of *morality*, not supererogation. And due process does all this negatively, as it were: by its abstentions and inhibitions.

4. I would say, without elaboration, that some of the arrangements or structures (as distinguished loosely from procedures) of constitutional democracy can be analyzed for their intrinsic value. In American constitutional democracy, the separation of powers, checks and balances, judicial review, the federal division of powers, and a written fundamental law all may be prized for more than the valuable outcomes they were established to attain or do, in fact, attain.

5. In discussions of the intrinsic value of procedures, the question always arises, and rightly, as to how to compare the relative importance of the values contained (the intrinsic value) and the values attained. It is helpful, but not sufficient, to acknowledge that procedures are valuable apart from the valuable ends they attain. One must go on to reconnect procedures with their ends. The question is unmanageably big and amorphous. All I can do is to offer a few suggestions.

Obviously one can propose that the values accommodated, embodied, and expressed (all somehow added up) are less valuable, equally valuable, or more valuable than the values that the given procedure more or less regularly attains. Or one can simply say the procedures not only attain values, they also contain values, and then stop. Without being able to explain adequately my position, I believe that either way of talking is not the best way, even though it is useful and probably necessary. It is not only that the difficulties of comparing the relative importance of values is, in most cases, tricky, inconclusive, and maybe even misguided. In addition, talking in either way tends to create a disjunction between means and ends, procedures and outcomes, even as it tries to effect a connection between them. Of course, common sense is right to hold that means and ends can be judged independently of each other. What have I been doing so far in this paper, if not examining procedures independently of their outcomes? How could it be in any way objectionable to do as simple a thing as to judge a method for its own sake, while reserving to oneself the right to look also at its results, and then enter a judgment on them, too?

The paradoxical and therefore tentative answer is that though the need to attain some end is (conceptually) at the origin of a means (method, procedure), a means, once established, may come to be seen as the only morally right and permissible means, and that the valuable ends thought to be attained by some other means are not really the ends they are supposed to be but rather a shadowy or parodied form of those ends. To consider the value of procedures apart from outcomes is only a first step and is made necessary by the prestige of the view that the procedures of constitutional democracy are neutral instruments. The real aim is to show that outcomes cannot be valued apart from the procedures that have attained them. The intrinsic value of the electoral system and due process is not merely great, or greater than any particular outcome or pattern of outcomes; it is unique and incommensurable. Albert Camus's remark that the means justifies the ends is not a cheap reversal but another way of making our point.[12]

Rejected, on this line of argument, are two views: first, there are many means for attaining the end of, say, humane governance or dispensing legal justice; and second, the view that the best means may truly turn out to be those of constitutional democracy (the electoral system and due process), but they could as easily have turned out to be other ones. What I propose is not a new view but one that may still be thought extreme or muddled. This view is that without the electoral system as the modern basis of governance, governance lacks legitimacy; and it is therefore governance only in a manner of speaking. Without due process as the basis, legal justice cannot be done. Without the electoral system all sorts of ends may be attained, but respect for persons (in the full sense) has been denied. The ends attained cannot, for that reason, be considered as ends that serve human persons, but only, at best, human creatures. Without due process, legal justice has been attained at the expense of certain individual rights, and hence of justice, and is, for that reason, a contaminated legal justice. (Some want to say that the only guilt is legal guilt and that the only way of ascertaining legal guilt is through due process.) To put it analogically, when you change the form, you change the content.[13]

The electoral system is a *frame* for action: almost any particular result attained within it is acceptable, just as the characteristic types of ends it attains, like welfare and social innovation, are valuable. Due process is a *sieve*: almost any particular verdict that survives its abstentions and inhibitions is acceptable, just as its characteristic end, legal justice, is valuable. Both procedures, like games, create the activity they confine. The inexact metaphors of frame and sieve are intended to suggest the difference between a procedure that is used joyously and one that is used reluctantly. Indeed, though both procedures convert, as we have said, a necessity into a moral opportunity, we would not, in good conscience,

[12] See Albert Camus, *The Rebel* (1951), trans. Anthony Bower (New York: Vintage, n.d.), 292.
[13] See Packer, 166.

lament the evaporation of the necessity for due process. We would rather have a world without crime, provided it remained a world of persons and not of sheep. On the other hand, insofar, but only insofar, as government makes electoral politics possible and necessary, we could not imagine a world of persons without government. And the only legitimate (modern) government is that formed by the electoral system.

In sum, when we consider political and legal procedures, we may insist that these are the only permissible means and that they alone really attain the ends we posit. The fundamental reason for this unyielding position is that the values contained in these two procedures are necessary to establish the principle of respect for the human dignity of individuals in society as a whole, in all its relations and institutions. The values these procedures accommodate, embody, and express are necessary to the existence of persons. (Also necessary are other guarantees and conditions: most especially, an "absolutist" First Amendment.) The means are the only means and they are more than means.

Ends certainly matter when we consider the interests of a society as a whole. In smaller groups, it may very well be that almost all that mattered was, say, the quality of participation or the quality of personal relations. In forsaking ends small groups may convert life into art. A society of tens of millions cannot be theorized in this way. Our subject is procedures in such a society. But I want to be able to say that we are allowed to look at the ends only after we have looked at the means. The ends are not secondary: rather, they are not the ends we think they are unless they are attained by intrinsically valuable procedures of the sorts we have been discussing.

6. The foregoing position is shaky, I am sure. One cannot just turn away from the serious charges that have been made against both the electoral system and due process on the grounds that they fail to attain what they are supposed to attain or that they accommodate, embody, or express vice or irrationality. The principle of the indissolubility of procedures and outcomes which I have put forward can be accepted, and the charges still made.

It could be said that it takes no great wit to see that the outcomes of the electoral system and due process are open to *systemic* criticism. It is not that on occasion both procedures lapse. It is that their outcomes compose a pattern that cannot withstand moral scrutiny. If that is so, then it is likely that the procedures accommodate, embody, and express vice and irrationality. Granted that the connection between procedures and outcomes is essential and not slight or accidental: that is precisely the trouble. We are familiar with the leftist critique of the electoral system: roughly, the procedure of energy is a procedure that accommodates deception, manipulation, corruption, and irrationality; that embodies relationships of unchanging inequality between the government and all citizens and among all citizens; and that expresses values no better and really not different from those it accommodates and embodies. The electoral system is rigged in behalf of various kinds of privilege, but especially wealth. When it does not serve as an empty ritual that distracts attention from those unelected people who wield the basic power in society, it works with an irreversible bias toward the preservation of privilege. Its contests, struggles, differences, choices, debates all take place within a preposterously narrow range—especially preposterous because falsely thought indefinitely wide. The electoral system in a capitalist society is an instrument of elite dominance.

We are also familiar with the rightist critique of due process, a critique summarized in Packer's "Crime Control Model."[14] Enlarged due process (what I have been calling due process) accommodates the distortions and withholdings of lawyer and client, the general sophistry and trickery of counsel, and the irrational pedantry of old, complex, and inconsistent rules; it embodies relationships of irresponsibility, evasion, and egocentrism; and it expresses the general idea that it is all right in everyday life to go easy on yourself, to get away with anything you can, to use any method to gain an advantage, to misrepresent yourself, and to avoid merited penalties. The upshot, inevitably, is that guilty people go free or are punished much less severely than they deserve; while individual victims go unrequited, and the whole of society suffers from a legal procedure that encourages crime itself, not just noncriminal selfishness.

(A rightist critique of the electoral system and a leftist critique of due process have also been made; but at the present time they are less intimidating than the two I have just mentioned, and I can do no more here than refer to them.)

Another line of criticism challenges the indissolubility of procedures and outcomes, and the hesitations I have indicated concerning my view partly derive of course from awareness of this line. At issue is the

[14] A general defense of this model is found in Macklin Fleming, *The Price of Perfect Justice* (New York: Basic Books, 1974); and since the early 1970s in various opinions by (among others) Chief Justice Warren E. Burger and Justices Byron R. White, William H. Rehnquist, and Lewis F. Powell. Of course, elements of this tendency are found in countless other court opinions on various levels through the years and in many announcements by lawyers and officials.

constant possibility that a procedure—understood rightly as a mode of human activity—must fail on not infrequent occasions to attain ends that are worthy of that procedure. This is not systemic criticism. All it asks is that we remember that human agency is imperfect. The defense of an enhanced view of procedure should not, in its turn, repeat the inadequate idea that procedures work with an impersonal agency. Once we recall that, we are enabled to retain the right to examine the outcomes and judge them independently of the procedure that attained them. That is, we should be allowed to say that some outcomes are so gravely wrong (evil done or not prevented or not rectified) that the intrinsic value of the procedure cannot outweigh them. Impossible as it is, the effort to compare the relative importance of the values attained with the values contained must be undertaken. Ordinarily, we go along: we accept the outcome just because it is the outcome of an intrinsically valuable procedure that is preponderantly nonatrocious in its outcomes—and is nonatrocious precisely because of the nature of the procedure and the values it contains. But there are supervening occasions of individual or constitutional conscience when rejection is the rightful response, especially in regard to the political procedure.

The last line of criticism I point to is reducible to the insistence that some outcomes, actually end results or steady conditions, are attainable variously. They do not gain their identity from the procedures that bring and keep them in being. Some examples are the preservation of life; the reduction of violence; the avoidance of war; the successful conduct of diplomacy and war; the provision of the means of subsistence; the prudential toleration of many religious, intellectual, cultural, and technological endeavors; and many other policies. Specifically, governments not constituted by the electoral system may attain all these end results. In addition, the "Crime Control Model" or, indeed, some other legal procedure, may, despite all sophistry to the contrary, be able to ascertain guilt and innocence. A murderer is a murderer.

Full answers to these several lines of criticism are beyond me. To the last one, I can only concede the point. Some ends are variously attainable. But then I would insist that the status and activity of citizenship remake the world in which they exist. Life is life, peace is peace; but there is no truth in modern constitutional and democratic theory if we would be right to settle for order and security on any terms. We are not supposed to want any benefit if it is imposed, when we can have that benefit as well as an entirely transformed conception of benefit in general without nondemocratic imposition. Constitutional democracy promotes a way of life, and its distinctive features constitute its claim to moral superiority. These features are accommodated, embodied, and expressed in its political and legal procedures. On due process, specifically, no other legal procedure does justice justly. That is its specific claim to moral superiority. A murderer is a murderer, and due process will find him out without having the government itself perpetrate wrong by refusing to recognize the murderer's rights. A government loses its status as government when it does unnecessary wrong in pursuit of good; good ceases being good when unnecessary wrong has produced it.

The first two main lines of criticism are more vexatious. What they have in common is the demand that any defender of an enhanced notion of procedure pay attention to the context, to the social reality in which the procedures work. If in some respects political and legal procedures are like games in that they seem to constitute a whole world, gathering all our interest into the play, we would be mistaken if we were to lose sight of the elementary fact that a political or legal procedure is not a game. The social world is not constituted anew every day. It is there day after day in its overwhelming presence and it will intrude on the playing of a game (or the performance of any self-contained activity). Indeed, "intrude" is too remote a word, too connotative of aestheticism. Procedures absorb or "process" what is external to themselves, problems and issues; and do so because they exist to do so. Procedures have a reciprocating influence on the society that influences them. Games do not, or at least not nearly to the same degree. History and nature and culture do their mysterious work to create interests, attitudes, commitments, prejudices, traditions, passions, and reasons. People become what they are. And they, after all, are the agents and experiencers of the procedures, and the ones who are influenced by them inwardly and who benefit or fail to benefit from the results of their working. It cannot but be the case that the same procedures will, in different circumstances, yield different results. But to say that is not only to readmit the rightness of judging the procedures and the outcomes independently; it is also to say that social reality substantially affects every aspect of a political or legal procedure. I think this consideration applies with special force to the political procedure.

In America, the political procedure coexists with and preserves a condition in which many people live below the socioeconomic level of a decent life. The result is that the procedure's integrity is impaired. To revert to our analogy, the content spoils the form because the context is not wholly appropriate to the form.

Yet this point marks the limits of the concessions I would make to the view that procedures and outcomes may be judged independently. The (conceptual) right to judge in this way is a sign of the serious imperfection of social reality. With lesser imperfection we would be entitled—or more entitled—to insist on the indissolubility of means and ends, procedures and outcomes. This is not to say that the means morally outweigh the ends, but that the ends are really the ends because the only morally permissible means have attained them.

I hold on, then, to the belief that, ideally, the social reality of constitutional democracy could be such as to permit its great procedures to be perfectly themselves, untrivialized or undistorted by the degradation of millions and other deficiencies. That society does not exist in America, except approximately, or in some sectors, or in recurrent phases, or for some groups. However, only that society is genuinely a constitutional democracy, the developed civilization of constitutional democracy. Far from being neutral, the great procedures must be at the heart of thought about the moral nature of that civilization.

Democratic Individuality
and the Claims of Politics

There is common agreement that the individual is the moral center of American life. Tocqueville was one of the first to inject the word "individualism" into discourse about the American character,[1] but the feelings and attitudes that support and grow out of the centrality of the individual had of course to precede his brilliant depiction. Furthermore, American political and judicial institutions were implicated from the start in the enterprise of surrounding individuals with guarantees and protections, just as economic institutions housed individual acquisition. The general sense radiated by the actuality of the American democracy is that the individual is important or prior or precious or sacred. It may be that democracy as such must from its very nature accord such primacy to the individual. The possibly nonindividualist experience of democracy outside America must be treated circumspectly. It is an open question as to whether the Athenian democracy regarded the individual as the center. What is remarkable is the degree to which the student of American democracy can recognize America in Athens—especially in Plato's satiric-affectionate-elegiac-denunciatory account in the eighth and ninth books

I thank Morton Schoolman for his continuous encouragement, and Barry O'Connell, Michael Sandel, and Ronald Beiner for their critical remarks. This chapter is a revised version of a paper presented at the APSA in 1983.

[1] See the discussion by Steven Lukes, *Individualism* (New York: Harper & Row, 1973), 32. For accounts of earlier and later uses of the word, see Koenraad Swart, "'Individualism' in the Mid-Nineteenth Century (1826–1860)," *Journal of the History of Ideas* 32 (January–March 1962), 77–90; and Gregory Claes, "'Individualism,' 'Socialism,' and 'Social Science': Further Notes on a Process of Conceptual Formation 1800–1850," *Journal of the History of Ideas* 47 (January–March 1986), 81–93.

of *The Republic*. For all the force of such considerations as the enclosed quality of the polis, the hold of kinship, the pre- and antidemocratic past, the comparative underdevelopment of individualizing capacities that were made possible only later by Christianity (especially the encouragement of private conscience), and the existence of a *demos* (a permanent majority of the less advantaged set off against a permanent minority of the unreconciled), the Athenian democratic individual seems at least a distant cousin of the American. On the other hand, except for the United States, the major industrial democracies of the modern world—precisely because of the unpurged past—may not truly be the homes of the democratic individual, or may be so in only a significantly mixed or ambiguous manner. Thus, it is a cardinal fact that the individual is the center in the most modern democracy, the democracy least continuous with nondemocratic systems—in short, in the American democracy.

To speak, therefore, of individualism is to speak of the most characteristically democratic political and moral commitment. It would be a sign of defection from modern democracy to posit some other entity as the necessary or desirable center of life. There is therefore nothing special (much less, arbitrary) in assuming that the doctrine of the individual has the preeminent place in the theory of democracy. I would like to propose that the richest presentation of the doctrine of democratic individuality is found in the work of Emerson and his two greatest "children," Thoreau and Whitman, each also, like him, a genius. In this body of work we find the doctrine of the individual in a democracy carried to its idealist perfection. But because the word "perfection" threatens the very sort of premature closure derided by the Emersonians, let us say, instead, that their work is the best yet, the best by far.

Any philosophical consideration of the individual (or the person or "subject") which does not take this contribution into account simply ignores the richest set of ideas belonging to the field. What is at issue is the doctrine of *democratic* individuality and the way in which democracy's most elevated justification lies in its encouragement of individuality. The further possibility is that individuality's meaning is not fully disclosed until it is indissociably connected to democracy. From a democratic perspective, the Kantian tradition is seriously deficient. It cannot be taken as the sufficient doctrine of the individual because its republicanism is not culturally democratic. Even when Mill's invaluable contribution is somehow joined to that of the Kantian tradition, the doctrine of the individual must strike a democrat as incomplete. Indeed, the third chapter of *On Liberty*, "Of Individuality," is as much a defense of the individual against popular government and middle-class society as it is anything else. Similarly, the beautiful and invaluable conceptualizations found in English and German romanticism are not usually democratic in their moral and existential coloration, but rather aristocratic, and sometimes antisocial altogether. Perhaps democratization enhances them. In any case, it is completely unaccidental that the doctrine of *democratic individuality* found its modern voice in America, and that the intensification of the democratic impulse accompanied the flowering of the theory of democratic *individuality*. The relation has always been dialectical but neither term is ever superseded, or could be. These developments mark the Jacksonian period and after.

More than anyone else, Whitman strives to understand this connection between "en masse" and the individual. At times, he warns that the spirit of democracy may suffocate individuality; and therefore his writings, insofar as they *defend* any moral idea, defend individuality as the stranger idea, as the idea in need of greater elaboration and sympathy. The defense is all the more powerful because it manifestly emanates from an extreme democrat. Yet it would be mistaken to think that Whitman—or Emerson or Thoreau—ultimately believes that democracy and individuality are foreign to each other and that one can flourish only at the expense of the other. The meaning of the theory of democratic individuality is that each moral idea needs the other, both to bring out its most brilliant potentialities and to avoid the most sinister ones. A good tension would mark the relationship between these mutually dependent and mutually refining ideas. Whitman expresses it memorably:

> For to democracy, the leveler, the unyielding principle of the average, is surely join'd another principle, equally unyielding, closely tracking the first, indispensable to it, opposite, (as the sexes are opposite), and whose existence, confronting and ever modifying the other, often clashing, paradoxical, yet neither of highest avail without the other, plainly supplies to these grand cosmic politics of ours, and to the launch'd forth mortal dangers of republicanism, to-day or any day, the counterpart and offset whereby Nature restrains the deadly original relentlessness of all her first-class laws. This second principle is individuality.[2]

It is noteworthy that the ferocious modern or recent onslaughts on the doctrine of the individual often pay no attention to the fact that there is

---

[2] Walt Whitman, *Democratic Vistas* (1871), in *Leaves of Grass and Selected Prose*, ed. John Kouwenhoven (New York: Modern Library, 1950), 485.

such a thing as a doctrine of democratic individuality, and confine their attention to an unqualified individualism, a doctrine of the individual without a democratic connection. This is not to deny that the overt or implicit critiques of individualism (conceptually unconnected to democracy) made by, say, Marx, Nietzsche, and Freud, and by their followers and sympathizers (class theorists, structuralists, and deconstructionists, among others) have immense power to sow profitable doubts among adherents to democratic individuality and thus to improve the nature of their adherence and the nature of what they adhere to. But surely the discussion would be helped along if participants acknowledged that there is a moral idea of individualism other than an unqualified individualism, that democracy radically transforms the doctrine of the individual, and that the most profound expressions of the idealism of democratic individuality are found in the work of the Emersonians. Of course, repudiation of actual democracy, or at least a serious skepticism toward it, often accompanies the critique of unqualified individualism. But then, democracy is understood as the rule of the *demos* or mass or mob or herd, or as a facade for the rule of the few or of the wrong few, or as a technology of insidious regulation. It is not then understood in its connection to individuality any more than individuality is understood in connection to it. (Foucault's radical questioning of both democracy and individualism and his perception of their entwined and deceptive actuality are specifically discussed in Chapter 9.)

I also wish that the phrase "the liberal self" were used solely as a synonym for the democratic individual, in order to avoid the unhistorical, tendentious, and stultifying conflation of liberalism with either the Whig tradition or the theoretical consecration of the private life of property acquisition within the uncitizenly safety of undemocratic rule (whether absolute or constitutional). The renovation of liberalism should not be undertaken, as it usually is, in complete disregard of Emerson, Thoreau, and Whitman. Their writings are indispensable. In general, the renovation of liberalism is the renovation of both the theory of representative democracy and the theory of democratic individuality, and of the effort to connect these theories.

The view of the Emersonians on democratic individuality is not sufficient or free of difficulties. In fact, a more nearly complete and more nearly suitable theory would have to make use of other doctrines of the individual, including uncitizenly, aristocratic, and antisocial ones. There is no doubt that such other doctrines played a clear or vague part in the formation of the Emersonian view, as they played a part in the creation and development of the American democracy. Just as the powerful, modern critiques may work to ward off complacency, so other doctrines of the individual may assist the theory of democratic individuality. I believe that the most valuable addition to the Emersonian tradition would take the form of elaborating the implications of Tocqueville's concept of democratic despotism (from the second volume of *Democracy in America*) and Mill's concept of individual sovereignty (from especially the first, fourth, and fifth chapters of *On Liberty*). Present here are the substantial beginnings of a theory of individual integrity, a theory that is even more urgent now than it was in the middle of the nineteenth century. On this matter the Emersonian tradition is innocent because of its inexperience. When it turns premonitory it fears the entrepreneurial excesses of the market economy, not the statist and welfarist responses to those excesses. This notion of integrity is, of course, not the concern solely of adherents to democratic individuality: in all societies individual integrity is under constant assault; and in some societies the assault is systematic, is systemic. At the same time, we could say that a developed notion of individual integrity is the necessary foundation of the theory of democratic individuality. The political and legal realization of this notion helps to secure the preliminary conditions for democratic individuality, but it is also valuable in itself, is never superseded, and remains as a continuous standard for judging the whole culture.

The defense of individual integrity is the effort to repel, on the one hand, certain tendencies on the part of government (and other agencies of power) and, on the other hand, certain tendencies in practical thought concerning the nature of rights and duties. The two tendencies often strengthen each other but also may work separately. One governmental tendency ("democratic despotism") consists in the gradual creation by democratic government of painless oppression. It knows individuals through and through: their behavior is observed and studied, their wants are anticipated, their hurts are assuaged, their lives are mapped out. Everything is permitted but initiative. Paternalism reigns. Another governmental tendency consists in enlisting all individuals in centralized projects and thus converting them into mere members or mere means. Lives are lived as it were by permission; private lives are lived as it were on loan; and the justification is that the feeling of "community" ensues. The corrosive tendency of thought consists in the idea that rights are not attached to individuals as individuals but are granted (by society or government) on condition that they be used well or virtuously or productively or for the sake of a common purpose. Rights are thought to need justification. This tendency may be utilitarian. When it is, it is more easily fought. The more dignified hostility to rights as intrinsic to individuals, the more dignified demand for the justification of rights, is found most memorably in the work of T. H. Green, even though Mill formulates the essence of the position earlier in the fourth chapter of *On Liberty*, in order to criticize it. (We must also say that the mere fact that Mill devotes chapters two and three to justifying the liberty of *self-regarding* conduct he finds admirable represents an immense concession in itself to those who are not inclined to respect rights.)

Obviously if respect for rights characteristically resulted in havoc or in utterly trivial uses of these rights, the question of why rights (or a particular right) should be respected would legitimately arise. But the question is forced into existence usually because a particular matter or some specific condition seems to beg for a remedy that respect for rights is thought to obstruct. This forcing of the question is a sign that there is no underlying respect for rights on the part of those doing the forcing. They want some other kind of society than one in which rights are respected. To keep on demanding an answer to this question—even to ask it as if it were just another question that could be reasonably argued about—is already to be on the way to abandoning respect for rights. It is exemplary that the Bill of Rights contains no rationale.

The emphasis here, however, is on the contributions that Emerson, Thoreau, and Whitman made. I propose to give only a sketch of these contributions. I also take up one of the most serious difficulties in the overall theory: the uneasy relation between the defense of political activity and the affirmation of a more perfect democratic individuality.

Emerson, Thoreau, and Whitman (and Lincoln) are the second generation of intellect, the true inheritors of the founding of the American polity. They disclose the fuller meaning of the founding. I do not think that there has been a third generation. It may be that there has not been the need or opportunity for it, though it is impossible to know what is missing. In any case, I believe, just to speak of Emerson, Thoreau, and Whitman, that we have not fully explored their exploration of the full meanings of the founding. Their moral universe is not exhausted, or exhaustively known, though I know many persons would disagree. Of those many, a good number aspire to something less individualist and more collective.

As I have said, they are three independent geniuses, but there are influences and affinities among them. That means there is some extensive common ground, which I try to indicate by piecing together a general argument, a mosaic. I have to exclude a great deal that is related to our subject, and I do not dwell on the differences among these writers. These very differences—of emphasis, nuance, and focus of sensitivity—are indubitably instructive. It would be beneficial to emphasize them and thus try to say which writer is best on which point in the theory of democratic individuality. Even better would be the effort to keep these differences alive as essential to a theory whose power (and even coherence) allows, and may even require, unresolved tensions. I just hope to suggest the basic theory of democratic individuality which emerges from these writers.

They all encourage *democratic* individuality, not individualism pure and simple. They all try to liberate human energies; they all call their readers to live more intensely. They all find the pursuit of status and wealth the greatest of all hindrances to living intensely. They do not, however, find very much in the practice of citizenship which contributes to democratic individuality, as we shall see. But the broadest point, beyond their censure of economic life and their skepticism toward political life, is that their encouragement of democratic individuality is motivated by the fear that people do not see clearly and unrelentingly enough that all social conventions are, in fact, conventions—that is, artificial; that they are changeable; that conventions have in fact changed through time and are different from place to place. No human life can exist without conventions. But people tend to take a given network of them as natural, as nature itself—as imperative and therefore sacred; with the result that people—even in a democracy—are too timid, too unadventurous, too conformist. Consciously, half-consciously, or unknowingly, people engage in their activities and play their roles, as if no other possibilities of life existed. In "Experience," Emerson says, "It is very unhappy, but too late to be helped, the discovery we have made that we exist. That discovery is called the Fall of Man."[3] But even democratic people tend to act as if they were merely natural, as if the consciousness

[3] Ralph Waldo Emerson, "Experience" (1844), in *The Complete Essays and Other Writings*, ed. Brooks Atkinson (New York: Modern Library, 1950), 359.

of existence did not sever them from the rest of existence, as if they—we—had not therefore fallen (and hence were not capable of rebirth). They are guilty, therefore, of what existentialists later call bad faith or inauthenticity—a forgetting or attempted forgetting of our nature, which is not only natural.

All three writers begin with the knowledge that some persons actually try to live more fully as democratic individuals and that the culture as a whole is unmistakably marked by evidence of this idealism. America is not a mere repetition of the Old World. Its difference derives from its (flawed) commitment to democratic individuality. Nevertheless they also know how difficult their idealism is, and how most persons fall quite short of it. They do not, to be sure, expect that all will ever be individuals in the full democratic sense. In any case, democratic individuality is not an ideal that one can ever be certain to have reached. It is not meant to be so unequivocally defined as to be unambiguously reachable. It is not a permanent state of being, but an indefinite project. It allows of degrees, approximations, attenuations. Still, some persons try harder than others; some try *deliberately*. The strange result is that the egalitarian ideal is lived unequally; the cultural ideal is lived fitfully; the *telos* is often avoided. That is why the ideal must be advocated, yet the only appropriate advocacy is philosophical or poetical.

Though of the three writers only Whitman is explicit on the point, their work is suffused by the sense that the political arrangements of democracy conduce to a people's ability to glimpse—if only hesitantly or occasionally—the merely conventional nature of conventions, of most rules and most laws. All pay tribute to the American political system, despite their continuous guardedness. In an early and brilliant speech, Emerson talks with feeling and subtlety about the meaning of town meetings, with Concord particularly in mind.[4] More decisively, Whitman emphasizes that the skeleton of democracy, the electoral procedure, is the key to liberating democratic individuals from servility to conventions.

He compresses this sentiment in the Preface of 1855 to *Leaves of Grass*: "the terrible significance of their elections—the President's taking off his hat to them not they to him—these too are unrhymed poetry."[5] In support of his claim that "I know nothing grander . . . than a well-contested American national election," he points to the tonic effects of

[4] Emerson, "Historical Discourse" (1835), *The Complete Works of Ralph Waldo Emerson*, ed. E. W. Emerson (Boston: Houghton, Mifflin, 1903–6), 11: 27–86.

[5] Whitman, Preface, 1855, in Kouwenhoven, 442.

the electoral *agon*: "Political democracy, as it exists and practically works in America, with all its threatening evils, supplies a training-school for making first-class men. It is life's gymnasium, not of good only, but of all. We try often, though we fall back often. . . . Whatever we do not attain, we at any rate attain the experiences of the fight, the hardening of the strong campaign, and throb with currents of attempt at least." Yet it is not so much the exhilaration of involvement as the subtly powerful moral and existential message embodied in the democratic political system which matters most to Whitman:

> The purpose is not altogether direct; perhaps it is more indirect. For it is not that democracy is of exhaustive account, in itself. Perhaps, indeed, it is, (like Nature) of no account in itself. It is that, as we see, it is the best, perhaps only, fit and full means, formulater, general caller-forth, trainer, for the million, not for grand material personalities only, but for immortal souls. To be a voter with the rest is not so much; and this, like every institute, will have its imperfections. But to become an enfranchised man, and now, impediments removed, to stand and start without humiliation, and equal with the rest; to commence, or have the road clear'd to commence, the grand experiment of development, whose end, (perhaps requiring several generations) may be the forming of a full-grown man or woman—that is something.[6]

Present in the thought of all three, even if not pronounced thematically, is finally, the knowledge that the "mere" fact that all important political offices are filled by contested elections, and for a limited term, and in a way that both judges the past conduct of officeholders and provides general instruction for future ones, is a strong dissolver of the mystique of authority, first in the public realm and, ineluctably, in all others as well. The laws are changeable (even if their basic principles are not, and should not be) and are made by changeable officeholders. If the laws are such, so must be other sorts of rules and conventions. If officeholders are such, then all figures of authority endure the ordeal of scrutiny and judgment. All fathers "suffer a sea-change." Democracy is the culmination of radical protestantism.

In sum, I do not think that it is possible to understand the attacks on conventions in the name of democratic individuality except against the background of these writers' quiet celebration of the regular workings of the democratic system. Democracy unsettles everything (though not all

[6] Whitman, *Democratic Vistas*, 482, 480, 476.

at once) and therefore permits the slow growth of individuality. But it unsettles everything for everyone, and thus liberates *democratic* individuality.

Ranged against addiction to the existing conventions, the encouragement of democratic individuality is thus a call to *honesty*, to acceptance of the dangers and opportunities of being self-conscious creatures, able to see ourselves, see through and around ourselves, and thus able to reject identification with any role or set of conventions. Individuals are detached from even the conventions they accept and are free to change conventions. Let us not be afraid of self-consciousness, they urge: democracy will thrive on it. Democracy is, in secular terms, the realization of the grand historical effort to sustain social life without bad faith, and without superstition, mystique, and misdirected religiousness.

The theorists of democratic individuality want to maintain the attitude that because of the self-consciousness that democracy encourages, people can no longer pretend that they are totally enclosed within any system. If one learns to talk about one's life as if from a distance, one can at the least partly separate oneself from what one does and who one is and maybe even change one's life. The life of honesty is the critical and self-critical life, but aspiring to new release, to what Emerson, in "Circles," calls "abandonment," not to justifying old inhibitions on a new basis.

Emerson's essay "Self-Reliance," from 1841, remains the great starting point for thought about liberating the self from a religious or superstitious or unconscious bondage to roles and conventions. He says, "Society everywhere is in conspiracy against the manhood of every one of its members." But the conspiracy could not work unless we allowed it to—we take each other in. We conform. "Well, most men have bound their eyes with one or another handkerchief, and attached themselves to some one of these communities of opinion. This conformity makes them not false in a few particulars, authors of a few lies, but false in all particulars. Their every truth is not quite true. Their two is not the real two, their four is not the real four; so that every word they say chagrins us and we know not where to begin to set them right."[7] Emerson preaches self-trust, trust in one's spontaneity and hence in one's intuitions, because they come from Nature—that is, they are not predictable

---

[7] Emerson, "Self-Reliance" (1841), in *The Complete Essays*, 148, 150–51. A memorable expression of the contrasting view is given by F. H. Bradley in "My Station and Its Duties": "If you could be as good as your world, you would be better than most likely you are, and that to wish to be better than the world is to be already on the threshold of immorality." *Ethical Studies*, 2d ed. (Oxford: Clarendon, 1927), 199.

social responses; and they may be thought prior to all conventional roles. He says that there is a ray of beauty even in trivial or impure action if it has the least mark of independence. And one should respect one's involuntary perceptions and idle reveries: my social will is "but roving" in comparison with the genuineness of the spontaneous. The power that resides in every man is new in nature, he says. And the great aim of self-reliance is to avoid having one's *force* scattered: self-trust makes new *powers* appear.[8] Conformity makes one dishonest, therefore, in this two-fold sense: intellectually dishonest because one subscribes to the lie that things as they are have to be that way and have always been that way; and existentially dishonest, because one subscribes to the lie that one is merely the totality of one's conventions, and could be nothing more, that one should accept the view that one is merely the net result of all that has happened to oneself as one has grown up in society and acquired its conventions.

Analogous to this resistance to self-loss in conventions is the uneasy obedience to the laws advocated by these writers. This attitude is codified in Emerson's famous sentence in his essay "Politics": "Good men must not obey the laws too well." This sentence is the culmination of a number of sentiments found in this essay and in many others. The pervasive sense is that individuals are likely to be better than the laws, because "every actual state is corrupt."[9] Private moral feeling, when the individual stops and takes time to think in the forum of his individual mind, is likely to be better than the moral feeling embodied in laws that are made by a process of publicity, exaggeration, competition, and compromise. Even the contents of good laws are damaged by being contained in laws, because good sentiments are damaged by being expressed in the imperative mood, by being translated into commands and backed by sanctions to ensure that they will be obeyed. Good persons are insulted when they are commanded, because they know better than those who command them what is right and wrong. That the laws, in a democracy, have their ultimate source in the group that must obey them cannot totally cure the laws of their intrinsic injury to individuals. The only thing that deserves to be obeyed well is the true source of good law: the highest moral feeling.

---

[8] Emerson, "Self-Reliance," 155, 150, 162.

[9] Emerson, "Politics" (1844), in *The Complete Essays*, 427. See also Henry David Thoreau, "Civil Disobedience" (1849), in *Walden and Civil Disobedience*, ed. Brooks Atkinson (New York: Modern Library, 1950), 636–37.

Obviously such an uneasy relation to law is a sign that the sphere of politics is morally dubious.

The logic of this attitude toward obedience is advocacy of limited government. In "Politics," Emerson says, "Wild liberty develops iron conscience. Want of liberty, by strengthening law and decorum, stupefies conscience. . . . the less government we have the better—the fewer laws, and the less confided power." He reminds us, "The law is only a memorandum."[10]

In the essay on civil disobedience, which Thoreau himself published under the title "Resistance to Civil Government," this advocacy of limited government is fully present. Confine government to what is expedient, says Thoreau. But if government tries to promote moral improvement by continuous activity it will degrade the people whom it is trying to improve by treating them as objects in need of repair. "That government is best which governs not at all." More important, if government commands what is seriously wrong—as, for example, maintenance of slavery, or the extermination of Indians, or an unjust war of conquest, then it must be disobeyed. He says, "I was not born to be forced. I will breathe after my own fashion." And he says that if government "is of such a nature that it requires you to be the agent of injustice to another, then, I say, break the law. . . . What I have to do is to see, at any rate, that I do not lend myself to the wrong which I condemn."[11]

Thus, these writers—Emerson and Thoreau especially—defend the individual against regulation by any agency that is starkly and publicly distinct from the individual, and against regulation by any less specifiable force that seems to permeate society and threatens to take in the susceptible individual.

I now propose a little scheme in order to distinguish the elements of democratic individuality present in the work of these writers. The categories do not have sharp demarcations but I think we need to make distinctions. The rubrics and phrases are mine.

The encouragement of democratic individuality, in the face of conformity and the wrong kinds of obedience, is the encouragement of three aspects of individuality.

[10] Emerson, "Politics," 429, 431, 423.
[11] Thoreau, "Civil Disobedience," 286, 281, 296, 290.

First, *negative individuality*, which is the disposition to disobey bad conventions and unjust laws, by oneself, and on the basis of a strict moral self-scrutiny, self-examination. The aim is not to lend oneself, one's powers, to wrongdoing, to cruelty and atrocity. The irony is that, as Thoreau puts it, "the broadest and most prevalent error requires the most disinterested virtue to sustain it. Those who, while they disapprove of the character and measures of a government, yield to it their allegiance and support are undoubtedly its most conscientious supporters, and so frequently the most serious obstacles to reform." The dutiful sinner is the object of Thoreau's wrath precisely because such a person perverts virtue by having it enlisted in the work of evil. The true individual is truly virtuous—the truly virtuous person must be prepared to disobey, and also be prepared, disposed, to engage in other forms of disobedience, like heresy, dissent, unorthodoxy, no-saying. Self-definition must proceed by way of refusal, but the motive is not that of Pontius Pilate: to wash one's hands of guilt ritualistically while standing by and letting falsehood or cruelty proceed. It is unfortunate that Thoreau urges, at one point, that one "wash his hands" of support for "enormous wrong."[12] Rather, the real motive of disengagement is to take a stand in order to encourage others to do so as well. Hence Thoreau's refusal to pay church tax and poll tax, his later help to runaway slaves, and his public adulation of John Brown.

It is worth noticing that Thoreau's acute sense of responsibility (he was a citizen of a nonslave state) is joined to an emphatic rejection of the idea that individuals exist in order actively to promote the well-being of others. What we call "do-gooding" earns the amusement and annoyance of both Emerson and Thoreau. It may be that Thoreau suspects his own strong tendency to "improve" things and therefore goes out of his way to distinguish the avoidance of involvement in wrong-doing from the use of one's energies in worthy ameliorative causes. He wants people to take care of themselves, not to be taken care of. In any case, the moral intensity of negative individuality is accompanied in Thoreau's case (it is typical) by the flat assertion that "I came into this world, not chiefly to make this a good place to live in, but to live in it, be it good or bad." Yet in living a life, in following one's pursuits, "I must first see, at least, that I do not pursue them sitting upon another man's shoulders. I must get off him first."[13]

[12] Thoreau, "Civil Disobedience," 288.
[13] Thoreau, "Civil Disobedience," 290, 288.

Second, there is *positive individuality*: the word "autonomy" catches part but not all of the content of this notion. We have already taken up the preliminary sense, the view that existent conventions repress or distort powers or potentialities for valuable experience and praiseworthy conduct. More positively, one must take responsibility for oneself—one's self must become a project, one must become the architect of one's soul. One's *dignity* resides in being, to some important degree, a person of one's own creating, making, choosing, rather than in being merely a creature or a socially manufactured, conditioned, manipulated thing: half-animal and half-mechanical and therefore wholly socialized. Living a life is not like going through motions. The encouragement of positive individuality is the encouragement of courage, so to speak: the courage to "live deliberately," as Thoreau puts it, so as not, when one came to die, discover that one had not lived.[14] We all benefit if each is not penalized, but allowed and encouraged to be himself or herself. To be oneself means to have the courage not to hide oneself from oneself or others (to get out of the closet, as we say nowadays), or to have the courage to persist in a certain direction and not tire too soon, or to break out of one's pattern and start over again.

Emerson's writings continuously advocate the idea of self as project. I would emphasize the essay "Circles" for this theme. Thoreau lived his theory by going to Walden Pond for two years and then wrote up his experience in his *Journals* and in *Walden*. And Whitman's poetry and prose celebrate the aspiration of each person to cast off embarrassment and feelings of self-rejection and emerge ever more fully as the being he or she is. He says in *Democratic Vistas* that after all has been said in behalf of subordination, deference, and duty, "it remains to bring forward and modify everything else with the idea of that Something a man is (last precious consolation of the drudging poor,) standing apart from all else, divine in his own right, and a woman in hers, sole and untouchable by any canons of authority, or any rule derived from precedent, state-safety, the acts of legislatures, or even from what is called religion, modesty, or art."[15]

Third, there is what I call *impersonal individuality*. The rupture with external regulation, when found narrowing and stultifying, is a necessary preparation for an openness to experience, for an ability to form a

---

[14] Thoreau, *Walden* (1854), in *Walden and Civil Disobedience*, 74. Compare the closing lines of Matthew Arnold's "Lines Written in Kensington Gardens" (1852): "nor let me die / Before I have begun to live."

[15] Whitman, *Democratic Vistas*, 471.

self out of all the materials that constantly impinge on the receptive soul. But this process of self-formation is itself not the thing of highest value, though it is indispensable as a mark of rejection of society's—even democratic society's—claims about itself. There is something better than the achieved or ever self-changing particularity of the individual self; there is something beyond individuality or personality or character or even individuation. What is it? The soul. What is the soul, in their view? It is of course impossible to say. I do not know what they knew or claimed to know. But there is some sense that there is divinity in each human being—some kinship with either the creator or all creation— something indestructible or inexhaustible that may, at least metaphori- cally, be called immortal. To think oneself immortal is to think oneself something more than social. That is to be reborn. To be reborn is to acquire a new relation to all experience, which may be called either a philosophical or a poetical relation to reality.

Emerson describes it in his first book, *Nature* (1836):

> Crossing a bare common, in snow puddles, at twilight, under a clouded sky, without having in my thoughts any occurrence of special good for- tune, I have enjoyed a perfect exhilaration. I am glad to the brink of fear— In the woods is perpetual youth. Within these plantations of God, a decorum and sanctity reign—and the guest sees not how he should tire of them in a thousand years. In the woods, we return to reason and faith. There I feel that nothing can befall me in life—no disgrace, no calamity (leaving me my eyes), which nature cannot repair. Standing on the bare ground—my head bathed by the blithe air and uplifted into infinite space—all mean egotism vanishes. I become a transparent eyeball; I am nothing; I see all; the currents of the Universal Being circulate through me; I am part or parcel of God—I am the lover of uncontained and immortal beauty. . . . In the tranquil landscape, and especially in the distant line of the horizon, man beholds somewhat as beautiful as his own nature.[16]

To believe in the immortality of one's soul is to be glad the world exists, and exists as it exists; is to know that no matter how long one lived (in tolerable health) one would never run out of sentences to say and write about the nature and the course of life. Immortality is another name for the possibility of infinite responsiveness. The soul would be literally immortal if the body could last.

To be beyond egotism is perhaps to *abandon* positive individuality. The

[16] Emerson, *Nature* in *The Complete Essays*, 6.

idealism certainly moves beyond Mill's hope (too pagan, too aristocratic) that the end state of developed individuality would be that "human beings become a noble and beautiful object of contemplation."[17] Being such an object is being permanently at one with oneself, present to oneself. This condition is not celebrated by the theorists of democratic individuality. Of course living experimentally matters immensely, but as much for its indication of courage and for its deflation of prevalent conventions as for itself. By the time we think through the idea of impersonal individuality we may find that it seems to relegate positive individuality to a secondary status, a necessary stage on the way to a philosophical or poetical loss of self. Impersonal individuality is still individuality only in the sense that sociality is transcended now and then, and something godlike (and childlike) is approached. (Negative individuality, on the other hand, is the sort of self-concentration, of presence to self, that is not secondary, and not to be superseded. Resistance is a perpetual possibility, because the public commission of atrocity is.) It may even be that our fuller analysis would find that the accompaniment of positive individuality is such a solemn self-possession that it impedes the growth into impersonal individuality. If the Emersonians do not emphasize the ultimate incompatibility between positive and impersonal individuality, we may. But these writers certainly incline this way. The preference for impersonal individuality over positive individuality would be, in sum, a preference for consciousness over action, for the indefinite over the social, for the intense over the well-rounded, for the episodic over the uninterrupted, for uncertainty over a false sense of completion, for the true over the fictional.

Notice, Emerson says, "all mean egotism vanishes." This impersonal individuality is thus achieved—if only in transcendent moments—when one rids oneself of the possessive grip of those qualities in oneself which one has tried hardest to acquire as distinctive, which one is proudest of. Even if they are not merely socially induced characteristics, but the attainments of a positive individuality, they are minor in themselves and serve only by their socially alienating effects on individuals to open them to possibilities beyond individuality.

In a passage in "Self-Reliance," Emerson makes another attempt to express the nature of ecstatic contemplation. He says, "Prayer that craves a particular commodity, anything less than all good, is vicious.

---

[17] John Stuart Mill, *On Liberty*, in Marshall Cohen, ed., *The Philosophy of John Stuart Mill* (New York: Modern Library, 1961), 257.

Prayer is the contemplation of the facts of life from the highest point of view. It is the soliloquy of a beholding and jubilant soul. It is the spirit of God pronouncing his works good." But if joyous contemplation is the only true prayer, this prayer transforms all it contemplates. It changes the way the world looks, and does so precisely by making all human activity appear as prayer: "He will then see prayer in all action. The prayer of the farmer kneeling in his field to weed it, the prayer of the rower kneeling with the stroke of his oar, are true prayers heard throughout nature, though for cheap ends."[18] "Though for cheap ends" cannot really diminish the trans-moral result of Emerson's philosophical embrace.

Whitman uses the idea of immortality as a way of sponsoring a poetical relation to reality which may be richer than the view of Emerson and Thoreau. For him, to believe in one's immortality is to begin to acquire the only real moral virtues, courage and generosity. And these virtues, in turn, sustain continuous and receptive involvement in life. He says in the 1855 Preface to *Leaves of Grass* that "the known universe has one complete lover and that is the greatest poet." Each of us, inspired by the poet, may become to some degree or at some moments, poets ourselves, by learning to love. The poet (and anyone in a poetical state of being) "judges not as the judge judges but as the sun falling around a helpless thing."[19]

"The perception of beauty is a moral test" says Thoreau;[20] and Whitman's life work may be said to be an elaboration of that thought. He wishes to perfect the idealism already present, though imperfectly, in democratic life, especially in the city, in New York City, the most fully democratic society in the world in his lifetime. What is already present there needs further definition and advocacy. The perfected poetical relation to reality is the content of impersonal individuality and has three elements.

The first is aesthetic: to see all persons as beautiful, even when by conventional definition they are not; to see everyone as having a style or trying to have one, and to complete or perfect it in one's own observing eye; to see a self displaying itself instead of some fragments, useful or hurtful, ugly or strange. The aesthetic thus becomes indistinguishable from the moral.

The second is overtly moral: to see all persons as human, as able to

18 Emerson, "Self-Reliance," 163.
19 Whitman, Preface, 1855, 447, 445.
20 Quoted in Joseph Wood Krutch, *Henry David Thoreau* (New York: Morrow reprint, 1974), 176.

suffer, and to sympathize with them in their ardors and their travails. He begins *Song of Myself* thus:

> I celebrate myself, and sing myself,
> And what I assume you shall assume,
> For every atom belonging to me as good belongs to you.
>
> (Sec. 1)

His *Song of Myself* is a song, a poem, every self could sing about itself, as each makes the effort, inspired by this poem, to extend himself or herself, to try to see life from the perspective of another, to know others because one knows oneself, and to identify with others because all are human, even though diverse.

> Do I contradict myself?
> Very well then I contradict myself,
> (I am large, I contain multitudes).
>
> (Sec. 51)

Included in the multitudes contained in himself are all the despised and the persecuted, not only the vigorous and the excellent. They, too, are to be understood by being seen as already part of "myself."

> I am the hounded slave, I wince at the bite of dogs,
> Hell and despair are upon me, crack and again crack the marksmen,
> I clutch the rails of the fence, my gore dribs, thinn'd with the ooze
>   of my skin
> I fall on the weeds and stones,
> The riders spur their unwilling horses, haul close,
> Taunt my dizzy ears and beat me violently over the head with ship-stocks.
>
> Agonies are one of my changes of garments,
> I do not ask the wounded person how he feels, I myself become
>   the wounded person,
> My hurts turn livid upon me as I lean on a cane and observe.
>
> (Sec. 33)

Of course, another's agonies are not one's own. Empathy cannot abolish distance, only reduce it. Then, too, a certain theatricality seems to infect Whitman's empathetic impersonations. But I read Whitman as intending by this theatricality to encourage each to observe his or her own agonies as from a distance and to abstract the self from them as much as possible.

The third aspect is existential and pertains not only to how one should perceive and understand but also to how one should act. A belief in one's inviolability allows one to take chances, to transform dead seriousness into serious play.

> People I meet, the effect upon me of my early life or the ward and city
>   I live in, or the nation,
> The latest dates, discoveries, inventions, societies, authors old and new,
> My dinner, dress, associates, looks, compliments, dues,
> The zeal or fancied indifference of some man or woman I love,
> The sickness of one of my folks or of myself, or ill-doing or loss or lack
>   of money, or depressions or exaltations,
> Battles, the horrors of fratricidal war, the fever of doubtful news,
>   the fitful events;
> These come to me days and nights and go from me again,
> But they are not the me myself.
>
> Apart from the pulling and hauling stands what I am,
> Stands amused, complacent, compassionating, idle, unitary,
> Looks down, is erect, or bends an arm on an impalpable certain rest,
> Looking with side-curved head curious what will come next,
> Both in and out of the game and watching and wondering at it.
>
> (Sec. 4)

This last line—"Both in and out of the game and watching and wondering at it"—indicates a kind of detachment that is meant to energize one's involvement by freeing it of a sickly self-interest and blinding anxiety for success.

These three elements of impersonal individuality can be extended from a poetical relation to human reality to a poetical relation to all Nature. Whitman's poetry would have us see, first, that all things in nature are beautiful, even repellent creatures and destructive natural forces. Second, all beings, animal, vegetable, and mineral are kindred to humanity, as humanity is the culmination of everything animal, vegetable, and even mineral. He goes so far as to write:

> I find I incorporate gneiss, coal, long-threaded moss, fruits, grains,
>   esculent roots,
> And am stucco'd with quadrupeds and birds all over,
> And have distanced what is behind me for good reasons,
> But call any thing back again when I desire it.
>
> (Sec. 31)

Third, all the vast universe is a game, a show of energy, a veil of illusion covering an indestructible core. Reality is in and out of itself.

One might say that the impersonal individual aims to acquire an indefatigable capacity to know and love impersonally. The view of all three writers is that a democratic society is best justified as a preparation for this individuality and is indeed justifiable as the only society in which such individuality can exist as a possibility for all. It makes possible what goes beyond it. This is not a doctrine of spiritual elitism, and it does not defend a way of life in which some toil so that others may perfect themselves. As long as misery is absent, all may aspire to be reborn: to be reborn must not be a special privilege for the few, any more than it should be a consolation for the wretched (despite Whitman's contrary moment in the above citation).

If, then, the theory of democratic individuality is made up of these components and is defined against a background of opposition to the life of economic pursuits (as well as skepticism toward political involvement), certain frequent criticisms directed to some general idea called "individualism" cannot be directed to it. More exactly, the criticisms pertain to *some* of the untransformed preliminary elements of the theory of democratic individuality. It is not to be denied that though all three American writers despise and lament the life of economic pursuits— Whitman calls the life of "moneymaking" "the great fraud upon modern civilization"[21]—they assume the desirability of the institutions of owning, of private ownership. Whitman says that "the true gravitation-hold of liberalism in the United States will be a more universal ownership of property."[22] Their idealism is thus not congenial to economic collectivism, even if it were possible to imagine that collectivism could exist without the pathologies of bureaucracy and the related pathologies of *étatisme*. Really, democratic individuality shuns too much closeness, too much "togetherness." How could it be *individuality* otherwise? Recall Emerson's reproaches to the Brook Farm experimenters and Thoreau's gesture of isolation. Whitman, of course, speaks warmly of "adhesive love," but this notion is unrelated to tight collectivity. To the contrary, Whitman's great concept of the life of the open road is antithetical to

---

[21] Whitman, Preface, 1855, 454.
[22] Whitman, *Democratic Vistas*, 478.

community (in the usual sentimental sense). The whole idealist endeavor is to confine economic pursuits and to try to avoid having them give their coloring to all of life. Thoreau goes so far as to advocate voluntary poverty.

Thus, in the first instance, the theory of democratic individuality is not to be confused with the theory of possessive individualism. Up to a certain near point, the right of possession is the guarantor of democratic individuality; after that point, it becomes the greatest adversary by accommodating indefinite acquisitiveness, and by inspiring, in reaction, redemptive collectivist proposals.

It should also be clear that democratic individuality is not an incitement to the life of intimacy, or to a domestic privatism, or to a cult of "personal relations." It is quite remarkable, for instance, to see Emerson use the same formulations interchangeably for romantic love and for friendship: the "pathos of distance" is accepted. Of course, Emerson and Thoreau (unlike Whitman, whose imagination thrives on giant scale and effects) think that the smaller the scale of human relationships, the likelier the avoidance of confusion, dishonesty, false abstraction, and the dissipation of intensity. Yet, in a famous passage in the essay "Friendship," Emerson could say, "Every man alone is sincere. At the entrance of a second person, hypocrisy begins." Even with one other person, all the perversities of unmastered conventionality may do their insidious work. (I grant that Emerson, at least here, omits the terrific possibilities of lying to oneself, when one is alone or not—one theme in Sartre's extended discussion of bad faith. It is a theme of considerable importance to the theory of democratic individuality.)

All in all, the proclaimed self-development (what I have placed under the rubric of positive individuality) can proceed with any emphasis, more private or less. The ambition is to combine an introspective capacity with any sort of engagement in life. The introspective is not the same as the intimate or the narrowly personal. Naturally, it may turn out that the insistence on introspection, on self-observation, on self-watchfulness, precludes a wholehearted loss of self in playing any social role. But this effect is desirable. The grotesque solemnity of unironical performance in the unauthored play known as social life tends to disappear. Democratic individuality is not suited, on the one hand, to efficient functioning. To the spirit of Plato, the democratic individual says, What I do is never good enough, I must always try to do better; and what I do, no matter how well, is not the only thing I am able to do, or even to do well. On the other hand, democratic individuality is not suited to the maintenance of customs and habits, of as it were congealed social relations, no matter how beautifully solid they could be in the absence of encouraged individuality. For that reason, the social observer doubtless sustains an aesthetic loss. But Whitman, especially, promises that an altogether new aesthetic will emerge—provided the theory of democratic individuality is enacted rather than fled from in cowardly panic. The beauty of the democratic surface is in the exuberance or in the reticent vagueness of individuals, not in their rehearsed discipline. "The great poems, Shakespere included, are poisonous to the idea of the pride and dignity of the common people, the life-blood of democracy."[23] New great poems are needed by and induced by the people's more robust acceptance of the theory meant for them, and that they already live in part.

Relatedly, the theory of democratic individuality found in the Emersonian tradition is not committed to a monadic conception of the "subject." Though in the second volume of *Democracy in America* Tocqueville wrote a number of acute pages on the natural Cartesianism of the American individual, we must be cautious in the way we consider this matter. Indispensable to the ideal is the individual's disposition to examine the beliefs and opinions that are offered, especially in a society overwhelmingly rich in the means of dissemination, publicity, and public relations. The three American writers are fully aware of the danger that individual independence could be a mere pretense, with the public mind owned or manipulated by an anonymous "public opinion" or coerced by demotic pressures. But even in the absence of such factors, the theory of democratic individuality makes only certain claims for the subject. Notice again that Emerson says, in the passage quoted above from *Nature*, that the intermittent moment of philosophical ecstasy carries the surprised soul to a point where "all mean egotism vanishes." Self-possession is only preliminary to loss of sense of self. But the loss of self is not equivalent to immersion in role or function, but to some philosophical or poetical apprehension. These moments are to be understood as leaving a residue, as influencing the course of one's life. They are a rebirth: only in that sense is the democratic individual self-caused. The self can never again be clutched, can never again be possessed, as it had been earlier. Just as self-watching accompanies activity, so too does the recollection of ecstasy. At the same time, Whitman is particularly fertile in suggesting how each self is many selves; each person does actually "contain multitudes." No individual is indivisible. If the self has a core, it is not

[23] Whitman, *Democratic Vistas*, 482.

anything private or social, natural or cultivated. Though Whitman does not express his thought in our idiom of the unconscious, we could also say that much of what he suggests is congruent with the idea that the self is, in some ways, a conduit for, or a passive receptacle for, "forces," whether internal or external. The self is not always master in its own house. The very notion of house—a place with a shape and frame—is not appropriate to Whitman and hence not appropriate to the theory of democratic individuality.

Nevertheless, there are limits to which any believer in democratic individuality can go in making concessions. The radical thesis, stated in recent days by such otherwise diverse writers as Althusser, Barthes, Foucault, and Derrida, is that the self (the subject) is *only* an effect of language,[24] or that it is constituted *only* by the "calling" or "hailing" of a person by a (suspect) authority,[25] or that it is created *only* as a result of the deliberate or unmeditated intervention of those who wish to impose obligations or to strengthen the hold of their domination and who therefore spread a false estimate of individual powers in order to block collectivist cooperation. The subject is a "pseudosovereign," says Foucault.[26] If all this were true, there could be no theory of democratic individuality because there could be no individuals. There would be only "products of the environment." The radical anti-individualist thesis is that, to use Sartre's formulation out of context, individuality "does not break the chain. It is simply one of the links."[27] But the excesses of this tendency of thought (which is traceable, of course, beyond its recent statements, as far back as Plato's *Republic*, at least) rest on the view that because the self is not self-created it can never be anything but totally dependent. It is as if a human self were nothing but an "it," or as if all of mental life had the involuntariness of dreaming, or as if there were no difference between being a child and being an adult. Extreme claims for the individual have been met by the extreme counterclaim that no individual could say or do anything that was not deliberately or indeliberately "programmed." Language is converted from the possibility of freedom into the instrument of

[24] Roland Barthes, *Roland Barthes*, trans. Richard Howard (New York: Hill and Wang reprint, 1977), 79. I am not sure that Barthes is here saying what I attribute to him: the word "subject" is ambiguous.

[25] Louis Althusser, *Lenin and Philosophy*, trans. Ben Brewster (New York: Monthly Review Press, 1971), 170–83.

[26] Michel Foucault, *Language, Counter-Memory, Practice*, trans. D. F. Bouchard and S. Simon (Ithaca: Cornell, 1977), 221–22.

[27] Jean-Paul Sartre, *Being and Nothingness*, trans. Hazel Barnes (New York: Washington Square Press, reprint, 1966), 275.

self-deceived bondage. But the warrant for this conversion is never given.

In sum, the theory of democratic individuality must be criticized for what it is. To insist on its substantial distinctiveness, in relation to other doctrines of the individual, is not to try to exempt it from criticism or to deny its need for revision or for further enrichment. It is only to say that much common discourse on the inadequacies of individualism do not take up the richest formulations of one particular doctrine, the theory of democratic individuality as expressed in Emerson, Thoreau, and Whitman.

Let us now turn to the claims of politics—that is, of political involvement.

These writers fully know the indebtedness to democratic society of their refashioned doctrine of the individual. But the question remains: What is the connection between this self and involvement in political life? We have already seen that Thoreau counsels a readiness to disobey. Both he and Emerson insist that the only legitimate government is one that does as little as possible, and that, indeed, though it may have to coerce, it should not presume to improve the people because it thinks itself better or aspire to run things because it conveniently assumes that people in society are incompetent to run them. If it governs, it barely governs; it certainly should not rule, as the Old World state rules. This mistrust of government as such and this desire to deflate and limit it as much as possible inhere in the view that democratic individuality is to be encouraged.

But there is more to be said. The mistrust of government and the desire to deflate and limit it point to a general disparagement and depreciation of the whole realm of politics. That is to say, not only is the idea of government as a distinct entity, apart from the people and regulating them, rejected; the idea of limited and constitutional democratic government itself comes under ineffaceable suspicion. One conceptually necessary result is that the activities of continuous and regular citizenship—the citizenship of officeholding—must also come under suspicion. Relatedly, sustained involvement in political movements is regarded in an unkind way. These views are especially strong in Emerson and Thoreau but are also present in Whitman.

They seem to think that regular political involvement is not fully compatible with any of the kinds of democratic individuality which I have schematized. They seem to think that this involvement brings out the worst in selves but does not, in compensation, bring out the best, and actually distracts from their best those who engage in it. Schematically put, regular political involvement, in the forms of officeholding (on the one hand) and joining a movement in order to work associatively for social change (on the other hand) will violate the moral rigor that is intrinsic to (what I have called) negative individuality; will not contribute opportunities for valuable experience and valuable expressiveness that may benefit the cultivation of positive individuality; and will mean no more than any other kind of activity to the soul that has had experience of the absolutely best moments, which are those of an enraptured contemplation. Political activity has more nobility than careerism and moneymaking; but to grant that much is to grant very little.

Two considerations stand out. First, the claim is that the morality of both officeholding and involvement in a movement is too low. Second, holding office or being a leader in a movement is to assume a superordinate position and hence to offend against *democratic* individuality. That the subordinates may accept the situation in any spirit but that of shame condemns them. This condemnation of superordinate position is the "internal" reason for the tension between democratic individuality and political involvement. In Emerson's essay "Politics" we find both considerations concentrated.

Low moral quality. The characteristic impositions of those above on those below are manipulation, the tyranny of appearances, and general dishonesty and even charlatanry. The lie is the core of politics. Further, those who seek office are swollen with vanity; those who hold it are coarsened by power. On the other hand, those who enlist in a movement lose their selves in the imperatives of association: they become thoughtless, swept away by their passions or interests; they fail to accord justice to others because of the vehemence of their partisanship; they become morally insensitive or blind in their zeal to prevail. (On the last point, Emerson insists that those who try to reform others will fail unless they reform themselves first; and if they reform themselves, they are not likely to retain confidence in the ability of laws and policies to improve others.)

Superordinate position. Emerson says:

But whenever I find my dominion over myself not sufficient for me, and undertake the direction [of another person] also, I overstep the truth, and come into false relations to him. I may have so much more skill or strength than he that he cannot express adequately his sense of wrong, but it is a lie, and hurts like a lie both him and me. Love and nature cannot maintain the assumption; it must be executed by a *practical* lie, namely by force. This undertaking for another is the blunder which stands in colossal ugliness in the governments of the world. It is the same thing in numbers, as in a pair, only not quite so intelligible. . . . When a quarter of the human race assume to tell me what I must do, I may be too much disturbed by the circumstances to see so clearly the absurdity of the command. Therefore all public ends look vague and quixotic beside private ones. For any laws but those which men make for themselves are laughable.[28]

And being led unofficially is scarcely better than being commanded legally.

When this hostility to unequal position is brought up to date, especially to be shunned are those offices that call on their holders to wield discretionary power; or nakedly to issue orders; or engage regularly in secrecy, manipulation, or propaganda; or undertake activities of surveillance and "intelligence." Executive offices are, therefore, particularly dubious. They not only signify the greatest superiority over others, they also do the worst damage to the integrity (see above) of subordinate individuals. Furthermore, the idea that one person can now press the nuclear button is simply the most recent extreme form of wielding powers that in their giantism dwarf those who wield them. Thus, the life of the modern American president, in its royalty, security-consciousness, and general surrealism and irreality must be the most odious to the theory of democratic individuality.

Yet these writers do not exactly abandon politics altogether. Whitman says, "Always vote," but then quickly adds, "Disengage yourself from parties. They have been useful, and to some extent remain so; but the floating, uncommitted electors, farmers, clerks, mechanics, the masters of parties—watching aloof, inclining victory to this side or that side— such are the ones most needed, present and future."[29] (Notice the resemblance between "in and out of the game and watching and wondering at it" and "watching aloof, inclining victory.") They have their contemporary heroes: John Brown, but Lincoln, above all. Though they are distant citizens, we may say they remain citizens. The citizenship, how-

---

[28] Emerson, "Politics," 430–31.
[29] Whitman, *Democratic Vistas*, 492.

ever, that is most congenial to them is participation by lecturing and writing. As for some other, more direct action, there is only Thoreau's personal resistance. The theory of his act is that the citizenship proper to democratic individuality is only episodic or intermittent in nature; does not require continuous associative commitments; lends itself to memorable words; is of an educative or consciousness-raising sort; and seeks to protest, prevent, or repair some clear and profound wrong. The key point is that by refusing to pay his poll tax, which was the most general tax, Thoreau meant to strike at the authority and majesty of the government of the Commonwealth of Massachusetts. Massachusetts was a nonslave state, but its general acquiescence made it culpable. This act is not exactly civil disobedience, because Thoreau thought that violent revolution was justified to rid America of slavery and hence that the Constitution was not a constitution because it allowed slavery, while civil disobedience is, by the usual definition, an act that tends to repair a basically legitimate government. But, to leave this matter aside, we can say that the typical politics of the theorized democratic individual is the politics of no-saying, in behalf of the claims of moral seriousness, whether such no-saying is legal or breaks some law that is directly or symbolically connected to serious wrongdoing. This kind of politics is not merely allowed but is required by negative individuality.

We could say that a modern equivalent would perhaps be the episodic citizenship of loosely and temporarily associated individuals who seek to protest and end great atrocities or who seek to protest and end violations of the Constitution, with special attention to defending the Bill of Rights and to warning against executive and bureaucratic lawlessness and overreaching.

Naturally the question arises whether this attitude, even when it is given a modern equivalent of the kind I just suggested, is adequate. (Indeed one could ask if it has ever been adequate.) Acting now and then to preserve the Constitution is not the same as acting regularly or continuously to give it life, to keep it in motion—to preserve it in some essential sense.

Notice the paradox. The constitutional democratic political system is acknowledged to be the presupposition for the emergence of the kind of self that is idealized. Yet it is thought that this system does not enlist the best energies of the ideal self, nor does it seem to require them for its successful functioning. On the one hand, the electoral procedure, the set of rules, is morally great. It embodies the great value of equal respect for persons. It radiates a strong influence beyond itself, in private and social life, by regularly chastising political authority. On the other hand, the regular play and action attached to electoral contests, and the play and action of officeholding and of other kinds of steady involvement—in short the political process—also radiates a great invigorating energy. It may also often lead to good policies. But it is not pictured as requiring the best human qualities—only those that are perhaps good enough and mixed with ones that are not so good, and ones that are stigmatizingly bad. To take part in it regularly, as something more than a voter or an episodic actor, is to take part in a great process whose greatness is not individual or personal, except on rare occasions. In short, by being indispensable to the electoral procedure, and in itself, the political process is indispensable to the emergence of democratic individuality. But it is as if this process is not *principally* valuable as a political process. It matters less as a Madisonian transmutation of base motives into golden outcomes than as an aesthetic artifice (or artifact) greater than its workers (the active political participants).

The main locus of the aestheticism of relations in a democracy is thus not social but political. The overarching form is not ritual but game. The rituals of the Old World call for the suppression of individuals for the sake of conformity to activity more beautiful, more valuable, than themselves. The democratic political game calls for some individuals to lend their less-than-best selves to activity whose meaning is not confined to itself but spreads outward to benefit all individuals.

What are the implications? From this perspective, the regular political participants are lost to sight as individuals, in their political vices and virtues. What is worse, the assumption is that they must leave their best selves at home when they enter the public realm. It is to be expected that the shrewdest participants know what they are about: they need not be mere dupes of the cunning of democratic political reason. Indeed, insofar as they *play* (play in Whitman's sense), and find in playing something at least as important as winning, they are not far from the sense that the deepest meaning of their involvement is to contribute to the maintenance of the system—in particular, to the daily re-creation of an artifice much greater than the human qualities it requires for its re-creation. The principal virtue of the participants is their willingness to take part, to play, while their vices are "put on," impersonal. Correspondingly, the artifice is much greater in the manifold ways in which it encourages democratic individuality than in the policies it enacts. The policies are necessary; they constitute the kingdom of real or supposed necessity. Ideally the normal gains and losses achieved in policies should never be terribly important. Otherwise the policies would count more than the process.

But the greatness of the process lies not in coping with necessity (harsh or not quite harsh) but in the fact that the electoral procedure could not do without it. Together, the procedure and the process constitute the system, and they embody and exemplify the highest values. In addition, the very publicness of these values is an incitement for individuals to spread versions and attenuations of them in all the relations of society. The embodied and exemplified values signify the chastisement of authority, and the changeability of rules and conventions. They thereby instill self-respect and courage. All this is indispensable to democratic individuality. Furthermore, by spreading the moral influence of its procedural and processive values to all the relations of society, the political system contributes to the general cultural sustenance of democratic individuality.

Suppose this argument begins to draw out the implications present in the three writers. What then? I do not think there can be any easy answer. "He who wills the end wills the means also" is too brutal a maxim to serve as a guide. It may be that if one is sympathetic to their idealism, one would advocate a somewhat sharper feeling of indebtedness toward the system that allows and encourages the aspirations that then disdain it, or at least outgrow it. What would follow from a sharper feeling? Could an appeal be made to the sense of duty? Is there a duty to do one's share in actively perpetuating the indispensable resource of democratic individuality? (Let us notice that the duty to defend the country in time of need, and to do one's fair share in general, is a separate issue.) I do not think that one could plausibly answer Yes. As long as there are countless people willing to take part, there can be no duty to do so, no matter how sharply indebted one felt.

Yet that is a cold answer. It would be good if people who are inclined toward the fuller realization of the democratic individuality conceptualized by Emerson, Thoreau, and Whitman were to feel ready to compromise with themselves a bit. (The writing of T. H. Green on self-denial is to the point.)[30] If by entering political life they enter a world lower than the one they leave, they may not perfect their democratic individuality; they may necessarily act inconsistently with their ideal; they may even hurt themselves with power. But because they enter it reluctantly, they may improve the chances that the political artifice that sustains their individuality will be safer. They can tell themselves that they help to sustain what sustains their best.

---

[30] Thomas Hill Green, *Prolegomena to Ethics* (1883) (New York: Apollo Editions reprint, 1969), 290–302.

A Note to
Chapters Four, Five, and Six

The following three chapters were written in the summer of 1984, part of a period filled with discussion of nuclear weapons and strategy. Some of that discussion contained a horrifying glibness and an easy contemplation of nuclear war. That government officials in a democracy could put forth doctrines that rationalized mass destruction of lives, both of their own people and of their enemies, is a permanently remarkable fact. I interpret this fact as symptomatic of a statist tendency that is not confined to nuclear doctrines but can show itself deplorably in many areas of public policy. In Chapter 4, I try to characterize the statist mentality.

I was persuaded that nuclear war harbored the possibility of human and natural extinction. I must acknowledge that the danger of great-power nuclear exchange appears highly unlikely now and in the foreseeable future. The possibility of nuclear extinction has therefore receded. Yet I believe that the perspective of extinction, the idea of attachment to existence as such, may have some use apart from the nuclear threat, if only as a thought experiment. The generally preservative tendencies of both rights-based individualism and democratic individuality are more sharply brought out when we imagine the threat of extinction. Their suitability to dangerous or desperate circumstances is made more emphatic. Besides, who knows whether the threat of extinction may not again arise from nuclear states or from some other human source? The perspective of extinction could once again be plausible.

Needless to say, arguments against any use of nuclear weapons have lost none of their relevance despite the collapse of the Soviet Union. The weapons abound and spread. Their use, no matter how confined, would be a trauma of unconfinable effects.

CHAPTER FOUR

Thinking about Human Extinction (I):
Nuclear Weapons and Individual Rights

In a poem called "Fall 1961," Robert Lowell wrote:

> All autumn, the chafe and jar
> of nuclear war;
> we have talked our extinction to death.

These words, provoked by a Berlin crisis, suggest that it is possible to kill a subject by anguished attention—indeed, to kill even a subject that is not a subject in the conventional sense at all.

Even this subject, which is infinitely more than a subject—the subject of human extinction—can become yet another source of boredom. It is not simply that anxiety from its very nature often gives way to boredom, or at least to an effort to become bored, so as not to let anxiety give way in turn to despair. It is also the case that the subject of human extinction lends itself more than any other to language that fails.

Lowell's few lines may escape that condemnation: they are memorable. The irony is that, of course, they do not discuss extinction; they only name it. They have a powerful indirectness: talk about the failure of talk. It may be, however, that this very indirectness is a great poet's way of instructing us in the foolhardiness of trying to say something about the subject of human extinction which does not kill it by boredom.

Still, such foolhardiness is needed. The subject that is not a subject must be discussed; words about it must be produced. We must reject the advice of those who in brief and undeniably interesting sentences advise us to keep quiet, so that we do not reveal the nuclear situation's true absurdity and thus somehow make the worst more likely to happen.

Allow that most of the thousands of words one has read on the encompassing theme of nuclear weapons, and the fewer words on the specific theme of human extinction, fail. They tend to be boring, even when well written. One often notices, as well, a recurrent unsteadiness in nuclear discourse: writers seem to regret what they said earlier or to lose or bury their point, or change their minds without seeming to notice. Yet we could not do without much of this writing. The deficiencies themselves teach lessons.

Even when the specific theme of human extinction is left aside, the plain fact is that the whole subject of nuclear weapons resists the effort of translation into language that is alive. The weapons are hidden; their effects on the two occasions of their use are scarcely assimilable; the theory of the possession and possible future uses of these weapons is often technical or arcane, and it is probably infected with jargon so as to discourage public discourse; the nuclear situation is covered over, in many parts, by secrets.

The whole subject is distant, invisible, unreal, except in an occasional moment of crisis. The subject of extinction, the subject that is infinitely more than a subject, is thus wrapped in the encompassing subject of nuclear weapons, which often emerges as less than a subject or, at most, as one more subject, one more item of policy in an immeasurable thicket of policies, foreign and domestic, which press for attention. To say it again, foolhardiness is needed. Praise to those who have succeeded in not killing the subject of human extinction, who have not, to begin with, made the whole subject of nuclear weapons just another issue.

Though a good number of writers help us understand the nuclear situation, only a few have manifestly set out with the sense that unless they made special efforts their language would fail them, fail their subject, fail us. I do not mean to read off an honor roll. But I must single out, at the start, Jonathan Schell's book, *The Fate of the Earth*, published in 1982. I would claim for this book the distinction of giving greater life to the subject of nuclear weapons than any other. The key to Schell's success is that he makes human extinction the center of the whole subject. He is not the first to do so. As far as I can tell, Günther Anders, the distinguished German philosopher, is the one who first insisted that adequacy to the subject required dwelling on the possibility of human extinction. But it is Schell, writing as a citizen of the first nuclear state, who has had the great effect on opinion.

Of course, not all who read the book praise it; indeed, some have complained about its prose, as if to say that Schell, more than most, "talks our extinction to death." I simply disagree with this adverse judgment. In disagreeing I acknowledge that there can be no common agreement on what words actually do give life to the theme. I would hazard the view, however, that anyone who thinks that moral philosophy has a place in the discussion of the whole subject of nuclear weapons is very likely to find Schell's book of tremendous value. Any moral philosophy is bound to place human extinction at the center of nuclear discourse.

In making human extinction the center, Schell is trying to force us to abandon the usual way of considering the subject. He is persuaded, even if he does not say it in so many words, that we cannot just inch up to the nuclear situation, so to speak. Because this situation is radically discontinuous with all other past and present dangers, those who think about it must create a break with any discourse that tends to make the nuclear situation resemble, or resemble too closely, any other danger or predicament.

So far are common sense and policy discourse from being adequate, they falsify the subject. At whatever risks, writers must take the subject away—at least for a while—from common sense and policy discourse and entrust it to philosophy, to the capacity of philosophy to disclose the obvious, to reveal the obvious, which otherwise remains hidden and obscure in the unreal familiarity inflicted on it by common sense and policy discourse.

Philosophy instigates a rupture and then tries to redefine the field. This is Schell's endeavor. At the same time—and I know it may sound frivolous to make this admission—he helps to enlarge moral philosophy. He compels its attention to a subject that, long before, professional philosophers should have addressed. Again, this success depends on the theme of human extinction. By bringing the nuclear predicament into conjunction with moral philosophy his words give a new urgency to both. Schell thus helps to open up the subject for exploration.

I would like to be able to show that, most generally, in the midst of the nuclear situation, individualism is easily the most powerful idealism, the one most able, when taken seriously, to elicit, articulate, and justify resistance—in the first instance, resistance to common sense and policy discourse. The doctrine of equal individualism, in some of its principal components is, I believe, the doctrine for the nuclear age. The origins of most but not all its important components lie in seventeenth-century

Protestant England and America; its career has been continuous in the English-speaking world (and elsewhere) since that time. Its influence has been preponderantly, if not purely, benign. I would like to be able to show, however, that its greatest benignity, its profoundest mission, is to be the most adequate idealism in a world radically discontinuous with the one in which individualism was born.

The usual view is that individualism, in any version and in all its components, is obsolete and that, when it is held on to in spite of the fact that the modern world is so different from the one in which individualism was born and perhaps played a benign part, it becomes obstructive and hence dangerous. Most of those who are sensitive to the radical discontinuity of the present time in relation to all preceding generations claim that the only adequate idealism must be collectivist. I think they are seriously wrong. My hope is to suggest some of the ways in which individualism holds within itself some great philosophical resources needed in the struggle to see the nuclear predicament truly and to protest and resist its perpetuation.

Put briefly, part of my aim is to suggest that certain individualist ideas in the realm of political theory (one sector of moral philosophy) point to the conclusion that no use of any nuclear weapon, of any size, for any purpose, by any country, is morally permissible and that those responsible for any use forfeit their right to remain in office, even where they duly hold office in a legitimate government. The abstract right of resistance, founded in individualist ideas, vindicates the effort to remove the officeholders responsible for the use. Derivative from this contention is the right of other governments and people to compel forfeiture when prudence allows, if the citizens of the responsible government do not or cannot move. These elements comprise the no-use doctrine.

In the next two chapters I begin the effort of showing that the relation to human and natural existence which individualism sponsors best conduces to the will to preserve existence in the face of the possibility of its nuclear extinction. The metaphysical aspirations intrinsic to certain forms of individualism, if taken to heart, fortify persons in the task of overcoming within themselves all that cooperates with the possibility of extinction.

The highest worth of Schell's book lies in his insistence that we should all contemplate the nuclear situation from the perspective of possible human extinction and be overcome by the obligation, no matter what, to try to avoid human extinction. Yet as Schell says, human extinction (as well as the extinction of most species in nature) is not the intention of anyone in power. What must be seen is that the absolute end can come about even though no one intends it. "We can do it," he says, "only if we don't quite know what we're doing."

Schell's work attempts to force on us an acknowledgment that sounds far-fetched and even ludicrous, an acknowledgment that the possibility of extinction is carried by any use of nuclear weapons, no matter how limited or how seemingly rational or seemingly morally justified. He himself acknowledges that there is a difference between possibility and certainty. But in a matter that is more than a matter, more than one practical matter in a vast series of practical matters, in the "matter" of extinction, we are obliged to treat a possibility—a genuine possibility— as a certainty. Humanity is not to take any step that contains even the slightest risk of extinction.

The doctrine of no-use is based on the possibility of extinction. Schell's perspective transforms the subject. He takes us away from the arid stretches of strategy and asks us to feel continuously, if we can, and feel keenly if only for an instant now and then, how utterly distinct the nuclear world is. Nuclear discourse must vividly register that distinctiveness. It is of no moral account that extinction may be only a slight possibility. No one can say how great the possibility is, but no one has yet credibly denied that by some sequence or other a particular use of nuclear weapons *may* lead to human and natural extinction. If it is not impossible it must be treated as certain: the loss signified by extinction nullifies all calculations of probability as it nullifies all calculations of costs and benefits.

Abstractly put, the connections between any use of nuclear weapons and human and natural extinction are several. Most obviously, a sizable exchange of strategic nuclear weapons can, by a chain of events in nature, lead to the earth's uninhabitability, to "nuclear winter," or to Schell's "republic of insects and grass." But the consideration of extinction cannot rest with the possibility of a sizable exchange of strategic weapons. It cannot rest with the imperative that a sizable exchange must not take place.

A so-called tactical or "theater" use, or a so-called limited use, is also prohibited absolutely, because of the possibility of immediate escalation into a sizable exchange or because, even if there were not an immediate escalation, the possibility of extinction would reside in the precedent for future use set by any use whatever in a world in which more than one power possesses nuclear weapons. Add other consequences: the con- tagious effect on nonnuclear powers who may feel compelled by a mixture of fear and vanity to try to acquire their own weapons, thus increasing the possibility of use by increasing the number of nuclear powers; and the unleashed emotions of indignation, retribution, and revenge which, if not acted on immediately in the form of escalation, can be counted on to seek expression later.

Other than full strategic uses are not confined, no matter how small the explosive power: each would be a cancerous transformation of the world. All nuclear roads lead to the possibility of extinction. It is true by definition, but let us make it explicit: the doctrine of no-use excludes any first or retaliatory or later use, whether sizable or not. No-use is the imperative derived from the possibility of extinction.

By containing the possibility of extinction, any use is tantamount to a declaration of war against humanity. It is not merely a war crime or a single crime against humanity. Such a war is waged by the user of nuclear weapons against every human individual as individual (present and future), not as citizen of this or that country. It is not only a war against the country that is the target. To respond with nuclear weapons, where possible, only increases the chances of extinction and can never, therefore, be allowed. The use of nuclear weapons establishes the right of any person or group, acting officially or not, violently or not, to try to punish those responsible for the use. The aim of the punishment is to deter later uses and thus to try to reduce the possibility of extinction, if, by chance, the particular use in question did not directly lead to extinction. The form of the punishment cannot be specified. Of course the chaos ensuing from a sizable exchange could make punishment irrelevant. The important point, however, is to see that those who use nuclear weapons are qualitatively worse than criminals, and at the least forfeit their offices.

John Locke, a principal individualist political theorist, says that in a state of nature every individual retains the right to punish transgressors or assist in the effort to punish them, whether or not one is a direct victim. Transgressors convert an otherwise tolerable condition into a state of nature which is a state of war in which all are threatened. Analogously, the use of nuclear weapons, by containing in an immediate or delayed manner the possibility of extinction, is in Locke's phrase "a trespass against the whole species" and places the users in a state of war with all people. And people, the accumulation of individuals, must be understood as of course always indefeasibly retaining the right of self-preservation, and hence as morally allowed, perhaps enjoined, to take the appropriate preserving steps.

As Locke wrote to educate people in the always radical belief that they are entitled to resist rulers who refuse to acknowledge individual rights, so we today must try to use the possibility of human extinction to alert each other to the new threat, a threat more dire than any Locke could have imagined. Locke thought that popular attitudes were the ultimate deterrent of tyranny and that only if people were used to entertaining a deep suspicion of their own inclination to docility would rulers think hard before asserting absolutist and arbitrary claims.

In the nuclear age, the deterrent effect of popular attitudes is much harder to estimate. And what, after all, could possibly serve as a deterrent, not to meditated policy but to a calamitous decision made by one or a few in a moment of rage or horror or panic or fear or confusion? Nevertheless, every effort must be made to cultivate the sense, and to disseminate it, and perhaps to spread it upward to officeholders, that using nuclear weapons puts users at war against the world, including the citizens of their own country.

No nuclear power has publicly taken into account, except casually and perhaps cynically, the possibility of extinction contained in any use whatever of nuclear weapons. Official rhetoric refers to massive casualties and massive destruction as the worst possible outcome, and then almost always as a result of a sizable exchange, not as a result of escalation from a special or limited use. We cannot say whether one day official rhetoric will systematically incorporate the perspective of extinction, and do so for some purpose other than justifying an intensified arms race. For the time being, let us assume that the possibility of extinction will be mostly ignored, or even derided, as Sidney Hook, for one, has already derided it. If that must be the case, then so be it.

Citizens, however, may find in the perspective of extinction a powerful impetus to think about the nuclear situation and to act as they can. But even they need not argue about whether extinction is a possibility. This is my crucial point. Citizens may, instead, challenge the right of any government, their own included, to threaten or to inflict massive casualties and destruction, or to act so as to risk or actually bring on such casualties and destruction to their own people. Citizens would insist, contrary to official nuclear doctrine, that a special or limited use is as unacceptable as a sizable use, because the potentiality of a sizable use is present in the other kinds. But beyond that, there is no need for further insistence on a point that governments ignore or deride—that is, the possibility of extinction.

All that citizens have to do is to focus on massive casualties and massive destruction. A theoretical barrier to such casualties and destruction is simultaneously a barrier to the nuclear source of the possibility of extinction (to leave aside such sources as biological and chemical warfare). Here then—in the possibility of massive disaster—is the theoretical battleground. And this is where the moral doctrine of individualism makes a noteworthy contribution.

Individualism is the name of many moral ideas. It would be a hopeless task to try to give it a tidy meaning. I mean to refer especially, at this point in my discussion, to moral-political ideas enunciated during the Puritan Revolution in England and in the next generation, ideas that naturally undergo both expansion and refinement in succeeding generations, in England and America. The hard theoretical work of moral-political individualism in the seventeenth century is done by the Levellers, Hobbes, and Locke. These figures are diverse, and looked at in retrospect they appear in contention with one another, whether or not they were or could have been aware of one another. Yet later generations can and did bring them in relation, and picked and chose elements from their thought, and worked on them and added to them. I would assert that some individualist ideas found in seventeenth-century English thought (which turns out to be Protestant in sensibility even where it is not Protestant in faith) alone underlie and inform the correct principles of political legitimacy and that these principles are, in turn, the very principles of the U.S. Constitution.

The American political system, as specified by the Constitution, is thus one case of political legitimacy. Or, at least, the rules and procedures specified in the Constitution accord perfectly with the principles of legitimacy, even if the American actuality, for one sort of large reason or other, shows only an imperfect, even though substantial, legitimacy. In any case, the point is that official nuclear policy violates the principles of legitimate government. Included in this overall contention is the consideration, advanced with great skill by Richard Falk and supplemented by Jeremy Stone, that the formulation and possible execution of nuclear policy are inherently undemocratic because they are substantially removed from the public political process and that they are constitutionally infirm because they suppose overriding executive power. I wish to reach to the individualist substratum of these arguments, and to their frame.

What is legitimate government? By definition a government that is *entitled* to make laws and policies, that is, to make regulations binding on all people in a society. Legitimacy is found when the form and procedures of government are such as to give as much assurance as is humanly possible that it can achieve the aims for which government exists and which only government can achieve. The principal aim of legitimate government is to protect persons against itself. Only that government is legitimate which in its form and procedures acknowledges and protects the rights of individuals against itself. In modern life, only representative and constitutionally limited government meets the standard of legitimacy.

One may distinguish simply between personal and political rights. The former are listed abstractly in the Bill of Rights or derived from it. They are rights of mind, expression, movement, activity, and association, and rights that pertain to suspects, defendants, and prisoners. Political rights involve the rights to vote and hold office.

The seventeenth-century theoretical work on individual rights contained the basic claims, the basic arguments, and, equally important, the articulation of the basic sense of human dignity which permeates these claims and arguments. The literature is rich in concepts and formulations. Just to mention a few:

(1)   The Levellers' insistence that every person has the equal right to be represented in the political deliberations that result in decisions and regulations that bind or affect everyone.

(2)   Hobbes's conception of the unrenounceable right to self-preservation, his notion of the right of every individual to transfer allegiance if his safety depends on it, his emphasis on the moral priority of avoiding premature, violent death, and his troubled reluctance to vindicate conscription.

(3)   Locke's notion of having property in oneself, his notion of the person as including one's motions, actions, and exertions.

(4)   Further, the idea that political society is founded in an agreement of individuals made for the sake of acknowledging and protecting rights—rather than in a sacralized inertia or inheritance or in kinship or ethnicity or any other nonindividualist mode—is crucial to all three political theories.

I do not say that any of these ideas is free of the need for elaboration, adaptation, revision, or correction. That work has been going on since the first statements of the seventeenth century; it continues with great vitality today. What I mean to suggest is that as long as we take the problem of political legitimacy seriously, and as long as we take the U.S.

Constitution as the specification of a legitimate form of government, we will be taking the individualism of individual rights seriously. And in doing that we enable our challenge to nuclear policy.

I have rehearsed platitudes. The justification is that these platitudes of individualism are not really platitudes. They are fundamental considerations that can wither through complacent or irritable inattention. In their withering, the way is eased for massive ruin and for the possibility of extinction. From these considerations—presumably the considerations that guide our lives—the absolute impermissibility of using nuclear weapons emerges. Individualism in the form of personal and political rights bars a government whose legitimacy rests on acknowledging and protecting those rights from acting in any way that risks or causes massive ruin at home or that threatens or inflicts it abroad.

The emphasis is on the death of millions of individuals. The subjects of illegitimate governments—for example, the people of despotic states—are covered equally by this imperative: the claim to individual rights is not an enclosed, parochial matter, but universalist in nature. Even though their own government does not acknowledge and protect their rights, any legitimate government which has an effect on them must do so insofar as it can. (Michael Walzer has already made this point in *Just and Unjust Wars* [1977].) Above all, in dealing with foreigners, a legitimate government must not inflict massive ruin. The theory of the just war and elementary notions of common humanity may disallow any policy that risks or causes massive ruin, but the underlying moral principles of the American political system independently and clearly do so.

If officials of a legitimate government use nuclear weapons or threaten to do so, and whether or not their people suffer retaliation, the officials have so grossly violated the principles of the system that they must be understood as having intended its moral destruction and therefore to have created a situation in which a revolution against them is abstractly justified in behalf of the very system they have subverted. They are the real revolutionaries.

Notice what underlies the pretended right to use or threaten to use nuclear weapons. In the case of the United States, government rhetoric invokes freedom as the value that may be defended by nuclear weapons. Freedom is the term used to refer to all those rights to which the U.S. Constitution is devoted. Yet how can there be consistent faith in rights when masses of people become passive victims? American citizens would not be *acting* to defend their freedom; they would simply be enlisted in mass death. Further, how can there be consistent faith in rights when mass death is inflicted on others? The theory of rights recognizes no difference between one's fellows and foreigners so far as negative moral entitlements are concerned: everyone has an equal claim not to have rights violated, even if positive claims to increased well-being may be nationally confined. If political freedom institutionally survived the use of nuclear weapons, its essence would have been spiritually maimed, perhaps destroyed irretrievably. The users of nuclear weapons would have engaged in a revolution against freedom.

But I think that there is a much deeper passion than a concern for freedom which underlies the pretended right to use or threaten to use nuclear weapons. It is a passion common to authorities and establishments of all states, whether they possess nuclear weapons or not. It is a passion that has come to infect even the officeholders in American democracy, even apart from nuclear policy, as if accession to office or position were like drinking from the river of forgetfulness—forgetfulness of the moral meanings of constitutional democracy. The modern energies fueling this passion are immense. The best name for the passion or the mentality is appropriately a foreign name and, also appropriately, a French one: *étatisme*. The English translation, statism, is rather pale and not at home in the language. Still, let us use it, all the while hearing *étatisme*. All executive and administrative officials, or almost all, tend to be statists, whether they are initially disposed to be or only become so after a while in office.

The constitutional tragedy is that the American political system has always been animated by a dread of statism and by a calculated effort, reinforced by strong common feelings, to avoid its importation from the Old World. "State" is not a constitutional word; its conventional use has been confined to foreign policy, where the United States is one sovereign entity in a world of sovereign entities. The conventional use is totally dissimilar from statism. Thus when we notice the presence of statism, overt or implicit, in the rationalizations of nuclear policy offered by American officials, we are thrown into a world not recognized by the Constitution. Put most broadly, it is not a world recognized by the moral ideas that underlie and inform the principles of political legitimacy. Statism is totally at war with the culture and practice of individual personal and political rights.

What is statism? From a broad range of possible meanings, we may confine ourselves for the moment to the sense present in nuclear rhetoric. Let us say that this statism is the belief that a government is not a mere government but a state and that as such it is the locus of identity of a society; that it is not only distinct from but above society; that it has rights (not merely duties); that its survival can be secured at any cost to its own society or to others. We ordinarily associate such thinking with absolute monarchy or with modern party and military dictatorships. We certainly do not think that such a belief is compatible with the Constitution or with the moral ideas connected with political legitimacy in general. Statism is a vision of life in which people are means to the end of the survival of power, in which society is understood as one great quasi-military organization or power base and in which the state is seen not only as a society's leadership but also as its reason for being.

Officials may not recognize their rhetoric and themselves in this description. But I do not see what the expressed determination to risk or engage in a sizable exchange of nuclear weapons could mean except that the idea of statism has been accepted. This point becomes especially evident when we see that American nuclear rhetoric explicitly refers to a protracted nuclear war and thus to the readiness to accept massive numbers of American deaths. Even if we choose to leave aside the rhetoric concerning limited or special nuclear uses, and also to leave aside the massive numbers of deaths in other countries, we are compelled to take in the fact that the American government says it is willing to have the American people endure countless deaths.

This willingness, in turn, can only mean that officials think that as long as the executive upper echelons survive intact, and with them a corps of military and police, the only other need is enough people left alive to supply the means necessary for the government—that is, the state—and its purposes. Its purposes are one: to remain and continue to bear the true existence and meaning of society, even when millions have been passively victimized unto death. I do not see what other implication can be drawn from any rationalization of the use of nuclear weapons in a sizable exchange. If we insist that even a so-called special or limited use carries with it the immediate or delayed possibility of escalation, then we simply say that the rationalization of any use of nuclear weapons is the most extreme form of statism and therefore is the most extreme form of illegitimate or anti-constitutionalist doctrine.

Individualist moral ideas, as they get translated into political theory, preponderantly allow for conscripted participation, if necessary, for the common defense. But the object of defense in American terms is the Constitution. The Constitution, if it is understood in a way that stays faithful to the moral ideas of individualism which underlie and inform it, certainly does not allow millions of individuals to be passively sacrificed for any purpose. Such sacrifice is no part of any agreement between consenting individuals, no part of the social contract that creates and sustains a legitimate government. A government is guilty of genocide committed against its people when it causes passive multitudes to die. Acceptable sacrifice, on the other hand, is supposedly what preserves the rights of individuals, and if some die, they are imagined to die with the sense that without their sacrifice the rights of their fellows—all of whom share the risk equally—could have been lost.

The social contract allows only defensive war for the sake of rights. (A hypothetical war to compel foreign officials who have used nuclear weapons to leave office is a derivation from this conception.) When the purpose is to defend the state at whatever cost, then one should say that nuclear doctrine has passed altogether out of the sphere of our political theory. If the use of nuclear weapons would be a revolution against the Constitution, the rationalization before the use is, in itself, an abstract revolution against it. I believe that only a renewed insistence on the individualist basis of legitimate government can begin to dismantle the nuclear rhetoric of American officials.

Alternatively, it may be said that the implicit meaning of this rhetoric is not, Let society perish as long as the state survives, but, Even if millions die the people lives on. Thus the survival of the government is here conceived as only the means to the continuation of the people, but the people is not simply the numerous individuals who comprise it. The people is the flow of generations who possess a constant identity, derived perhaps from kinship or ethnicity or race or religion or culture or history or some other bond preexistent to any individual and meant to outlast every individual. Indeed the meaning of an individual life is supposed to come from incorporation into a body that has a superindividual existence and destiny.

When the matter is put thus, it soon becomes apparent that such a way of conceiving of a people does not answer to American experience. Even more than statism this conceptualization is alien, of the Old World. Just as American government is not a state, so the American people are not a body. The American collective identity exists only through the Constitution, understood as an agreement of consenting individuals who give their consent as they grow up into adult citizenship.

The ties of citizenship are not mystical or transcendental. An association of strangers and immigrants is made civil by adherence to the idea and practices of individual rights. Individuals never lose their identity as individuals; they are never transformed into mere members or parts of a totality. Their relations are fundamentally abstract, even though entailing severe sacrifices on necessary occasions. If I have to die in doing my duty, I nevertheless am the one who dies. I die my own death. I must therefore eschew the idolatry that consists in thinking that I survive in a superindividual body. I must eschew folk mystique.

The agreement, the social contract, is made and sustained for the sake of individual rights. We do not exist for each other; that truly means that we all do not exist for the sake of a mystique. We owe each other respect, with all the duties attaching to such respect. If one gives up everything, it is not for the people, but for the rights of other individuals, including the unborn.

Really, folk mystique is so theoretically repellent in an American context that we need not make the effort of determining whether it may be the underlying meaning of official nuclear rhetoric. At the same time, unfortunately, it is clear that other nuclear powers (or possible or potential ones) share to varying degrees in folk mystique. I would simply say that this tendency constitutes a fertile source of ruin. As long as some groups of people feel that, no matter how many of them die, as long as some survive the people survives—and that, furthermore, a people is what it is by contrast with others, with other peoples—the road to massive destruction is more easily traveled.

The strength of folk mystique decreases with the strength of the moral ideas of individualism. Individualist forms of self-love may help to check the horrors of group self-love. The extension of this point is to say that just as the idea of the state, where it exists in a constitutionally limited representative democracy, is a serious and perhaps fatal predemocratic impurity, so the idea of the people is a pernicious atavism.

The moral ideas underlying and informing the political system that is acclaimed as the only legitimate one in the modern age—namely, constitutional representative democracy—exclude absolutely both sets of superstitions. From a long historical perspective, individualist ideas are recent and hence seem odd or aberrant. But we might say that they have come just in time. If taken seriously they erect theoretical barriers (reinforced by common humanity and perhaps the theory of just war) to the right of any would-be legitimate government to claim that it can ever use nuclear weapons. It is theoretically enough that any use is likely to lead to sizable uses and that sizable uses cause massive ruin.

That massive ruin carries with it the possibility of human extinction gives citizens the most drastic incentive to resist all policies that lead to massive ruin and death, even though, so far, government apologists and others deny or deal cynically with such a possibility. Well, then, let us engage nuclear doctrine on the subject of massive ruin. Of course, theories by themselves cannot act, but action is always imbued with theory in some rough form or other, and with the feelings and passions that are aroused by theory and that, to begin with, help to arouse theory. The point is to try to remind people in all democracies that their very principles—ultimately individualist—must, if taken seriously and purely, set them in opposition to all governments, including their own, especially their own, when they claim the right to use nuclear weapons.

I have said that statism is one of the main ideas that are implied in official (and lay) rhetoric rationalizing the use of nuclear weapons. But the role of statism in the nuclear situation is not confined to this function. In another form it makes another contribution. The form is best called—once again a French name is most apt—*dirigisme*, the unremitting direction by the state of all facets of life. Let us translate the word as "state activism." The contribution is indirect but insidious and pervasive, and consists of the general tendency to leave citizens in a condition of dependence which borders on helplessness. The virulent practitioners of state activism are, of course, the police state, tyranny, despotism, and totalist rule in all their varieties.

Whenever a nuclear power is also one of the latter regimes, then the disposition among a compliant population is to get used to the idea that the state, as the source of practically all benefits and penalties—all those outside the intimate sphere and many inside it—has the right to dispose of the fate of the people in any way it sees fit. The way it sees fit seems the unavoidable way. Such compliance strengthens the readiness of officials to think seriously about using nuclear weapons. Just as the people are used to the idea that the state has the right to dispose of their fate, so the state gets used to the idea that it may even use nuclear weapons in disposing of its people's fate.

My concern here, however, is not with the mentality of unfree societies but rather with that of democratic societies. I propose the idea—it is no more than a hypothesis—that the growth of state activism in a democracy is the growth, as well, of that compliance creating and resting on dependence which makes it easier for the government to think of itself as a state—not only in our earlier sense of an entity whose survival is held to be equivalent to the survival of society itself, but in the related but separate sense of an entity that is indispensable to all relations and transactions in society.

The state, in this conceptualization, is the very life of society in its normal workings, the main source of initiative, response, repair, and redress. Society lives by its discipline, which is felt mostly as benign and which is often not felt as discipline or felt at all. The government becomes all-observant, all-competent; it intervenes everywhere; and as new predicaments arise in society, it moves first to define and attempt a resolution of them. My proposed idea is that as this tendency grows—and it is already quite far advanced—people will, to an increasing degree, come to accept the government as a state. The tendency of executive officials (and some in the legislative and judicial branches) to conceive of government as a state will thus be met by the tendency of people to accept that conception. People's dependence on it will gradually condition their attitudes and their sentiments. Looking to it, they must end by looking up to it.

I believe the "logic" of this tendency, as we say, is that officials become confirmed in their sense that they, too (like their counterparts in unfree societies), may dispose of the fate of the people. Entrusted with so much everyday power, the entire corps of officials must easily find confirmation for the rationalization of the use of nuclear weapons proposed by the foreign-policy sector of officialdom.

There may be a strong, if subterranean, bond between the state as indispensable to all relations and transactions in everyday society and the state as entitled to dispose of the fate of society in nuclear war, even though officials receive no explicit confirmation of this bond by the people. Under pressure, however, a people that habitually relies on the state may turn into a too easily mobilizable population: mobilizable but otherwise immobile. My further sense is that a renewed understanding of the moral ideas of individualism is vital to the effort to challenge state activism.

I say this, knowing that some aspects of individualism do help to push democratic government in the direction of becoming a state, and to push the state into state activism. Tocqueville's prescient analysis of democratic despotism must never be forgotten. Even more important, we must not forget that he thought that democratic despotism was much more likely in those democracies in which individualism was narrowly or weakly developed and in which, therefore, the power of a full moral individualism had never corroded the statist pretensions of political authority. His main anxiety was for France and the Continent, not for America. Thus, following Tocqueville, we may say that *anti*-individualism provides no remedy for the deficiencies: the remedy is to be sought from individualism itself.

One task of a renewed and revised individualism is to challenge everyday state activism. Remote as the connection may seem, the encouragement of state activism, or the failure to resist it, contributes to nuclear statism and thus to the disposition to accept and inflict massive ruin and, with that, the unwanted and denied possibility of extinction. In the nuclear situation, one must be attentive to even remote connections that may exist between human activity and human extinction.

There are no certainties of analysis on these possible connections. And so far the worst speculative connection is not exemplified in American society. I only mean to refer to the hypothesis offered independently first by Hannah Arendt and then by Michel Foucault; namely, that where the state is regarded both by itself and by the population not as a mere protector of life against domestic or foreign violence but as the source of contented and adjusted and regularized life (through its welfarist policies and other interventions), it is subtly empowered to take the next step and become the source of mass death. What it gives it can take away, like God. But though still short of this extreme, American society is full of serious tendencies of state activism which indirectly cooperate with the possibility of extinction.

By continuously expanding the scope of governmental activity, these tendencies work against one of the principal constituent elements of individualism, the idea that each person should be subject to the smallest possible amount of government regulation. The protection of rights and the restriction of governmental activity are jointly at the service of an individual's free life.

One's life is not supposed to be arranged or designed by government or have meaning or coherence given to it by government; nor is one supposed to be helped too much, or saved from oneself, or looked at closely or continuously. One is supposed to be free, autonomous, self-reliant. Individual rights are not always abridged when government acts to substitute itself for the individual and tries to lead our lives for us. Government may abide by the constitutional limitations on itself and nevertheless fill up too many vacant places in a person's life, thus leaving too little raw material out of which a person develops on his or her own. This ideal of free being is under relentless attack, but the attack could not score its successes unless we cooperated. In cooperating we forget the ideal, or let preliminary aspects of it, like the pursuit of interests, exhaustively define the whole ideal. The very notion of rights becomes bloated because of obsession with interests and turns false to itself.

Resistance must be offered from within the ideal, not from collectivism or communitarianism, which are both on the side of making a people systematically docile and ready for mobilization. Even if nuclear weapons did not exist and there were no possibility of extinction, the fight against state activism would have to be carried on. But the link between state activism and extinction suggests itself, and a cultivated individualism must be enlisted against such activism and in behalf of avoiding massive ruin and the possibility of extinction.

———————————————

We may distinguish several kinds of inspiration to state activism. Each kind has numerous sources, some of them commendable, some petty or sordid, some of them arising from society, some instigated by the power interest of public bureaucracies. All look like responses to genuine, sometimes profound problems. All of them seem plausible and are perfectly understandable. Yet all of them conduce to transforming government into the state and to getting people into the habit of looking up to it. The individualist disdain, the well-bred contempt for authority—I do not mean complacent cynicism—is gradually forgotten. All these tendencies are therefore at the service of a potentially lethal dependence and compliance. All help to furnish the mental universe in which nuclear statism is at home, and hence unwittingly and maybe even paradoxically prepare the way for massive ruin and the possibility of extinction.

I wish to mention not particular policies, and the motives and interests behind them, but some main ideas that inspire the policies that give state activism its fields of intervention. Among these disaster-laden ideas are:

ecological holism or humanism: the view that the state must treat society as one great source of excess, waste, and pollution;

society as discipline: the view that the state exists to transform superfluous or
  otherwise ungovernable masses into docile and productive creatures;
paternalism: the view that the state is expected to remain indifferent to no sort of
  behavior, no matter how private, but must endorse what it does not penalize
  and must become the moral parent and preceptor of otherwise wayward,
  weak, self-indulgent, or stubbornly transgressive creatures;
instrumentalism: the view that every individual right is only provisional and
  probationary and may be abridged when not put to virtuous or commendable
  or socially productive uses;
therapeutic welfarism: the view that the state must go beyond relieving misery to
  nurturing, healing, and cultivating the masses;
cultural illiberalism: the view shared by conservatives, radicals, and a few others
  that the state should somehow make up for the lack of community in modern
  life and the alleged presence of pathological alienation and anomie.

Common to all these ideas is what Foucault refers to as the problem of
the modern plebs, the solution to which is the creation of order by the
training and enlistment of energies that threaten gross disorder. Indeed,
the overwhelming passion in these ideas is a passion for order, for
stillness, for regularity, for predictability, for a coherence that can exist
only as the result of a drastic purification of human inclinations and
actions, and a continued exercise of fundamentally undemocratic authority in every area of society.

One might think that there was a latent death wish in this passion,
something akin to the death wish present in utopian thought. But apart
from this direct if dreamlike connection between the sources of state
activism and the will to deathlike stillness, I would suggest that the
various encroachments of state activism help to do the awful work of
subtly, indirectly, but inexorably emboldening officials to think with an
ever-deepening seriousness the nuclear thoughts they express publicly,
and of conditioning people to depend, comply, go along, trust, even to
the extent of accepting policies that threaten massive ruin and the possibility of human and natural extinction.

It is hopeless suddenly to reverse these tendencies of state activism in
the United States or other nuclear democracies. There may be something
quixotic in even thinking to challenge them. But if there is any resource
at all—in regard to the United States—it lies in the renewal of that
component of individualism which prizes noninterference in the life of
the individual for the sake of his or her exploratory self-making, for the
sake of what I call democratic individuality. Even short of the full

expression of that ideal, the challenge could be in the name of what Mill calls (in the first chapter of *On Liberty*) individual sovereignty. We would call it a modest free being. If individuals do nothing truly and gloriously individualist, if indeed some of them behave foolishly or disreputably, government must nevertheless not treat them as if they were only machines made to function smoothly. It must treat them without such contempt, if it is not to dwarf them. Mill's theory of individual sovereignty is all the more relevant in the nuclear age: the dwarfing inherent in state activism serves nuclear statism.

At least, one could hope that state activism would be discussed more and that obstacles to its almost noiseless spread would be interposed more often. The threat is all the greater because the injury to individuals inflicted by state activism can remain unfelt. Injury to the dignity of free being can be subtle, hard to talk about. It would be well to insist on talking about it.

Yet, looked at globally, the problems of overpopulation, ecological damage, and poverty seem so immense that, as I have admitted, state activism appears attractive. In fact, state activism carried out by disciplinary dictatorships can appear doubly attractive, as it does to even so magnanimous a soul as Hans Jonas in his important book *The Imperative of Responsibility* (1984). The further horror is that there might be fantasies in which the gravest problem becomes the Swiftian solution to other grave problems, in which nuclear war becomes the solution to many of the problems of overpopulation. Thus the possibility of nuclear extinction would become most real when the urgencies of economic survival had become most imperious, and the individual most pitilessly dwarfed.

CHAPTER FIVE

Thinking about Human Extinction (II): Nietzsche and Heidegger

It is often said that a change of heart is needed if humankind is to avoid its nuclear doom. Usually the call for a change in heart is made because of a dread of massive ruin. But the possibility of human and natural extinction has also figured in the call, thanks to Jonathan Schell's book *The Fate of the Earth* and conjectures concerning a "nuclear winter." The instincts behind this call are, in my opinion, right, despite the challenge to the nuclear winter hypothesis. I now explore one hypothetical meaning that a change of heart could have. I would like to see what resources individualist moral philosophy may contain for such a change.

I interpret a change of heart in the nuclear age as the cultivation of those thoughts and feelings that would drive people to do all they could to avoid the possibility of extinction. The dread of massive ruin can and does change hearts, of course. But it may be that the greatest change can take place if the possibility of extinction dominates reflection. Resistance to this possibility can and must take many forms. Whatever the forms, the struggle is not only hard but seems impossibly hard. No nuclear government has so far, except incidentally, acknowledged extinction as a possible outcome of any use of nuclear weapons, not even of a sizable exchange. Certainly no nuclear government wills extinction. It is therefore hard to join the issue directly with those who rationalize the use of nuclear weapons. On the other hand, there are thoughts and feelings—indeed, habits and passions and loyalties—inside almost everyone which offer their own resistance to a change of heart. Just because nuclear discourse is characteristically boring, it is easy to go along with nuclear policy and to remain enclosed, if bemused, within the world of words constructed by officials and apologists. A change of heart must mean, first of all, offering resistance to oneself.

I would propose that the thoughts and feelings that would drive people to do all they could to avoid the possibility of extinction are those that create an attachment to existence. This last phrase is simply a more positive way of putting the matter. I know that the idea sounds simple-minded, perhaps pious in a bad sense. It is reducible to the platitude that earthly existence should go on. The fact is that this is not now a mere platitude to those who ponder the possibility of extinction. To them, the seeming platitude is the beginning of inner conversion (or "turnabout," as Schell calls it platonically). Its power can be felt, and felt ever more deeply, only as a result of exploring its meaning in the nuclear age. The nuclear situation thus forces us to talk earnestly about things we maybe would rather keep silent about, and to talk about them in ways that seem all the more clumsy in contrast with decorous silence. But if existence is at stake, how can we keep silent? How can we keep silent about the ultimate reason for attention and resistance? What is involved here is not primarily one's love of life, of being alive, or attachment to one's own existence as a treasure of inestimable worth. Those feelings may help. In truth, an insistence on one's own existence as a treasure of inestimable worth is one of those components of individualism which are indispensable to challenging nuclear statism. Yet that is not the whole story. An attachment to existence must be understood as a will to see humanity and nature on earth preserved. One's own preservation is included, but only for a brief lifetime. Properly attached to existence, one wants to be survived, but not only by one's kin or fellow citizens. One wants the career of humanity and the processes of nature to continue indefinitely, forever. Oneself matters, but not as the preservation of humanity and nature matters. A change of heart consists in coming to think and feel that nothing matters as much, nothing matters in the same way as, the preservation of humanity and nature: not as abstractions but as indefinite histories taking place outside oneself and one's circle (no matter how enlarged). As Schell puts it, "The meaning of extinction is . . . to be sought first not in what each person's own life means to him but in what the world and the people in it mean to him."

The role of individualism as the supreme defensive idealism in the nuclear age is not exhausted by its usefulness in the challenge to both nuclear statism and the auxiliary of nuclear statism, state activism. I believe that individualism in some of its developments after the seventeenth century contains the substance of many saving thoughts and feelings. The great work of Emerson, Thoreau, and Whitman comprises the main development, and the phrase "democratic individuality" perhaps best names their idealism. It grows out of the individualism of personal and political rights and out of the related idea of individual sovereignty or free being, but it also represents their completion and ultimate greatness. This crowning work turns out to be central to the task of conceiving an attachment to existence which withstands all temptations to go along with policies that may lead to human and natural extinction. It offers itself for an enlistment never imagined by its devisers and propounders.

Furthermore, when elements from other individualist doctrines— actually, antidemocratic individualist doctrines as hinted or expounded by Nietzsche and Heidegger—are mixed in, then we may have the outlines of a more complete preserving or saving attachment. We may have it in theory, if not yet in the heart. Notice as well that the process of conceiving a saving attachment to existence may also yield philosophical truth, as if to indicate that the truth could come only in our most desperate condition. Whether the truth saves because it is the truth, or whether what saves is only coincidentally the truth, is an open question. But it may be that the answer to Nietzsche's question in *The Gay Science*, "To what extent can truth endure incorporation [into life]?" can be answered without reservation. It must be incorporated fully if life is to go on. Let us reverse Nietzsche and say that we possess truth lest we perish of art (the wrong sorts of aestheticism). I set down the following reflections only as pointers, not as the content itself of a more complete saving attachment. The content can be developed only by many people over time, by those blessed with powers that one does not have, that, of course, I do not have. Let us be students of the thinking of a number of geniuses who, for the most part, did not dream that literal extinction was possible, yet who, in their philosophical struggles, engendered ideas that give us the best assistance. We must tear their ideas out of context. Except for Heidegger, none of the others lived in the atomic situation. We must be ruthless and force their ideas into use, and we must use any ideas from other writers which seem suitable. To repeat: my contention is that the best defensive idealism is individualism, especially in the form of democratic individuality as conceived by Emerson and his two greatest American intellectual children, Thoreau and Whitman. Support and revision also come from another kind of individualism—thoughts in Nietzsche (Emerson's greatest European heir) and Heidegger (Nietzsche's greatest heir), both adversaries of democratic individuality, yet vital to its improvement. This discussion is dominated by the irony that a seemingly self-centered sense of life is most truly itself when it loses sight of the self for the sake of becoming newly attached to existence. The self-surpassing of individualism is the unique source of a selfless and saving attachment.

The preserving attachment to existence will consist, I think, in a spectatorial or observant or contemplative relation to existence as such. A change of heart is a change in the way of seeing, which then will energize action that strives to avoid extinction, and will not be only a truth that one possesses for its own mental sake. The power of this contemplative, perceptual attachment should irresistibly impel into action, as existentialists say all genuine thinking does. The hope is that many will come to share and spread it. It is of course set in motion, to begin with, by horror at the thought of incalculable nuclear suffering, but the possibility of extinction elicits a feeling different from this horror, from this inalterable moral indignation. Schell's work should cause us to feel again the meaning of massive nuclear ruin, but it also makes us think that there is something else that is not worse than massive ruin but altogether beyond it: the possibility of extinction, the murder of the unborn, the possibility of "the second death"—a phrase, but not a sense, traceable to the Book of Revelation. The main elements of a new relation to human and natural reality grew in Emerson and the other thinkers as the result of their effort to imagine what it means to live truthfully. But in the nuclear situation, as conceptualized by reference to the possibility of extinction, one's susceptibility to the teachings of the theorists of democratic individuality and of the antidemocratic individualists is given a direction and an intensity that is distinct.

Properly attached to existence as such, one wants it to go on forever; one cannot bear the thought that it may end forever. Schell suggests that we try to take the perspective of the unborn and strive to ensure that they will be born and thus given a chance to live life and even enjoy it, for all its sin and suffering, and to feel gratitude to predecessor generations for not having blocked all future chances for earthly existence. This suggestion is fine. But there is also a less humanist perspective—existence as that which must go on apart from any blessing future generations bestow or fail to bestow. It must go on because one cannot bear the thought, here in the present, that it would cease. Not that one wants it to go on for one's own sake or for the sake of one's pleasure in life. Indeed, it is not impossible that, with Socrates as the distant model, one is not especially in love with one's own life, *and for that reason*, though not inevitably so, one is all the more disposed to be attached to existence as such. One wants existence to go on for considerations that may not or would not matter to most people, living or unborn. One who is attached to existence by contemplating it in the way urged upon us by philosophers of individualism may even be cut off from other considerations that attach people to their existence but do not attach them to existence as such. (I think, however, people of a democratic culture are closer to sharing an attachment to existence as such than other people are. I shall take up this point later.)

Put minimally, to be attached to existence as such is to want human and natural existence on earth to go on forever, for time out of mind, apart from the value or glory of any particular thing in it, or number of particulars, and in spite of the immorality of many human particulars and the ugliness or odiousness of many natural particulars. Further, one is attached to existence at whatever cost to particular things one values. The keen sense that all valuable things are endangered must be supplemented by the keener sense that many valuable things are dangerous, insofar as they can be converted by officials and aroused populations into sources of hostility, war, and the possibility of extinction, including the extinction of these valuable things. On the other hand, many particulars may tend to strengthen attachment, just as, of course, some may threaten to weaken it. If attachment to existence as such is a philosophical attachment to what is indefinite, to what is not encompassable, actual particulars must nevertheless play an indispensable role in its sustenance. But these are particulars that offer themselves to contemplation; they are philosophically or poetically pondered and cannot be confined to the personal facts and events of one's life. And no particulars of any sort can be philosophically permitted to provide a sufficient reason for (or against) attachment.

This kind of preserving attachment must be cultivated; it obviously cannot be taken for granted. No one wants human and natural existence to end; no political actors are doing or preparing deeds with the intention of ending existence. Of course, everyone—just about everyone—wants existence to proceed. Not yet common is Bertrand Russell's sentiment that "the planet will perhaps be happier without us," referring only to human extinction. But as we know, the unintended can take place; and what contributes to its taking place must be recognized and resisted. The resistance must be continuously attentive, and will feel harsh and sometimes unnatural. A cultivated attachment to existence as such is therefore arduous, and all the more so because almost no one is working deliberately to end existence. From day to day resistance is undertaken under the guidance of political ideas—the political theory of constitutional democracy with its basis in the rights and integrity of individuals. The underlying commitment, however, is to human and natural existence on earth. This commitment need not figure explicitly in the politics of resistance, but it could be the deepest source of energy. A changed heart does not have to talk constantly about itself, but to itself it will return in order to remember why it struggles. Nevertheless, now and then it may be possible to appeal to people by expressing some of the considerations that lead to a philosophical attachment. I think that such an appeal is more easily heard and understood in a democratic society, and for individualist reasons that I will try to develop.

Now, I must admit that the change of heart sketched here may be open to the charge that it would take generations of unremitting cultivation to take hold (whether or not it is plausible or desirable). If the situation is urgent, such a time-dependent change would be irrelevant. On the other hand, if, after generations, it were to take hold, that could only mean that it had been unnecessary; after all, the world had repelled the possibility of extinction without recourse to any change of heart. I cannot satisfactorily answer such charges. All I can say is that the world—unpredictable though it is—may experience terrible nuclear events without a change of heart.

How then is an attachment to existence as such cultivated? To say it again, what is offered here is only the most sketchy outline: a partial assembling of relevant points that await their poets and philosophers. Only at an academic distance from an actual change of heart is it appropriate for me to go on, even though it may be thought inappropriate to be academic about the most fundamental subject—the subject that is not a subject. The risks are great no matter how one approaches it.

With this in mind, a start may be found in the contention that attachment to existence as such is not attachment to any kind of totality. If we insist that no particular should be sufficient either to attach us to existence or to make us cease caring whether existence goes on, we do not mean that particulars count for nothing in themselves and count for something only as parts or aspects of a defined or designed order or pattern. Thinking about attachment to existence in an age when existence is threatened with extinction is, concurrently, thinking about attachment to existence in an age when the death of God has been announced with adequate plausibility and when, furthermore, honesty in one's knowledge compels the additional judgment that existence on earth cannot be justified by any "internal" or human standard developed independently of a supposed divine authentication. That is to say, attachment cannot be cultivated by way of a theology that bestows meaning or worth on existence, or by way of a believable reconciliation to the facts of wickedness, suffering, waste, cruelty, obscenity, and death. The universe, not just the earth, is without sponsorship; and existence on earth fails every test that is strenuously pressed by moral or teleological inquirers. The point is that attachment is best cultivated when acknowledgment is first made that the inherited modes of translating the world into a story have been discredited—discredited, let us say, for some of us, for enough of us so that some new mode is needed. What is needed is precisely a mode that is content not to make the world—human and natural existence on earth—into a story, a picture, an order or a pattern, or a coherent part of a larger one—that is, into a self-adequate totality or into a necessary part of a transcendent totality. Indeed, the new mode must exult in the impossibility of the inherited modes and insist that attachment to existence is most preserving when the inherited modes are discarded.

If, however, some say that attachment to existence requires either a more-than-human sponsorship or a justification honestly arrived at that satisfies a conscientious humanism, then I, for one, think that such attachment must remain more precarious philosophically, despite appearances to the contrary. In my judgment, indications present in Nietzsche and Heidegger combine to suggest that existence will *eventually* be more secure because both the more-than-human and the humanist are in the course of being discredited. The trouble is that Nietzsche feared that most people needed what new philosophers, in their strength, could do without and, in their honesty, had to do without. The spreading beliefs that God is dead and that life is morally unjustifiable, indeed condemnable, produce despair, which then may turn life denying and life destroying. Nietzsche's thought thus contains the paradoxical notion that the presence as well as the absence of both theological and humanist doctrines contributes to the weakening of attachment to existence and, even more, to a destructive despair. Great global calamities must result, he thought, from the working out of these elements. Only a few individuals, a few philosophical spirits, radically unlike and cut off from most people in society, can make themselves immune to the blindness of doctrine and the ravages of its absence.

Heidegger enriches and revises these suggestions but seems to retain Nietzsche's spiritual elitism, the conviction that only a few individuals, here and there, can be counted on to understand. For them both, individualism, from its nature, must be deviation from, or discontinuity with, the social norm, enabling an ascent to superiority, but not to any platonic transcendence or Archimedean point, only to detachment from the social. They retain the platonic separation between the social cave and the saving vision, but with the unplatonic aim of taking in, of being taken in, by appearances that are seen as no "mere" appearances. (This is a project beautifully captured, by the way, by Wallace Stevens in a number of poems—for example, in "Landscape with Boat.") In Nietzsche and Heidegger, only a few can acquire vision or truly see or apprehend.

I wish to emphasize that these two are individualist thinkers because they find no way into truth without an attempted if never fully successful abandonment of social being. I do not mean to say that their doctrine is permeated by a concern to affirm the sacredness of individuals. Indeed, unmastered fright or distaste seems to drive them to betray individualism by entertaining fantasy projects that use individuals collectivistically and ruthlessly. But their deepest teaching on a new attachment to existence is not social and is reserved for those few able to separate themselves from the social. In that respect, both Nietzsche and Heidegger are radical individualist thinkers.

Is it possible, however, that democracy is already built in part on the rejection (even if disguised) of the need to have either a God or a moral justification of existence? And that, therefore, an appeal made to democracy's innermost—that is, individualist—meaning not only can prevent theological and moral disappointment but can actually lead to the most preserving attachment to existence? Of course, neither Nietzsche nor Heidegger thought that possible. The irony is that though Nietzsche and Heidegger are antidemocratic because they say only a few can see philosophically, nevertheless a good deal of the content of their vision bears a strong resemblance to that of the theorists of democratic individuality.

Before considering democratic individuality, I wish to explore some hints in the thought of Nietzsche and Heidegger. I believe that, more than any other philosophers, they have tried to think about a preserving attachment to existence as such, even though Nietzsche could not address the technological possibility of literal human and natural extinction, and Heidegger only rarely did so with any explicitness. Nietzsche, however, refers to human self-destruction, and such a thought exerts some (strong if mostly hidden) pressure in Heidegger's later work. Nietzsche, especially, wrestled with the spirit of human destructiveness, and what he suggests and implies about this nihilism is of the greatest relevance to my theme. One need not follow Nietzsche in thinking that in the nuclear age the source, or even one of the main sources, of the possibility of extinction is the nihilistic will to destroy, the "will to the end," born in religious or moral fanaticism or uncertainty. One may nevertheless learn from him about ways of cultivating an attachment to existence as such, whatever may threaten it. And Heidegger, though locating the danger to existence in Western rationalism's compulsive effort to convert all nature, and man himself, into something manmade, also contributes to thinking about attachment to existence. One does not have to adopt completely his analysis of the trouble to benefit from his sense of what a change of heart would be. I admit that in separating out various elements from two thinkers who are deliberately elusive I run the risk of misconstruing and misusing them. I grant that this risk is increased when one feels, as I do, that practically every direct remark on politics by either Nietzsche or Heidegger is silly or wicked, and that practically every effort made so far to distill for reconstructionist uses—apart from the nuclear predicament—a political theory or a vision of the good society from their work ends up fascistlike, or reactionary, or communitarian-conservative, and self-deluded to boot. These writers matter politically only for a certain politics, actually the most important politics—the politics of attachment to existence in our age (and coming ages, if there are any) which contain the possibility of extinction. Their saving implications must be wrested from them almost violently.

One could say that Nietzsche's life work is dedicated to the philosophical effort to ward off disgust with life and find fresh sources of attachment. The disgust is that of one who feels too keenly the sufferings of others and also feels a disquiet arising from a sense of universal pointlessness. He knows the seductiveness of the ancient adage that it is best for someone never to have been born and second best to die young. He also insists that Christianity spread throughout the world those thoughts and feelings that heighten the sense of suffering while trying to impose an interpretation that redeems the suffering and the seeming general pointlessness. I suppose that Nietzsche is saying that even when it tries to help humanity with its picture of the world, Christianity makes things worse. It arouses expectations that, with time, it loses ever more surely the ability to satisfy. Its picture of the world as God's design grows ever less persuasive, but its induced demand that human life (and even natural life) pass a strict moral test and also show some general point, some coherence, some progressive or redemptive tendency, continues, and even becomes more fierce as its theological mooring is cut. The failure to find a new picture, a new way of reconciling people both to the horrors of human and natural life and to the seeming pointlessness of existence, leads to nihilism, a disposition to destroy and to take a solacing satisfaction in the spectacle of ruin and the imagined spectacle of total ruin, of nothingness.

No doubt Nietzsche is prepared to speed up the process of despair and to do so by enlisting his genius in the task of further discrediting all the remains of the Christian world picture. He is a tactical ally of the nihilistic disposition. But that is only to clear the way for something new—a new affirmation, a new attachment to existence that is constantly attentive to anything that threatens the hold of humanity on it. His aim is a philosophy that does not arouse expectations that later thinking is able to discredit. He thus wishes to avoid repeating the Christian pattern of producing a latently destructive but temporarily preservative relationship to existence. I know that he does not believe that the sense he wishes to impart should be called the truth. But I nevertheless incline to say that he thinks it truthful. I myself think that it is truthful or, at the least, that it contains the beginnings of the truth, the philosophical truth, a truth that also contains the beginnings of a preserving attachment to existence as such. If I am not persuaded by Nietzsche that Christianity, in both its ascendancy and its decline, promotes disgust and destructiveness, I can still agree that an attachment to existence is greatly strengthened when every system of belief, every theology and every metaphysics, whatever the content, is made to give way and go under.

Nietzsche teaches that God is dead. Others may have said it before him, or all but said it. But he really means it. What does he really mean? It is often said that Nietzsche is not a simple atheist. That may be the case: what we attribute to him depends on the definition of atheism. Yet certainly he does not believe that the personal God of the Jewish and the Christian Bible exists. There is no God in whose image mankind was made; there is no God who made the universe; there is no God who is father, judge, rewarder, intervener, upholder, and sustainer of all existence. Nietzsche does not believe in the epistemological possibility of revelation. If such denial is not atheism, then let it be called something else. The growth of science has discredited Jewish and Christian theism. That Nietzsche thinks that science itself is constructed out of human conventions of understanding does not, it seems to me, affect his religious denial. Nothing is gained by saying that Nietzsche is not holding that God is dead but only that belief in him is dead (or dying). He gives not an inch even to a concept of God which remains mystically or agnostically void of content.

Nietzsche unsystematically but nevertheless powerfully draws out the implications of God's death. What holds all these implications together is that the death of God is the loss of the "not ourselves" (in Matthew Arnold's phrase), the more-than-human, which, though not human, is connected to humanity, cares for it, speaks to it, understands it. The death of God is the loss of the ability to believe that there is an otherness standing in intentional relation to humanity, an entity, distinct but not totally dissimilar, that is superior to humanity in knowledge, even if most of this knowledge is inaccessible to humanity. The pictured God made some of it accessible. In supposedly making it accessible, in revealing it or in inscribing it in the human heart, God did not leave humanity alone, did not leave it without word from outside itself and able to talk only to itself. But God is dead. In truth, belief in God was never tenable. Without quite knowing what it was doing, humanity was always and only talking to itself. The death of God is not the death of a truth but rather of a successful untruth. We are cut off from all previous human life because it was built on untruth. All that humanity can do now is *consciously* invent, construct, see, and understand from an anthropocentric perspective, or from various particular cultural or individual perspectives. Morality is left without the fiction of sponsorship. Whole ways of life are left without the disguise of unwilled principles to inspire and organize them. But for our discussion the most important implication of God's death is that no answer to the question of the value of existence is believably traceable to anything outside and above humanity. It therefore cannot be answered; at least, it cannot be answered except from within, by groups of human beings, now this way and now that way, and always arbitrarily. As Nietzsche says in *The Twilight of the Idols*: "One would require a position outside of life, and yet have to know it as well as one, as many, as all who have lived it, in order to be permitted even to touch the problem of the *value* of life: reasons enough to comprehend that this problem is for us an unapproachable problem."

Nietzsche's point is, in the first instance, epistemological. For humanity to know the value of human life it would have to know itself. To know itself means, as Hannah Arendt says, to know *what* humanity is. That, in turn, requires that it be seen from a distance, from what she calls an Archimedean point—and indeed to see its indefinite process as completed, and perhaps see all its experience at once. The constructed God was generally given such powers and such knowledge. By his death, humanity is left in the impossible position of being judge in its own case. It may be that the Incarnation, the son of God who became man, was supposed, precisely, to give flesh to the abstract idea that something more-than-human, yet intimately human, could know what humanity is. But that God is dead: his true cross is modern science. There is no way by which humanity can reach an Archimedean point, can stand within and outside at the same time, can be only itself and yet know itself as another would know it. In any case, even if this more-than-human other existed and deigned to communicate with humanity about what humanity is and, correspondingly, about the value of human existence (and natural existence, too), such knowledge would have to be a matter of submissive acceptance, a matter of childlike mimetic knowledge. Humanity could not know itself as God knows it, because it could not know God as God knows God. The death of God is the end of childhood, the end of gullibility, a fall from pretended knowledge into truthful ignorance. The enchanted world was a duped world. Thus the human epistemological ambition must be redefined. As Wallace Stevens, an eminent heir of both Emerson and Nietzsche, writes in "Chocorua to Its Neighbors":

> To say more than human things with human voice,
> That cannot be; to say human things with more
> Than human voice, that, also, cannot be;
> To speak humanly from the height or from the depth
> Of human things, that is acutest speech.

But the death of God is not only (as Stevens says the death of Satan was) "a tragedy for the imagination" or the cause of an apparently hopeless epistemological quandary that makes knowing humanity and estimating human life impossible. Just by these two effects, Nietzsche holds, it weakens attachment to existence. The heavenly void induces nihilism, a destructive despair that comes from the imaginative shrinkage and the epistemological quandary left by the withdrawal of belief in a personal God. Even more devastating, in Nietzsche's view, is the way in which human self-esteem is felt as lost, as if being creatures made by a more-than-human power is the key to dignity rather than the sign of dependent and reliant inferiority. He says in *The Will to Power*, "At bottom man has lost the faith in his own value when no infinitely valuable whole works through him; i.e., he conceived such a whole in order *to be able to believe in his own value*." Nietzsche tried to tally the costs of the death of God before finding joy in it, and the possibility of renewal.

He does not make another point that I should mention: namely, that if the death of God includes the death of the belief in human immortality after bodily death, an insouciance about life may develop that is especially poisonous in the nuclear age. That is, if being dead means nothingness, no consciousness, the loss of one's life cannot be regretted and death is not to be feared. Similarly, if humanity is extinguished forever, what does it matter? There is no consciousness on which extinction can register and be regretted. Thus, what would be unfelt may cause no present dread: eternal nothingness may cause no dread. An idea that underwrites personal courage in the face of death (as, say, with Socrates) can be translated into a nihilistic recklessness concerning the perpetuation of humanity. It can thus give a spurious legitimacy to the absurdly murderous idea that we can deprive others of what, once lost, they would not miss, and do so for some reason of our own, or for no reason, as Camus's Stranger kills.

It does not matter that Nietzsche may make too much of the nihilistic consequences of the death of God. The problem is not really so much that people sicken of the world as that they are joined to it in a dangerous way. They are in their own world as if it were the whole world (and the only possible world). Such partiality can, in the nuclear age, promote the possibility of extinction. One must be attached to existence as such at the cost, when necessary, of the attachments of ego and group ego.

Despite any dispute over whether nihilism is actual and urgent, I still think that Nietzsche's contribution to our reflection on the possibility of extinction is uniquely precious. His particular kind of antitheism helps us devise an attachment to existence as such that may dispose us to overcome our passivity and complacency in the face of a movement to extinction which is not willed but which should be all the more horrible to the emotions because it is not willed. He shows how the death of God, for all its dangers, clears the way for an attachment to existence which is proof against disappointment and which is also strong with a passion that no theism can arouse.

Nietzsche is famous for calling for a revaluation of all values, famous for advocating the return of something more aristocratically pagan and the banishment of all that is envious, resentful, vindictive, sour, gloomy, energy hating, and life hating. But this revaluation is an argumentative move made within the family of human conceptions of how to live. Here, too, he is instructive for those who try to conceive attachment to existence anew. I mean to touch on this matter in a moment. I believe, however, that the notion of a revaluation of all values has a meaning—at least for us—which is prior to any argument made in the civil war or even in the friendly dispute of conceptions of how to live. That meaning is that we must grow radically suspicious of all values. More exactly, Nietzsche is saying that those few separated individuals who are capable of doing so should become radically suspicious of all values. The true revaluation is to move beyond good and evil. It is only in this way that anyone can resist the destructiveness in himself or herself, the only way in which, indeed, anyone can cease being so life denying as even to want to imagine nothingness in the place of earthly existence. In the nuclear age, our worry is not primarily nihilism but the possibility that realist power politics, in its superstitions and abstractions, will unintentionally lead to human and natural extinction. But the beginnings of adequate response to our worry concerning the preservation of existence coincide with elements in Nietzsche's strategy for the avoidance of destructive nihilism. If one is not to abandon the world, one must establish some sort of distance between everything in it and oneself; if one is to grow attached to existence as such in the face of any sort of threat to it, one must become in some sense detached from everything and every value in it. The point is one must try to become attached to the particulars in one's own life in a new poetical way, without narrowness, exclusiveness, and obsession, in order to make room for a nonparticularist attachment to existence as such. To put the matter bluntly: there is no straight road between possessive attachment to the persons and things of one's world and poetic attachment to them or to other particulars, or between such possessive attachment and attachment to existence as such. Possessive attachment can block both poetic attachment and wonder at existence. The lesson is as old as Job or Plato.

Nietzsche wants to affirm existence, yet he knows that the death of God leaves the certainty that humanity is merely talking to itself about itself and able to talk only anthropocentrically about the rest of nature and the universe. How to affirm all life, and yet not go against one's sense that humanity cannot objectively evaluate its own life or the life of the rest of nature? A formulation, ripped out of Wallace Stevens's poem "Flyer's Fall," gives the direction: "We believe without belief, beyond belief." (The "will to believe," in William James's religious sense, must be discouraged.) If we did not face the possibility of extinction, and if we took the epistemological implications of the death of God seriously, we might wish to remain silent about existence as such. Or if we spoke, we would speak knowing that any evaluation we made of existence as such was a mere perspective, a construction, that might serve or hinder some human purpose or other.

But neither of these responses will do in the nuclear situation. To affirm existence as such is to go beyond good and evil; it is to will its perpetual prolongation for no particular reason. To affirm existence is not to praise it or love it or find it good. These responses are no more defensible than their contraries—no more defensible than calling existence absurd, or meaningless, or worthless. All such responses are appropriate only for particulars. Existence does not have systemic attributes amenable to univocal judgments. At least some of us cannot accept the validity of revelation, or play on ourselves the trick of regarding existence *as if* it were the designed work of a personal God, or presume to call it good, and bless it as if it were the existence we would have created if we had the power, and think that it therefore deserves to exist and is justifiable just as it is. No: these argumentative moves are bad moves; they are hopeless stratagems. The hope is to go beyond the need for reasons, to go beyond the need for justifying existence, and in doing so to strengthen, not weaken, one's attachment. Earthly existence must be preserved whatever we are able or unable to say about it. There is no other human and natural existence. The alternative is earthly nothingness. Things are better than nothing; anything is better than nothing.

At the same time, to say what I have just said is not to single out humanity for special praise as the sole bearer of self-conscious and philosophically responsive capacities. We cannot praise ourselves: what standing would such a judgment have? We cannot follow the chorus in *Antigone* and assert, "Many the wonders but nothing walks stranger than man." In talking about ourselves we are only talking to ourselves. The talk is as it were one-dimensional, even though it is indefinitely and inexhaustibly various. It is infinitely interesting—to at least some of us. But it cannot discover the objective reason for wanting existence to go on forever. It is not even, in itself, the reason for wanting to see existence go on forever. There is no reason that existence must go on, but it must go on. Nietzsche helps us to walk along this road of thinking. So does Jonathan Schell.

Yet to repudiate the very idea of giving reasons for wanting existence to go on forever, and of casting these reasons in the form of an evaluation equivalent to a justification of existence, is not to leave oneself with nothing to rely on. To abandon reasons is not to abandon considerations of a certain sort. These would be considerations that incline us to be attached to existence even though they do not add up to a complete case or necessarily entail a preserving attachment. They refer to, and take into account, features, particulars, of humanity and nature. An attachment to existence as such must be sustained by particulars—actually, by a philosophical or poetical contemplation of particulars. But such contemplation can go only so far; it cannot reach the impossible destination of sufficiently justifying existence and hence attaching us to existence as such for good reasons. Certain considerations abet what they nevertheless cannot carry by themselves.

In the case of Nietzsche, the initially efficacious consideration is aesthetic. One of his most famous sentences, found in his first published book, *The Birth of Tragedy*, is that it is only as an aesthetic phenomenon that existence and the world are eternally justified. (This thought is darkened later in *The Gay Science*: "As an aesthetic phenomenon existence is still bearable for us.") He is saying that only if we imagine ourselves and everything else as necessary elements in the composition of a great artist, and adopt that artist's point of view, can we justify existence. What he means, above all, is that life on earth cannot be *morally* justified. Existence cannot satisfy any strict moral standard. There is too much cruelty and waste in human life and too much blind predatoriness in nature. Nietzsche especially fears the relentless utilitarianism of Bentham's impertinently honest question as to what life is good for, if not for the pleasures it procures. *Of course* there are more pains than pleasures. Just so, there are more defects than virtues.

To affirm existence is to try to suppress the inevitable human response of moral complaint. To exult in the death of God is, then, among other things, to believe that because the world is not designed it should not engender the tremendous moral disappointment that would be suitable only if it had a creator. To go beyond good and evil is to be willing to spare existence moral condemnation, to find it innocent (in Nietzsche's word), not because one judges it innocent but because one knows one cannot judge it at all. To include within the definition of going beyond good and evil a heightening of aesthetic responsiveness is to move emphatically away from such condemnation. This is not to say that one wants existence as such to go on forever because of its beauty. The tendency of Nietzsche's thought is to move away from the epistemologically impossible task of estimating the worth of humanity or of the rest of existence. We should not dwell on his reference to justification in the sentences from *The Birth of Tragedy* and *The Gay Science*. Rather, the point for Nietzsche is to try to cure oneself of any response to existence which allows one to join forces with destructiveness. The point for us is that we must try to move away from any response that does not positively strengthen our will to resist complacency and compliance in the face of the possibility of extinction, *unwilled* though that possibility is.

Nietzsche says in *The Will to Power*, "Insofar as we believe in morality we pass sentence on existence." His sense is that even when people cease believing in a personal creator-God they do not cease believing in measuring existence by a moral standard that would be suitable only if a personal creator-God existed. Indeed, the hypertrophied moral sense is the strongest and most long-lasting residue of the lapsing faith. But if allowed to rule, the moral sense places a curse on life, and human beings sicken from their grievance over suffering that is in fact irremediable.

It would seem that Nietzsche is truly an immoralist and that the meaning of going beyond good and evil is to become what the Christian world calls evil, so immoral as to be totally indifferent to moral principles and thus aspire to the amorality of a liberated anti-Christian. Nietzsche clearly encourages his readers to construe him in this way and to see the very word *evil* as narrow and ideological. But I do not think that immoralism is his most searching thought—at least, not from the nuclear perspective. His great hint is that individuals should cultivate their sense of beauty and come to admire the radiant look of things which so abundantly presents itself when one knows how to see. We may go on to say—even if doing so means departing from Nietzsche—that the sense of beauty cannot be an attachment to existence as such: no perspective derived from particulars can be. Even apart from the nuclear situation, the total substitution of a sense of beauty for a moral sense leads only to cruel stupidity. That existence is as "truly" beautiful as it is good, as Emerson suggests in "The Poet," cannot mean that evil, too, is beautiful. The usable hint from Nietzsche—and it is a hint that is found earlier in the theorists of democratic individuality, as well—is that the sense of beauty must assert its rights precisely so that the moral sense not give up on the world. He says in *The Gay Science*, "For anyone who grows up into the heights of humanity the world becomes ever fuller; ever more fish-hooks are cast in his direction to capture his interest." But this need not mean that we must stop using the word evil or that beauty outweighs evil. The point is to remain in incommensurability, disposed neither to forgive nor to think forgiveness is necessary.

One can stop short of Zarathustra's embrace of eternal recurrence: of wanting to live forever, even in eternal repetition, like a soul in Dante's hell; of joyously willing, even though one does not live forever, the eternal existence of all elements in life, including the terrible ones; of joyously affirming the recurrence of the same stale or awful meanings in life. We are driven by the moral sense away from such joy, but the sense of beauty is always there, in turn, to prevent the moral sense from cursing life.

It may also be the case that if, in its strife with the moral sense, the sense of beauty must sometimes yield, it should be allowed—by the conscientious individual—to influence the moral sense. Here I mean to point to the notion that if the moral sense is aesthetically unenhanced, it will tend to engage in dualistic thinking, to believe that every struggle is between a wholly good and a wholly evil adversary. Nietzsche's strategy is to try to demonstrate that seeming opposites are genealogically inter-twined, especially that the roots of what is esteemed good are lodged in something evil or bad or not good. To understand that suggestion is not necessarily to find goodness spurious or to celebrate evil. It is, instead, perhaps, to go beyond good and evil in the additional sense that one sees moral shades and nuances everywhere. One can admire more. One grows more tolerant. In one's tolerance, the sense of beauty may strengthen, and in its greater strength it may make affirmation of exis-tence as such more likely. But to say it again, the idea is not that one becomes attached to existence as such just and only because one manages to see and feel every particular in existence, all of existence, as beautiful. Rather, one is kept by the sense of beauty in an attitude that it is best able to keep us in; but it cannot by itself suffice to create or vindicate that attitude. Not even beauty should be allowed to pose as the reason for wanting existence to go on forever. Perhaps we can pass with Schiller beyond the beautiful to the sublime of quantity and the sublime of unas-similable confusion, but we arrive at no theological or quasi-theological sublimity that other thinkers have offered to locate beyond beauty.

To sum up the lines of thought that Nietzsche starts, I suggest first that it is epistemologically impossible for humanity to arrive at an estimation of the worth of itself or of the rest of nature: it cannot pretend to see itself from the outside or to see the rest, as it were, from the inside. Second, after allowance is made for this quandary, which is occasioned by the death of God and the birth of truth, humanity, placed in a position in which it is able to extinguish human life and natural life on earth, must simply affirm existence as such. Existence must go on but not because of any particular feature or group of features. The affirmation of existence refuses to say what worth existence has, even from just a human perspective, from any human perspective whatever. It cannot say, because existence is indefinite; it is beyond evaluating; being undesigned it is unencompassable by a defined and definite judgment. (The philosopher Frederick A. Olafson speaks of "the stubbornly unconceptualizable fact of existence.") The worth of the existence passed on to the unborn is not measurable but indefinite. The judgment is minimal: no human purpose or value within existence is worth more than existence and can ever be used to justify the risk of extinction. Third, from the moral point of view, existence seems unjustifiable because of the pain and ugliness in it, and therefore the moral point of view must be chastened if it is not to block attachment to existence as such. The other minimal judgment is that whatever existence is, it is better than nothing. For the first time, in the nuclear age, humanity can fully perceive existence from the perspective of nothing, which in part is the perspective of extinction.

The contribution made by Nietzsche's heir, Heidegger, is immense. It is also extremely difficult and liable to numerous and competing interpretations. But if a ruthless and selective reading of Nietzsche is allowable, then perhaps such a reading of Heidegger is, too. I believe that, in the context of the theme of possible extinction, Heidegger's thinking (especially in *Being and Time*) enriches Nietzsche's. I am able only to mention a few indications of why that may be so.

Heidegger says that the fundamental question of metaphysics is, "Why are there beings rather than nothing? . . . Why is there anything at all, rather than nothing?" In that form, this question was first put, apparently, by Leibniz in the seventeenth century; but its equivalents are as old as metaphysics, and constitute it. It would be unlike Heidegger to answer this, or any question, directly. Yet I think that by the time one is finished reading *An Introduction to Metaphysics* (in which Leibniz's question is the center) and other writings by him, especially "The Principle of Ground," one may conclude that Heidegger finds the question unacceptable, and does so because every answer to it presupposes that the universe is created, that it is the designed work of a purposive creator or maker, that monotheism or monism is the true story. The reduction to its essence of the idea lodged in the question is that the universe is rational and that man, as the sole rational agent in it, can comprehend it: his intellect is nature's mirror. Heidegger seems to be saying that rationalism is the founding sense of life in the West, from Plato onward, and that it underlies both Western religion and Western science. With the death of God, rationalism delegates its mission solely to science and to technology.

Science and technology will allow humanity to remake earthly life or to make it for the first time. Western religion has deposited the insatiable appetite to see the human world on earth as a coherent picture or artifice—an appetite that survives religion's demise; and if that world is not coherent to begin with, it will be made so. Western humanity is rapacious in its heroic or virtuosic or vengeful endeavor to make itself and the rest of earthly nature measure up.

Heidegger holds that this rapacity, this zealous rationalism, aspires to global mastery, that one or another nation will be the vanguard of such mastery, that the immediate result will be an inhuman life more dangerous in its manipulative power, especially genetically, than the risk of extinction itself, and that this very inhumanity will somehow engender its correction, the saving remedy. What matters more than any of this, however, is that Heidegger draws out of the death of God the possibility that a few will glimpse the truth, which is that all existence is not necessary, is an accident, is something arbitrary or contingent. There could have been, could be, nothing. Why is there anything at all, rather than nothing? The question is destructive because it presupposes that a rationalist answer of some kind must and will be found. And this assumption, in the age of science and technology, will lead humanity to force an answer by remaking its world to suit whatever master passion or intention now drives it, whether resentment of inequality in human endowment, or resentment of impairment in humanity, or resentment of imperfection in the rest of earthly nature, or simply an "insurrection" (as he puts it) against anything in nature which resists man's will or his effort to make all things bear a human look and serve a human purpose. To want the world to have been made, and made well, but to regard the given world as something that would be poorly made if it had been made at all, prompts the desire to make it over. This desire is preliminary to regarding it as disposable, to unmake it, to destroy it. (Analogous to this is the spectral sequence in which the state, seeing itself as the source and sustainer of human life, comes to feel licensed to destroy it in massive quantities.) As against such sequences, hope lies in seeing life on earth as inessential. To receive beings or a particular being adequately, one must always be mindful that they or it did not have to be. They were caused to exist by no supreme will. (It is true, contrastingly, that Marx held, in the *1844 Manuscripts*, that beings would have inessentiality [*Unwesentlichkeit*] only if a supreme will did cause them: it need not have, but chose to. Atheism begins the process of thinking that beings necessarily are.)

The thought of inessentiality, not remote from Nietzsche, is the heart of Heidegger's endeavor. He announces the death of God with his own emphasis. The world was not made; it is there, for no cause, reason, or purpose. It is there just "because," as a child would say when refusing to explain. I believe that this emphasis is seen better when contrasted to that of Richard Rorty, another theorist of the death of God. Rorty says in "The Contingency of Language," "For genuine novelty can, after all, occur in a world of blind, contingent, mechanical forces. Think of novelty as the sort of thing when a cosmic ray scrambles the atoms in a DNA molecule, thus sending things off in the direction of the orchids or the anthropoids. The orchids, when their time came, were no less novel or marvellous for the sheer contingency of this necessary condition of their existence." Heidegger is suggesting rather that things are contingent despite all local causal necessities, and are *all the more* marvelous for being contingent. Existence is unsponsored, unguaranteed, unguarded. Existence as such and in its indefiniteness is a source of unwearying astonishment or wonder, a wonder that altogether surpasses the immemorial wonder at nature's supposed order or harmony. We must learn to be "astonished especially about [a] being and that it is and what it is," "that it is as it is and not otherwise."

But human and natural existence on earth is now imperiled. To the Heideggerian thought that it is an accident that there is not nothing (I know that the word "accident" is inadequate, as any such word must be), it now depends on human choice whether, one day, there will be nothing. The death of God coincides with the birth of humanity-as-God-the-destroyer, able to choose to preserve what it did not and could not create, what was not created and did not have to exist. It is then possible to extend Heidegger's thought and say that the liberated sense of inessentiality, and the radicalized wonder that grows out of it when joined now to the novel sense of earthly precariousness, provides the scarcely namable passion that informs the affirmation of life and hence the disposition to feel a preserving, protective attachment to earthly existence as such in its ungraspable indefiniteness. I know of no philosopher who imparts such a vivid and saving sense of the inessentiality of things as Heidegger. To be sure, his sense that the source of the danger lies in man's resentment must be supplemented, though not necessarily abandoned. It is an enhancement of Nietzsche's notion of vengeful moralism. Yet even if resentment of the human condition had no conceptual place in the attempt to understand the nuclear situation, Heidegger's thought on the response to it would be of considerable importance.

But wonder at existence, at indefinitely so much existence (even when joined by a sense of precariousness), needs support. Support can come only from particulars, especially from particulars not one's own, not those of one's immediate world. Attachment to one's own world, to one's "little platoon" must be challenged and corrected.

Just as Nietzsche introduces considerations, especially aesthetic ones, which can help sustain us in an attachment to existence beyond all considerations, even aesthetic ones, so Heidegger, by suggesting a way of curing resentment, surpasses the question of resentment in the direction of an overall preservative sense. He explicitly repudiates aestheticism, but his philosophical call is to cultivate a sense that surely bears some resemblance to Nietzsche's sense of beauty. As I have suggested, Heidegger wants to avoid having to praise things in nature anthropocentrically—that is, to praise them because they already serve some human purpose or other, or because they seem to reflect outwardly some human likeness. He is steadfast in repudiating the Hegelian aesthetic project by which man is "to strip the outer world of its foreign stubbornness" and shape the world into a "reduplication of himself." This would be the aesthetic version of the crazed and lethal drive to remake the world which Heidegger sees latently in Western metaphysics and religion, and overtly in Western science and technology. The cure for resentment is found, rather, in letting things be, in *Gelassenheit*. Letting things be is taking each as itself and not coercing it into human use or human likeness. Not coercing is a strenuously self-denying act. Even when human beings make things, the spirit of their making should be of letting the materials they work on slowly reveal themselves. (Perhaps Heidegger's conception of letting things be can also be extended—but not as he himself seems to extend it—to relations between people, whether private or institutional.) Human beings must learn to stop forcing or projecting or imposing themselves on otherness; rather they must preserve it, guard it, shepherd it.

This receptivity attends to the "isness" or "thereness" of every particular. It is a kind of self-emptying, a living outside oneself, a living ecstatically. It is a cure for habitual immersion in a fatally thoughtless, if gratifying, life. At its most rigorous, Heidegger's hint is that the only person who is truly alive is one who is dead while still living—dead, that is, to what society calls life. In "dying to the world" one for the first time is able to be in the world and not in some fantastical simulacrum of it. One comes back from the dead and starts to live for the first time. One recovers. One lives as an individual, as one not wholly social. Constant awareness of one's literal mortality tinges one's sense of the inessentiality of all things. Thus cured of a driven anthropocentric purposiveness, which in the modern age is tantamount to resentment and an enraged desire to make the world over, one is withdrawn from the pervasive spirit of rapacity and hence from a blind destructiveness.

I read Heidegger to be saying that the disposition to let things be flows naturally from the cultivated sense that any particular thing and that all things are inessential. To allow a thing to present itself in its unmolested particularity is to accept fully the commitments implicit in the sense of wonder at the fact that the thing exists at all, when it did not have to, when nothing more-than-human decreed or arranged for its existence. I would like, however, to think that a protective attachment to existence as such does not have to go the length of *Gelassenheit* in regard to all things and that extreme *Gelassenheit* can be severed, if need be, from the primary element in Heidegger's thinking: the sense of inessentiality, the sense that the shadow of nothing adheres to any particular thing and to all things and should provoke wonder at the fact that it and they are there at all, that it and they are "not nothing." For nuclear readers of Heidegger, letting things be is only auxiliary to becoming protectively attached to existence as such. An enlarged receptivity that is not merely passive attaches us to many more particulars than we customarily notice, and we may rejoice in what we allow ourselves to take in, in a poetically active receptivity. Yet, whatever Nietzsche or Heidegger may say, the horror and the obscenity crowd in again and shove themselves forward; *their* existence cannot be denied or made glamorous. Existence is not confined to the beautiful. Condemnatory judgments will inevitably be made. Feelings of disgust and horror must shake the soul. But just because the earth is inessential, contingent, not necessary, just because there could have been earthly nothingness—to leave aside the philosophically disputable idea of literal universal nothingness—one must finally attach oneself to earthly existence as it is, whatever it is, and act to preserve it, not just because of its beauty and in spite of its suffering and wickedness, just as we are not allowed to jeopardize it for the sake of any value or purpose that arises within it.

I grant that the proposed attachment to existence as such is allied to an attitude that is aesthetic and antimoral. The attachment is quasi-aesthetic. I mean that persons must be schooled in beauty to acquire the disposition to sustain wonder that there is earthly existence rather than none. But wonder, in turn, strengthens the sense of beauty. More largely, one continues to feel such wonder partly because one is able to regard earthly existence as *interesting*—to use a deliberately academic word of no great standing, but a word with Keats's sanction, and Thoreau's too. Yet no particular feature accounts for the interest of existence, not even its beauty. Existence is profusion, overwhelming quantity. No one mind can think or feel or experience all of it. One knows that fact and exults in it. Thus the cultivated meaning of wonder is a substantive consideration but not a specific one. It is the indefiniteness, indefinability, inexperience-ability of the unpatterned, unordered, transcendentally unpurposive histories of human and natural existence on earth. To be possessed of wonder at both the inessentiality and the indefiniteness of earthly existence is to have a feeling not aesthetic, but assisted aesthetically. It is, of course, only a human feeling. Like the sense of beauty and the moral sense, it lacks but does not need a more-than-human or other-than-human warrant. Indeed, belief in God is death to such an idea. It must suffice philosophically when the fate of the earth is precarious; and if it suffices, it does so by either canceling or transcending every particular human consideration, every sort of attachment to particulars, if need be. There is no ordered whole greater than its parts. As Wallace Stevens puts it in "On the Road Home":

> In the sum of the parts, there are only the parts.
> The world must be measured by eye.

There is indefiniteness rather than nothing, and the human choice in the nuclear age is between indefiniteness and nothing. That sense leads to the tightest attachment—detached from (while of course not giving up) particulars in order to be attached preservingly to the thought of per-petual indefiniteness. Attachment to existence as such, when aided by the sense of beauty, is also a way of becoming newly attached to the par-ticulars one is already attached to, and of discovering new attachments.

In conclusion, I repeat only an earlier point about Nietzsche and Heidegger. They are both individualist thinkers. It is as if only individu-alist thinkers can open up preserving thoughts that philosophically per-tain to the possibility of human and natural extinction. They are individ-ualist in the sense that they locate the highest human possibility in a philosophical relation to existence. They believe that to be philosophical is necessarily to be nonsocial and antisocial at one's best, in one's best moments. If one is philosophical and also nonsocial and antisocial, one is therefore an individual. Only socially detached individuals can care about existence as such, though they must act with others. Nietzsche and Heidegger do not think that any but a few can aspire to this kind of philosophical caring; and they are sure that no society could ever live, even in some partial or attenuated manner, a philosophical way of life or be comprised of individuals. The challenge they throw down is enormous. The quarrel is not, for the most part, with their vision. Rather, one wants to believe that more than a few can attain, to some degree, what they hold out only for a few. One wants to believe that a democratic society may already be such as to dispose the people who live in it, despite appearances to the contrary, to sympathize with those considerations that set us in the direction of an attachment to existence as such. Perhaps an appeal to the full meanings of individualism in a democracy is the best support for the preserving sense of wonder.

CHAPTER SIX

Thinking about Human Extinction (III): Emerson and Whitman

I am trying to explore the possibility that individualism is the best defensive idealism in the age of nuclear threat. In the last two chapters I looked at the resources contained in individualism as the theory of personal and political individual rights and how it might be used to counter nuclear statism and its confederate, modern state activism. But I also asserted that one of the historical developments of the individualism of rights and free being, the theory of democratic individuality, is the substantial beginning of the needed change of heart. Thus, on the one hand, the individualism of rights and free being interposes a theoretical obstacle in the way of claiming that a democratic government may threaten or inflict massive ruin or may subject its people to the risk or actuality of massive ruin. On the other hand, the democratic intensification of individualism represents, I believe, an immense contribution to the cultivation of a new kind of relation to particulars, to persons and things. I do not say that everything needed for a change of heart is present in the original theory of democratic individuality. How could it be? If you think, as I do, that the greatest formulations concerning democratic individuality are present in the writings of Emerson, Thoreau, and Whitman, then it is obvious that the possibility of extinction could play no role in the founding texts. Furthermore, an inexpungeable religiousness permeates or seems to permeate the work of all three: it is pervasive even though it is nonbiblical, antibiblical, and heterodox by almost any standard of conventional religiousness. Yet I have tried to maintain that the death of God, the end of all religiousness, best serves the cause of attachment to existence as such. My view is that the original theory of democratic individuality is indispensable in the nuclear situation, but that it must be revised by the antidemocratic and antireligious individualist insights of Nietzsche and Heidegger. At the same time that we benefit from Nietzsche and Heidegger, however, we must aim to withstand their insistence that only a few can achieve the saving attachment to existence, and those few cut off from the public world. If the attachment is to work to preserve earthly existence from extinction, how can it be confined and cut off?

What is more, the principles of democracy improve the capacity of individualism to help us in the nuclear age. There are many close similarities between the (as it were) preliminary considerations adduced by Nietzsche and Heidegger to sustain their highest concern—attachment to existence as such—and the philosophical or poetical relation to particulars constructed by the theorists of democratic individuality. The resemblance is basic; its nature is aesthetic. Emerson is, of course, a decisive common individualist influence. But democracy helps Emerson and others to deepen the meaning of the elements of poetical attachment; it makes those elements seem more interconnected and less idiosyncratic.

The conclusion must be mixed. The democratic aesthetic attachment to particulars is deeper and better articulated than Nietzsche's aestheticism or Heidegger's *Gelassenheit*. But of course Nietzsche and Heidegger can remedy, by means of the death of God, the insufficiency of any aestheticism, while the still religious democrats cannot. Placed in conjunction, these democratic and antidemocratic individualist thinkers correct and enhance each other.

Now, I cannot possibly pretend that just by reading again the great texts of democratic individuality we acquire the weapons of successful struggle. There can be no immediate connection between any reading and political action. I wish to claim only that by renewing acquaintance with some of the democratic idealists of the mid-nineteenth century in America one may be led to welcome a change of heart and to try to encourage others in the same effort. We are not without indigenous resources. Actually, the matter is more definite. It would be well to remember that for the first time in modern times a handful of writers said that democracy was not only a form of government along with other forms but that just because it was a transformation of the very idea of government it would, or it could, make a more than political difference in human life. It could revolutionize human self-conception; it could engender a new relationship to the particulars of human and natural reality. It could give birth to a new way of being in the world. People—ordinary persons—could aspire to this way, the essence of which was that many, rather than a few, could aspire to it. Through and through, it was a democratic relationship to human and natural reality. To try to recover this sense of, this hope for, democracy would have been good for its own sake, for the sake of democracy, so long after its first articulation. But, beyond finding perhaps fresh inspiration in allegedly outmoded writings, one may feel that just because these writings appear outmoded to many, especially on the Marxist and non-Marxist left, they may have an additional remarkable power just now, in the nuclear situation—a situation, of course, as remote from the imagination of Emerson, Thoreau, and Whitman as any could be. It is possible to think that existence would be safer if only large numbers in the democracy moved closer to the way of being that is posited by these three writers, posited as the true purpose of democracy.

The premise is that democracy is a distinctive culture, made and kept so to a significant degree by its political system. That there is such a thing as a distinctively democratic way of being, a distinctively democratic relationship to the particulars of reality, and that it is sponsored and fostered by the democratic form of government—or, more exactly, by the constitutional-democratic form of government—are the premises of my discussion. The hoped-for but tentative conclusion is that democracy provides the best cultural preparation for a protective attachment to existence as such, that democratic individuals are at least potentially those most likely to be able in large numbers to understand and feel the meaning of becoming attached to existence as such and thus to overcome any obstacle in the way of avoiding human and natural extinction on earth. Appeal must be made to them: it is not the case that democratic individuals will resist the possibility of extinction out of a conditioned commitment to the deepest potentiality of their idealism. It is hard enough just to make the initial point that individualist idealism in the basic political form of personal and political rights, and of free being, is incompatible with nuclear doctrine and its rationalization of massive ruin. But at least the larger appeal, in the name of avoiding extinction, *is* to the deepest potentiality of the idealism they profess, an idealism that is already present in a subdued or attenuated form in the very lives they live. To use a formulation of Thoreau's in his call to resist the government that cooperated with the institution of slavery: the appeal is "from them to themselves."

The profound and immediate given—more purely in the American democracy than in any other—is equality. From this principle flows much of the defensive power of individualist idealism in the nuclear situation. To begin with, it is the foundation of democracy, both as a system of power and as a culture. Emerson, in "Politics," says, "Governments have their origin in the moral identity of men." He means that they should have; he knows that democracy is the only government that does have, just as he knows that he lives in the only society that respects the general claim he is making. The "moral identity" of persons has two meanings. First, governments cannot have their proper theoretic reason for being in any but a moral consideration and cannot be judged properly by any but a moral standard. Second, from the moral-political perspective, persons are identical; they have identical identities, so to speak. That is, persons count *equally* before society proceeds to judge them, in this way and that, as unequal. Their moral-political equality is prior to their individuation, their individualizing differentiation, even though such equality never impedes or cancels their individualism. Rather, it provides the frame within which the best individualism arises.

What matters for our discussion is that Emerson's phrase "moral identity" powerfully conveys the essence of democratic equality. To live in a democracy is to live in a society in which the most important judgment made about persons is that they are of equal worth just because they are human beings. It matters, but it matters less, "what sort of persons" they are and what their virtues and attainments or weaknesses and failings are, provided of course persons are able and willing to treat others as they themselves are treated. The unity of a democratic society lies in the acceptance of this insistence that all qualitative judgments are secondary. What is primary is humanness. The political system, insofar as it is democratic, is built on such acceptance. The recognition of the personal and political rights of all, and of their right to free being, follows. But the culture as a whole, insofar as it is democratic, will also show this acceptance in all relations, private and social, formal and informal, even when relations must remain unequal to some considerable degree. The greatest of all guides to the ways in which a commitment to moral identity, to equal humanity, permeates democratic society remains Tocqueville in *Democracy in America*, though one should not ignore Plato's depiction of Athenian democracy. (The most attentive and dignifying descriptions of democracy have come from skeptical aristocrats.)

Precisely because of an initial and ultimate acceptance of moral identity, a further acceptance develops. Obviously, morally identical persons are diverse; they are individuals. Yet to accept them as equals by what is held to be the most important standard (the moral-political) is already to accept them as individuals in their differences. Belief in moral identity is the very source of the tolerance of otherness. From the start, the other is not the Other—the foreign object of hostility. In effect, each is saying to the rest, Whatever you do, however you live your life, provided you accept me and others, I accept you. I may judge, and will like and dislike, admire and disapprove; but I will accept, I will tolerate. When I cannot celebrate your distinctive personality, I will nevertheless let nothing affect my underlying attachment to your humanness. Each of us not only counts equally in a moral-political way, but each has the equal right to become individual and therefore to be accepted as different. Democratic equality is a theoretical preparation for democratic individuality, though democratic actuality is full of forfeiture: many resent the efforts of others to become individual; many think they must morally condemn the effort to become individual; many are too diffident to try to become individual. The forfeiture is the subject of much commentary, perhaps of most of the commentary, on democracy. We also know, however, that forfeiture is not the whole story. Still, my major point is that a consistent acceptance of the moral identity of all, and hence of the equal right of each to become individual, is a schooling in the democratic sort of attachment to human (and even natural) reality which is the best beginning for another school-ing, the aim of which is to learn to become attached to earthly existence as such. The acceptance of otherness because of a prior acceptance of identicalness is an indispensable part of being attached to existence in a way that compels one to give one's overriding loyalty to it.

Restating the democratic donnée in this manner runs many risks. It exposes one to the charge of banality—also, and contrastingly, of unre-ality, certainly of philosophical vagueness. Whether the ideal itself has fallen from grace is an open question. I make no special claim for my restatement of it, in any case. But one cautionary remark is needed. The foregoing restatement seems merely to repeat the traditional Christian view (and perhaps the Stoic one as well) that all human beings are equally the children of God and are equally precious in His sight and that consequently all social distinctions and personal inequalities pale in comparison. There is no doubt that the democratic principle of equality echoes the Christian view and is even historically dependent on it. Nevertheless, it must be noted that democracy gives secular institutional expression to the ideal of human equality. This establishes a radical difference between democracy and those other societies which, while professing allegiance to the view that all human beings are equal in the sight of God, nonetheless institutionalize inequality in every secular form. If democratic equality owes much (though not everything) to

Christian equality, it is probably the case that a break with Christianity was necessary to release the full social power of the ideal of equality. To get started, the ideal of equality could not be political (that is, instantly dangerous); it had to be religious or metaphysical. But it had to cease being only a consolatory doctrine of the other world and the afterlife before it could begin to constitute a democratic system of power and a democratic culture. Thus, the foregoing restatement is not to be confused with a nostalgic fideism. The death of God was already slyly at work in the founding of modern democracy, as some cultural reactionaries knew.

A century and a half ago, Tocqueville found evidence of the commitment to human equality in every aspect of American life. For him, democratic equality was a reconstitution of human life altogether. Since then, the scale of things has changed: the population has vastly expanded, corporate capitalism has come into being, the federal government has become enormous, the United States has become a world power and an empire. The surface of life has changed many times. Yet I believe that though the United States has only an imperfectly democratic system of political power it remains the most democratic culture in the world. Everywhere we look we see traces and often more than traces of the fundamental commitment to human equality. At the least, democratic culture has weathered the onslaught of stupendous economic inequality and an immense and ramified governmental apparatus. It has so far weathered, more to my point, the ravages of acts carried out by (first and foremost) nuclear statism and the antidemocratic and anticonstitutional claims made on behalf of it. It has survived state activism, as well as the removal of day-to-day nuclear and foreign policy from democratic processing. What I wish to propose is that the survival of democratic culture in its espousal of both moral identity and democratic individuality is unthinkable without the functioning of the system of power—without the functioning of constitutional democracy—even though that system functions so imperfectly, so unequally.

One might wish that the people made the public political system function more democratically. Yet I think that the political system continues to sustain and to deepen the culture of democracy. The curious fact is that a political system so full of faults, when judged by the standard of the equal power of citizens, is incessantly encouraging individuals in all the nonpolitical sectors of life to claim a kind of citizenly equality and is also encouraging individuals to claim the general existential prerogatives of democratic individuality. Therefore, if the political system rests on an idealism of personal and political individual rights and of free being, and thus from its very nature would seem to disallow wars of massive ruin, its normal functioning, imperfect as it is, offers continuous incitement to realize its idealism more perfectly outside it, in nonpolitical life. Most important, it fosters the growth of democratic individuality as an existential condition. By the latter notion I mean especially the way an individual in certain moments or in certain respects withdraws from his or her immediate world in order to enter into a relation to the reality that lies beyond it. One stands contemplatively alone in order to regard the world that is not one's own. One's relation to one's own world is also thereby changed. One has the experience of impersonal individuality.

These cultural effects are the peculiar fruits of representative democracy rather than of direct democracy. The structured feature of representation, in its remoteness from actual equal political power of all citizens, is the very occasion of these effects. It inspires a general spirit of equality and then irritates it into seeking nonpublic outlets and expressions as compensation. But the democracy of everyday life, incomplete as it is, is more than compensation, while the contemplative moments of democratic individuality are so much more than compensation that they turn into a reason for attributing splendor to the political system.

I mean to suggest that constitutional democracy, especially but not only in its American version, radiates an immense influence on the culture as a whole. It is not only the case that the original commitment to equality expressed itself, from the start, in every feature of American life, as Tocqueville so resourcefully showed. It is not only the case that, to put it crudely, the culture feeds its interests, passions, virtues, and ideals into the political system and thus provides the system with its energies and its purposes—indeed, fosters the human beings and their particular traits that allow the system to function as it does. It is not only the case that out of the functioning come innumerable laws and policies that affect the life lived by individual citizens. It is also the case, and decisively so, that the system of constitutional democracy, understood as a system of patterns of action that citizens, individual citizens, may take part in only minimally and apprehend as from a distance, contributes in an indispensable and illimitable way to encouraging them to become democratic individuals. This system teaches, but does so without trying. As long as politicians and officials play their parts, the actual things they do matter a great deal, but their mere readiness to keep the system in motion also matters a great deal. The patterns of action, in their publicity and definiteness, constantly solicit democratic individuality. The very political system that, along with contrary systems, threatens the extinction of human and natural life on earth is, at the same time, the system that helplessly instigates the very democratic individuality that, cultivated and intensified as well as appealed to, may eventually lead to an overriding attachment to life on earth.

Now, the question of understanding constitutional democracy as a form of government can certainly be discussed by reference to the good sense of laws and policies made in consultation with and by the consent of the people, and by reference to the protection of personal and political individual rights and of free being that a constitutional democracy exists to provide. These are justifications in themselves for constitutional democracy in rivalry with other forms of government. But there are still other justifications. These are the ways in which the form and workings of constitutional democracy are instructive in themselves and make an immeasurable contribution to the development of democratic individuality. Mill in *Considerations on Representative Government* speaks of the "indirect effects" of governmental activity, and in *Democratic Vistas* Whitman says of democratic government that "the purpose is not altogether direct; perhaps it is more indirect."

The view that I am proposing is closer to Whitman's than to Mill's, even though Mill's guidance on these matters is fundamental. There are noticeable contrasts in their approaches. Mill is reviving the Aristotelian teaching that activity is to be judged, to a significant degree if not exclusively, by the human qualities it permits or requires the display of. Activity is the occasion for the display of qualities more than it is the pursuit of ends that matter apart from the qualities enlisted in their pursuit. The good life consists in the exercise of certain qualities, qualities that count as virtues. The Aristotelian concept is not entirely stable, but the foregoing idea emerges. What Mill does is to elaborate it into the contention that a form of government is to be justified by the contribution its workings make to the "general mental advancement of the community." This advancement will take place not primarily because the government enacts laws and policies that contribute directly to mental advancement, as, for example, laws requiring and subsidizing education for the people—though such laws are excellent. Rather, the continuing advancement, beyond all specific and temporary ones—the advancement that is intrinsic to representative government—is made because some of the best qualities of human beings are qualities of citizenship, and these qualities are, from the very nature of the political system, called forth, used, disciplined, and therefore strengthened. One's good powers are coherently employed in public purposes outside oneself. The system works because of desirable qualities of all the people, not just a few. The upshot is that the people are not passive recipients of the care of others; if benefits accrue as the result of governmental activity, the source of these benefits is the very people who enjoy them. But the greatest benefit is the opportunity the system grants for permitting the display of, and constant improvement in, politically relevant and desirable human qualities. Furthermore, Mill says that the involvements of citizenship will increase the general social level of benign energy in society: citizenship is a superb tonic because of "the invigorating effect of freedom upon the character." All aspects of life in society will show a progressive intensity.

Mill thus emphasizes the effects on character of citizenly participation, but he is not blind to the invigorating effect of political equality, of merely not being "left out of the constitution." Not wishing to depreciate the worth Mill ascribes to the workings of constitutional democracy, I do want to make more room for the view, present more decisively in Whitman, that the democratic political system has effects upon character other than those provided by the opportunity for actual involvement, great and necessary as that opportunity is. What counts in a major way for Whitman is the equal right to participate as a citizen, whether or not one chooses to participate. The status of equal citizenship, in which one counts equally with the rest, in which one knows that one is accepted by the rest on the sole condition that one also accepts the rest, each of them, equally—this is a status that in itself can transform the person. It is good and right that a person take part, even if minimally, in order that the status not remain a merely internal transaction between one and oneself. But more than the minimal acts of voting and observing political life are not strictly necessary for the almost transubstantiating power of the equal franchise to achieve its effects. Whitman says, "To be a voter with the rest is not so much; and this, like every institute, will have its imperfections. But to become an enfranchised man, and now, impediments removed, to stand and start without humiliation, and equal with the rest; to commence, or have the road clear'd to commence, the grand experiment of development, whose end (perhaps requiring several generations), may be the forming of a full-grown man or woman—that is something."

An essential aspect of Whitman's thought is that equal enfranchisement must be coextensive with the adult population, that democracy cannot exclude any segment of the population. If some are excluded, citizenship would necessarily induce arrogance toward the excluded and achieve effects different from those Whitman has in mind. And when everyone is included, the conscientious person can hope to feel that the political system will not produce evil results. The absence of systematically evil results allows the further hope that the system can be judged apart from its practical results, that it can also be judged for its effects on character. Specifically, one looks first to the effects on character of universal suffrage, and then one can go on to examine with a less morally troubled eye other "indirect" achievements of the system's continuous functioning.

Whitman encourages his readers in the effort to look upon the functioning of the constitutional democracy as a morally expressive system. In the Preface, 1855, to *Leaves of Grass*, he himself illustrates the "terrible significance" of American elections by "the President's taking off his hat to them [i.e., the people] not they to him." In *Democratic Vistas* he speaks of the way in which elections supply a "training-school," a "gymnasium" for attaining "the experiences of the fight, the hardening of the strong campaign," allowing people to "throb with currents of attempt at least." Those who take part only minimally and those who observe can be inspired to self-confidence and energetic endeavor: the effects on character do not register only on those who fully or continuously participate as officeseekers and officeholders or as their auxiliaries and assistants. Indeed, there is no guarantee that full-time players will not be damaged by their involvement.

Whitman suggests that, quite without the deliberate intention of any full participant, the system that enlists their participation is always emitting instructions to its citizens. It may be that theoretical observers, like Whitman himself, or even some of the more reflective participants, should now and then make the instruction more pointed, more explicit. Theorists, especially, should bring the lessons home by distilling them, by undertaking to show that the workings of constitutional democracy comprise patterns of action which should also exist, in some way or degree, in other situations and relations in life, even though we are sometimes blind to the relevance of the instruction. We may come, when theoretically enlightened, to see the relevance and then strive to introduce or deepen the same pattern where it has hitherto been missing or been too thin. The theorist, following Whitman's lead, thus translates public into nonpublic, carrying public lessons from the political system into the spiritual and practical life outside it, and does so by distilling the lessons and articulating them appropriately for this or that sector, or for social life in general. Naturally, people must already be susceptible to this translation for it to succeed, and Whitman assumes they are. The various institutions of democratic society show kinship and affinity, to varying degrees.

Indebted to Whitman, I propose that the functioning of constitutional democracy imparts existential teaching, not only patterns for nonpublic relations and situations. The political system teaches a new way of living in the world, of becoming attached to the particulars of human (and even natural) reality. The lessons taught by the political system are transcended altogether. And for us in the nuclear situation, it may be that this new kind of attachment is the best preparation for, and best auxiliary for, a saving attachment to existence as such. The essence is an aesthetically moralized or morally aestheticized relation to the particulars of reality. Democratic individuals aspire to be attached to social life and nature in a manner that takes advantage of an initial political and social decency in order to discipline moral considerations by aesthetic ones; but the aesthetic considerations are, to begin with, moralized. This sort of relation is not yet the quasi-aesthetic attachment that, as I suggested in the preceding chapter, would comprise attachment to existence as such; but it is a unique preparation in receptivity for the quasi-aesthetic, and it is the best sustenance.

The richest formulators of democratic aestheticism—Emerson, Thoreau, and Whitman—do not think that the whole American society is already made up of democratic individuals. Their passion is that it should be, and they urge a more complete realization; they preach to the half-persuaded. In the Preface, 1855, Whitman says, in a seeming paradox, "Of all nations the United States with veins full of poetical stuff most needs poets," and advises his readers that they should "come to us on equal terms. Only then can you understand us." "The soul of the nation" need only "go half-way to meet that of its poets." That is to say, the society of democratic individuals is and is not the society of democratic individuals. To arrive at its destination is to live more aesthetically, more poetically than it already does; and for that to happen, poets must help. This is not elitism on Whitman's part. He is a teacher who longs to see himself superseded by those who hear him. He is a teacher who insists that those who hear him already know what he says and that, in fact, he teaches them only what they taught him. His poetry is, as it were, a memorandum, as Emerson says the law is. His doctrine is for the "high average of men," and is "not restricted by conditions ineligible to the masses."

The elaboration of democratic individuality is the true work performed by Emerson, Thoreau, and Whitman. I can touch only on a few strands that promise most for the project of thinking about attachment to earthly existence as such. These strands manifest with a singular strength the influence on these writers of the functioning of constitutional democracy. Their imagination of democratic individuality is enhanced by the patterns of action, the political meanings of which are translated into general meanings that can guide the life of democratic individuality. Some examples follow.

First, as I have already observed, because every person can vote and will therefore be counted, the initial commitment to equality or moral identity is strengthened. The democratic individual is always encouraged to recognize others as being as real as oneself. The cultural effect of the political embodiment of moral identity is that the acceptance of otherness is dramatically consecrated no matter how like or how unlike any particular other person is to oneself. Just as the political system absorbs all individuals as equally worthy, so the democratic individual should absorb all other individuals. It becomes harder to overlook others with an easy conscience or to categorize them in a manner that excludes them from consideration. Whitman refers to the "adhesive love" that equal citizens may come to feel for one another. But adhesion may not be the proper connection between individuals. In any case, Whitman suggests other connections, the greatest of which is fellowship on the open road.

Second, the systemic cooperation of adversaries reinforces the lesson that otherness is to be prized because moral identity is affirmed, not in spite of the fact that moral identity is affirmed. If one sees that opponents need each other to achieve either a particular piece of work or to maintain a whole system, one can come to feel ever more genuinely—despite the difficulty—that one always needs opponents but even more that one's opponents are not finally one's opponents, that, in fact, in the words of William Blake, "Opposition is true Friendship." One's ability to accept is enhanced; one's tolerance of what seems to repel or be repellent slowly grows. Otherness can be uncomfortably other, abrasive, even irreducibly mysterious, and still also be felt as familiar.

Third, the degree to which, in the frame of constitutional democracy, action acquires the nature of a game moves one to new areas of experience with a less solemn, less literal eye. One looks for energy where the customary sensibility sees only purposive forces; one sees play rather than behavior. The world becomes lighter, more likable, less fatal. One is more disposed to become a player in one's life instead of an unconscious actor. And because the play is inconclusive, one's general tolerance for indefiniteness, for the incipient and inchoate, for the emergent and the novel, is expanded.

Last, and perhaps most important, the continuous changeability accommodated by the system of constitutional democracy imparts the lesson that change is the blessing in all life. In particular, the fact that those who make and administer the laws are regularly subjected to the judgment of those for whom the laws are made and administered teaches that even rightful authority is unstable. It is amazing that authority can be distributed amid balances and checks and broken into separate agencies, amazing that conflict between agencies of authority is intrinsic to the work of government, and more amazing still that offices must be fought for by means of contested elections on the basis of universal adult suffrage. Only an electoral victory can give title to office; and the title is for a limited duration, for limited purposes, and is revocable. Perhaps rightful authority is not quite rightful. The sense radiated throughout society is that all authority, in all human relations, is rightly unstable. Its instability is a sign that it is suspect, and all the more so the less it resembles democratic political authority. As Marx said in *The Eighteenth Brumaire of Louis Bonaparte* in reference to parliamentary division in France, "When you play the fiddle at the top of the state, what else is to be expected but that those down below dance?"

The systemic suspicion of authority teaches every individual to worry not only about authority exercised over oneself but also about the authority one exercises. The tentativeness of even rightful authority emancipates the capacity to become individual, to strain after independence or "self-reliance," to refuse to master and to be mastered. The further fact that the laws themselves change constantly (just as do the makers and administrators of laws) imparts the sense that, amidst constant principles, all rules and conventions are artificial and therefore changeable. Conventions are seen to be conventions. Only when this perception is regnant can individuals strain to become democratic individuals. Only then can large numbers of individuals become related to social life and nature in a moral-aesthetic way.

Within the common project of delineating the nature of democratic individuality, Emerson, Thoreau, and Whitman emphasize different elements. Tensions emerge between them when they are compelled to offer guidance in a situation—the nuclear situation—of which they did not dream. For all that, with a little exegetical violence, they all may be seen as working to deliver conceptions of democratic individuality.

There are numerous ingredients in the particular conception of each writer. For example, Emerson's work is full of incitement to the life of experiment and audacity in the face of inert or cowardly acceptance of convention, acceptance that exists even when convention is known to be (only) convention. Thoreau is strong in urging noncompliance with laws that inflict or sustain evil. Whitman begs his readers to shed diffidence and self-disesteem and to walk in life as if all arrangements were made for man, not man for them. Yet all three are transcendental: what they ask us to transcend is the social altogether, even if only in moments, so that one may enter into what Emerson calls "an original relation" to reality.

This is a transcendence even of self-expression. Democratic individuality gives way to moral identity—to, on a higher plane, a radical spiritual equality that in certain respects is shared with all natural existence. The embodiment of equality in the institution of universal suffrage promotes an even greater, nonpolitical equality. The point of the encouragement of democratic individuality is the transcendence not only of the social but even of the individualistic, and the attainment of impersonality. For Emerson, the word "personality"—often used synonymously with "individuality"—is a term that connotes unnecessary limitation. He sometimes even speaks of being individual as being limited, not yet philosophical, not yet "public."

To attain impersonal individuality is to become attached to particulars in a new way. It is to become attached with unreserved love. In the Preface, 1855, Whitman says, "The known universe has one complete lover and that is the greatest poet." Every man and woman can be his or her own poet. The attachment of love is a poetical relation to human and natural reality. Being loved as a poet loves is being seen as for the first time; it is being seen as beautiful. But in being seen as beautiful, persons and things are being seen accurately and honestly. The will to see beauty is the will to see truthfully. Thus, in *Nature*, Emerson says that though the poet proposes beauty as his main end and the philosopher proposes truth, "the philosopher, no less than the poet, postpones the apparent order and relations of things to the empire of thought . . . , The true philosopher and the true poet are one, and a beauty, which is truth, and a truth, which is beauty, is the aim of both."

The democratic aestheticism of the Emersonians directs itself toward reality as given. It finds beauty not only in deliberate art but in what is unintentionally beautiful, and finds it in more than the conventionally beautiful or sublime things and scenes of nature. Thus the sense of beauty is the same as an active generosity of perception and (in regard to human life) understanding. When one knows how to see, all things take on definition, distinctiveness; all creatures take on integrity. If human, they are understood as always innocent to themselves and possessed of adequate reason for what they do, no matter how odd or sick. Democracy of everyday life grows into the democratically aesthetic contemplation of all things and beings. Correspondingly, democratic aestheticism is conceived as everyone's way of seeing, if only in moments and to some degree. Every person has at least episodes of poetical attachment to things and beings, to everything in existence. The democracy of such aestheticism consists in its availability to all persons and their readiness to regard all that is outside them by its means.

To love the world for its beauty, to become attached to particulars poetically or philosophically, one must learn to see. To learn to see, one must first learn some detachment from oneself, from one's familiar attachments, without, of course, pretending to be able or wanting to abandon them. The aim is thus a detached attachment to one's immediate world, a disinterested interest in it. One must try to be connected to one's own world not much differently from the way one is connected to the rest of the world. Rootedness in social life precludes poetical attachment to social as well as natural life. In the nuclear age rootedness endangers existence by the compliance and conformity that always accompany it.

What fosters detachment? One principal encouragement to it is the fertilizing effect of the interminable and visible functioning of the political system of constitutional democracy. If one allows the deeper meanings of this system to penetrate one's sensibility, one can better learn detachment. I am certain that this system profoundly affected Emerson and Thoreau, not only Whitman. The curiosity is that a system that unleashes so much energy can exemplify detachment. Part of the secret is that the changeability of laws and officials teaches the lesson that the locus of ultimacy cannot be social relations. I place greatest emphasis on this systemic lesson. When laws and authoritative officials lose their mystique, people cannot honestly enter any determined relation as if it were inevitable or natural, much less as if it were sacred. There must be relations; there must be conventions. Indeed, many conventions in a democratic culture are undeniably good ones; but there is something above and underneath them, or off to one side of them. Supreme are individuals who can make and unmake their arrangements and make them again. One can learn to think, therefore, that one is always and only playing, no matter what one does. To accept that one is playing is to substitute conscious acting for unconscious mimesis, to substitute honesty for bad faith. The point of Sartre's formulation—one is what one is not, and one is not what one is—is most easily understood in a democracy. Honesty consists in the acknowledgment of this truth, the truth that no set of conventions exhausts any individual's human possibility and that every convention can be changed. No one can live without conventions, but Whitman says that there is a way of accepting conventions that is suitable for democratic individuals and that is to be "both in and out of the game and watching and wondering at it." Being in and out of a game is far better than being rooted in what is superstitiously regarded as reality. To watch the action as one acts is to play; to play is never to lose sight of others because of the mad zeal of one's undetached attachment to self. The player tends to adopt a spectatorial perspective on his own activity as well as that of others. When at rest, when engaged in contemplation or rumination, the observer feels with, sympathizes or empathizes with, those who act and suffer. Thus action allows itself contemplative moments, and contemplation is ravenously active. Democratic individuality radically changes both action and contemplation. Let us be clear that Whitman is not saying that aesthetic standards should regulate activity or that pragmatic standards should guide contemplation. What are involved, instead, are activity that is self-conscious and contemplation that quickens what it contemplates.

A kind of detachment from self is thus essential to democratic individuality, an individuality that goes beyond itself. The fruition of all self-assertion against conventions, of the whole passionate endeavor not to lose oneself thoughtlessly and unselfconsciously in any role or discipline, of the readiness to withhold some part of oneself from routine attachment, lies in the ability to see others (whether in one's world or outside it), to see otherness, and, in doing that, to empty oneself, to go beyond even a proud and cultivated individual personality. One becomes individual in the sense that one tries not to be merely social, tries not to be fully at home in one's social world. Only by such partial but studied disengagement can one at last truly see others, see them for what they truly are, which is beautiful, just because human; and in being human they are more than social, even if they do not try deliberately to be. Ideally, each has a turn in being the vehicle of democratic aestheticism. No one can constantly be so. The glorious but difficult work of democratic aestheticism is to be shared.

Whitman, for one, urges us to move beyond good and evil democratically. Every person is beautiful because the root of all conduct is some aspiration to be beautiful, especially in a democratic culture where many struggle against, as well as in behalf of, an ambivalently held social identity, role, or function. Every person is equally human. Democratic individuality is democratic precisely because, to repeat the point, it involves an openness to others who are granted a reality equal to one's own. One learns to see others in order to become properly attached to them, but first one must be somewhat detached from oneself.

Whitman's poetry is full of the persuasive effort to get us to see rather than to overlook, to accept rather than to disdain, to judge "not as the judge judges but as the sun falling around a helpless thing." The last phrase, from the Preface, 1855, is an unmistakable allusion to the sayings of Jesus: one should not judge; and in loving enemies—that is in refusing to have enemies—one imitates God who "maketh his sun to rise on the evil and on the good, and sendeth rain on the just and on the unjust." It took democracy to release Christianity from churches, though democracy is only paying its debt to its source when it releases Christianity. And Whitman, like Thoreau, extends his egalitarian attentiveness to the rest of earthly nature. He insists on the kinship of the human with other animals, but also with plant life and even inorganic matter.

It is also the case that the other lessons (besides that of changeability) taught by the functioning of the political system of constitutional democracy, when suitably absorbed, cooperate in the same direction. The need for otherness in the form of adversaries, who because needed are not merely adversaries, and the tentative, inconclusive, open-textured quality of the whole political process, contribute to the promotion of detached attachment. And in being entirely dependent on the daily renewal of acceptance and consent—not only on election day—the democratic political system plants the seeds of a vital lesson in the nuclear age, namely, that the continuation of earthly existence has come to be entirely dependent on the daily renewal of human choice. Statism kills all saving lessons and teaches, in their place, readiness to do or accept the worst: death and destruction.

Of special relevance to this project is Whitman's crystallization of the existential lessons, so to speak, of the democratic political system, and the main text is "Song of Myself," perhaps the greatest rendering of democratic individuality ever made. The poem itself is a great construction that Whitman asks every self to emulate, a construction always tending anxiously and joyously to some partial deconstruction.

The American democratic idealists help us see that democracy, truly understood, is a change of heart. Impersonal individuality, democratically formed, is a change of heart. Detached attachment, disinterested interest, indiscriminate love, are all indications of such a change. But we must add to and revise their great work in order to reach a point beyond democratic aestheticism so that we may return and repossess it. That would be the change of heart in full. Revision is needed because the formulations of democratic individuality in the middle of the nineteenth century are too exuberant, too prone to suggest that everything can be accepted, too eager for reconciliation. They share this tendency with Nietzsche (the partway Emersonian) and perhaps with Heidegger, too. But Nietzsche and Heidegger have the resources to correct it.

It is often said that Emerson and Whitman—to leave aside Thoreau— are innocent, that they go out of their way not to see evil. Their aspirations are incapable of assimilating and digesting atrocity, monstrosity, obscenity. In trying to encompass everything, they reduce and eliminate aspects of reality in order to make it encompassable or to make it lovable. They do not even go the length of Coleridge's Ancient Mariner in experiencing the disgust that must precede blessing the writhing creatures. I think that this charge has merit. There is too much in human and natural reality which cannot be accepted on its own terms; much less can it be loved. What we say against Nietzsche and Heidegger we must say against the American democratic idealists, but much more insistently.

Emerson, Thoreau, and Whitman share the conviction that the moral sense and the sense of disgust can be obsessive and therefore obtuse; that these two senses can paralyze one's active and appreciative faculties; that they are inadequate as arbiters of the quality of one's relation to human and natural reality. Thus, aestheticism is an ascetic chastening of one's exceptional sensitivity to suffering. But we must say that the moral sense and the sense of disgust must be allowed to reassert themselves, precisely in the name of the very honesty that these three writers demand and try to exemplify. Human reality altogether is not purged of the gross evils that perhaps democratic American life in the Northern states had managed to purge itself of in the nineteenth century. Nature is, too much, animals eating animals. The effect of these American writers is to discipline sensitivity to suffering by the sense of beauty, to extend our sense of beauty, to make us see, as democratic individuals, more beauty in the human and natural actuality than eyes not trained by democratic life are able to see. In truth, they moralize the aesthetic more thoroughly than Nietzsche does because of their democratic commitment.

Yet the most important attachment desired now must be attachment to existence as such, and this of course includes so much that is horrible that it cannot be transmuted by democratically prepared eyes. The demo-cratic aesthetic is the best general preparation and sustainer for what I have called a quasi-aesthetic attachment to existence as such. In turn, the quasi-aesthetic attachment can color the poetical reception of particulars, in social life and nature, and not only live by itself as the soul's connec-tion to the indefinite and the inessential. But the poetical reception urged by the American writers cannot suffice. Attachment to existence as such cannot sanely be only the attachment to particulars arising from a demo-cratically cultivated sense of beauty, of love.

Emerson, Thoreau, and Whitman all aspire to reach some reality that underlies or permeates or surpasses the particulars of social and natural life. Indeed, their transcendental beliefs help to uphold them in their democratic receptiveness to particulars, in their insistence that democ-racy can and should realize itself in impersonal individuality. Their religiousness, necessary as it was to their strength, now becomes for us, however, their salient weakness. None is a Christian believer. They think Christian orthodoxy too cramped, too inhibiting; and they do not think that either reason or the imagination can any longer find it truthful. They are not even residually Christian in any doctrinal sense. Still, all three are religious in that they cling to a belief or hope in the more-than-human, in the not-ourselves. They think that they detect in the world some force or spirit that though it may be beyond the human mind nevertheless also corresponds to it. The source of their wonder at exis-tence—a wonder they express in describing or imagining their moments of contemplative ecstasy—is still, to a significant degree, wonder at the lurking divinity of nature.

In a passage in his journal of 1838 (later reworked in "Self-Reliance"), Emerson gets it right: "In the highest moments, we are a vision. There is nothing that can be called gratitude nor properly joy. The soul is raised over passion." But he immediately spoils it religiously: "It seeth nothing so much as identity. It is a perceiving that truth and right ARE. Hence it becomes a perfect peace out of the *knowing* that all things go well." Religious pressure continues to confine and distort his greatest thoughts. It also seems that Whitman, for one, cherished a trust that the human soul was immortal. Certainly, his poem "To Think of Time" inclines that way. On the theme of the afterlife, Emerson slithers magnificently, but still slithers, in an essay (partly early, partly late) called "Immortality." Can we say that for these three writers God is not dead enough? A more modern soul is altogether less able to trust in its immortality or to detect some force or spirit in nature which corresponds to the human mind. If, then, finally, in the American idealist formulations, it is religiousness that helps to inspire (and is reciprocally confirmed by) poetical reception of particulars, even as it democratically coerces poetical reception into too much blessing, one may think it right to look for some other source of wonder at existence.

I believe that the wonder that stems from the Heideggerian sense of the inessentiality of all things and the wonder at the uncomposed indefiniteness that contrasts with nothingness constitute the right and true replacement for an untenable religiousness, glorious as it undoubtedly is, in the works of Emerson, Thoreau, and Whitman. This is the core of attachment to earthly existence as such. It may even be more consonant with the idealism of modern democracy than any religiousness, because the hidden source of modern democracy may always have been the death of God. But the sense of inessentiality and indefiniteness is certainly, at the least, compatible with the idealism of modern democracy. The precariousness of existence now deepens this sense, which, to begin with, came from antidemocratic individualism. On its basis, we then repossess the idealism of democratic individuality. The case that individualism in its contradictory variety is the best defensive idealism in the nuclear situation is thus provisionally made.

CHAPTER SEVEN

The Liberal Contract: Individualism, War, and the Constitution

The subject of individualism and the U.S. Constitution is a large one. It embraces all the ways in which the fundamental law is designed to protect individuals in their personal and political rights and thus to protect each person's claim to human dignity. Human dignity is to be protected, above all, against the tendency of government to injure it by oppressing individuals, by encroaching on their individual rights in either blatant or subtle ways. I shall concentrate on one particular right, the individual's right to life, especially in the form of the right not to be compelled by government to risk one's life or indeed to lose it; on the right to be free of the state-imposed danger of premature violent death. The right to life is the first unalienable right mentioned in the Declaration of Independence, and it figures centrally in leading theories of the social contract in the seventeenth and eighteenth centuries. My premise is that the Constitution is part of the social-contract tradition; it surely is the tradition's greatest actual and longest-lived achievement. My point is therefore that the Constitution understood as a social contract must be seen as devoted to, among other things, the protection of the individual's right to life against state-imposed premature violent death, the kind of death that is the defining characteristic of war. The Constitution's commitment to the preservation of life is not exhausted by provision for due process in criminal proceedings. The spirit of the Constitution has a very uneasy relationship to war.

What does it mean to say that the U.S. Constitution is best understood as a social contract? It means that we should be prepared to see the Constitution simultaneously as an agreement between individuals to live under a proper government and as a specification of the form, powers, procedures, and limits of that government. In its American reality, the social contract is therefore only a political contract; but just by being that, it is a social contract. In its origin the Constitution was, of course, ratified by states, not individuals. But this fact does not contradict my claim that the Constitution is best understood as a social contract between *individuals*. The reason is that the Constitution could have had its origin only through the agreement of individuals already organized into states. It is, however, noteworthy that in each state the people elected delegates to the ratifying convention, thus giving the state's decision an individualist basis. Ratification decisions were made by counting (representative) heads, not by negotiations between state governments. A referendum to ratify, in which individuals of all the states voted as one constituent body, would perhaps have presupposed its own result: the elimination of the several states' (though already qualified) independence. In addition, the common view was that every state was, in right, the result of a social contract between individuals. But the larger point is that by continuing in being, year after year, the Constitution unmistakably became after the founding generation a social contract between individuals. The federal government governs individuals. (The status of those who opposed ratification, or who urged secession later, is problematic, though made a bit less so by the right of emigration.)

Each adult, coming of age, must be understood as an individual who freely joins up with a group of individuals already contractually bound together by the innumerable free choices of those individuals. Though the states continue to exist, American membership (or citizenship) is national, no matter how strong one's affection for one's state. That has been irrevocably so after the Civil War and passage of the Fourteenth Amendment. I would add that all the people *renew* their contract, all together and at the same time, every election day. Government (and hence society) could not go on unless people regularly willed them into being by means of the electoral procedure. And they will the electoral procedure itself by using it.

I want to insist on the point that the U.S. Constitution is a social contract, and a social contract between individuals, because I think that this is the only political understanding that can serve to discourage the always present tendencies that threaten to enfeeble human dignity, which as I have said, I hold to be the true and underlying spirit of the Constitution, at its origin and throughout its difficult and at times tormented and self-inconsistent history. There is no Constitution without this spirit. But this spirit is under constant governmental assault. It is assaulted by the dragnet morality of techniques of mild discipline—for example, routine testing for drugs or roadblocks to ferret out drunk drivers; by the war on so-called obscenity; by the steady erosion of the rights of suspects and defendants; by the government's manufacture of crime in elaborate "sting" operations; and by techniques of intrusive surveillance—for example, prolonged wiretapping; as well as by brutal policies in foreign places. It has been assaulted by the daily behavior of the executive branch of the U.S. government, in its capacity as leader of the warfare state, which lives and thrives on secrecy, manipulation of public opinion, pursuit of covert policies, the encouragement of anxiety and the sense of alarm, and on a world of permanent and structural enmity. All these assaults show a certain contempt for the human dignity of people, of persons as persons, of individuals—no matter who they are, where they live, and what their nationality may be. The Constitution is a universalist, not a local, document. It is violated whenever any individual anywhere in the world is wrongly deprived of rights by acts done by American public officials and with or without the support or encouragement of the American people.

The violation most fateful occurs when individual lives are thrown away in wars or lesser military involvements, whether those lives are American or foreign. War is the sacrifice of what is infinite—the nature of any individual—for finite and often worthless ends. Against war and its waste of lives, the underlying spirit of the Constitution can provide a strong theoretical resource, as long as we understand the Constitution as a social contract between individuals, and as long as we understand what such a social contract really involves. In this chapter, I deal with the U.S. Constitution, but I believe that the arguments belong to a general theory of the social contract and individual rights.

I come to the general subject of war because I first did some thinking about the use of nuclear weapons or their threatened use in specific situations. The claimed right to use, or to threaten to use, these weapons represents the most extreme assertion by the state of its right to make war. The most extreme case may be so dire as to lead one to look again at less extreme cases, and not only because nonnuclear wars may turn into nuclear ones but also because the assumed validity of waging nonnuclear war does provide a cover and preparation for rationalizing nuclear war: war is war, it is thought.

No doubt changes in the world have temporarily reduced anxiety about large-scale war. But it would be foolish to think that perpetual peace has come to the United States or other countries. The political theory of war and peace, and even of nuclear policy, is hardly nugatory.

I do not approach the subject of war as a pacifist. To the contrary, I adhere to the ordinary view that it is consistent with morality for people to defend themselves and, at the limit, to kill so that they may stay alive. (The question, therefore, of conscientious objection does not figure in this chapter.) In fact, as one who admires but cannot accept pacifism, I approach the subject of war by putting individual self-interest or prudence at the center of thought about war—so far am I from urging a self-sacrificing pacifism. I am trying to take seriously the idea that in some matters the emphasis on self-interest serves a moral end, and does so with a force that a seemingly moral argument does not achieve. In doing so, I am trying to stay true to the individualist premises of constitutional democratic government. And when individual self-interest or prudence is put at the center of thought about war, a certain idea suggests itself, namely, that we may not have thought hard enough about the usual (though not exclusive) basis of modern war—conscription. There has not been much theoretical attention paid to conscription. Perhaps at a time when the United States is free of it, and free of a sense of national danger, it can be considered calmly.

I believe that conscription can be correctly described as a form of legally mandated self-sacrifice of a radical severity. I do not refer to the loss of time and civilian opportunity which serving as a conscript requires. Rather, I mean that conscription carries with it the claim that one can have an obligation to die, that is, to die for a purpose, whether that purpose is the preservation of others or of the body politic, or the promotion of some end. In many cases, in millions of individual cases, the obligation has been fully met: millions of conscripted young lives have been cut short violently. The question arises as to whether legally commanded self-sacrifice is morally justifiable. Is a legally commanded infringement on allowable self-interest, of a radical severity, moral? Can such an infringement be anything but a violation of a basic right? Most people, who would not hesitate to prefer themselves as natural individuals to others, who would not think it unallowable to save themselves even at the expense of other individuals, easily accept the idea that a person, as a conscript, can properly be commanded to risk death or to die. Those who marvel at the few who altruistically risk or destroy themselves or let themselves be destroyed feel little perplexity about the *system* of mandatory self-sacrifice which conscription is. If individuals in large numbers were told by the government to commit suicide, they would resist; but they do not wonder at conscription, much less imagine that it may often closely resemble an order to commit suicide.

I am disquieted by those philosophers who discuss so-called super-

erogatory acts—acts that are admirable (heroic or saintly) but not obligatory. In his famous essay "Saints and Heroes," J. O. Urmson writes as if
it went without saying that there was nothing morally out of the ordinary
in military duty, and instead he concentrates his attention on extraordinary acts of individual valor.[1] David Heyd, in his valuable book *Supererogation*, provides no sustained discussion of service in war. Both works
thus reinforce the psychology by which conscription is accepted as a
natural occurrence.[2]

I may be failing to see the obvious, but I find the situation very odd. So
I shall begin exploring the matter of conscription as mandatory and
ultimate self-sacrifice. I think that if we begin with individualist premises
as the premises of the U.S. Constitution and of all legitimate government
it is in fact possible to justify conscription. But justification can be made
for only a limited use of it, more limited than the use I mistakenly allow
in an earlier essay, now Chapter 4 of this book.

Let us look again at the old individualist idea of the social contract under
whose sponsorship the U.S. Constitution was created. Reduced to its
essentials, this idea holds that people living in an established society must
understand themselves as bound to one another by laws of political right
in order to avoid the peril and ruin of an uncontracted anarchy. They live
bound together so that they may live at all. Their association rests on the
conviction that unless a government exists, their preservation, could not
be guaranteed against those who threaten them, here or from the outside.
The Levellers—the spiritual founders of the American founding—suggest additionally that their social agreement allows not any form of
government but only a constitutional democracy. Security of life can be
had on terms that also achieve aspirations other than security and without cost to security; especially, acceptance of the claim to human dignity
made by every person in asking that a full range of personal and political
rights be recognized and then continuously respected by government.
Indeed, the right to life is all the more secure when other rights are
respected. If such terms can be had, they must be had. The Levellers'
understanding is the American understanding.

---

[1] J. O. Urmson, "Saints and Heroes," in A. I. Melden, ed., *Essays in Moral Philosophy*
(Seattle: University of Washington Press, 1958), 198–216.

[2] David Heyd, *Supererogation* (Cambridge: Cambridge University Press, 1982).

Indeed, the point should be made more forcefully. The theory of the social contract does not answer only the question of why government is necessary. In the versions of the theory closest to home, the need for a social contact arose (or would arise) from a revolutionary abolition of established oppressive or unjust government (not from primitive or un-political conditions of life). The fear that each would have of others, if there were no government, is for the most part a speculative fear. The mere existence of a functioning government is, in ordinary conditions, enough to make the fear of each by each only or largely hypothetical. The permanent fear, the actually constitutive fear, is that government, even after it is properly formed and limited, will become oppressive or unjust. The old wrongs will return, or new kinds emerge. The protector must always be suspected even when we choose officials for a revocable term. If, then, citizens fear crime more, fear one another more, than they fear *legitimate* government, the sense of the social contract is lost. If they need government very much for any reason whatever, that sense is lost or hurt. Government is then needed with a more than hypothetical despera-tion. Suspicion of it would diminish and its interventions and invasions increase. The doctrine of rights is a reminder to everyone and a warning to government, as well as a way of guiding the design of the government created by the social contract.

In sum, that which is meant to deter individuals from harming or killing one another—namely, government—must not itself become the source of the same sorts of harm (though inevitably magnified), or of yet other sorts that only a government functioning in a settled and complex society can inflict. This is our conception of the basis for society and for the form of government. Included in it is a resolute rejection of Aris-totle's scorn for the idea that society is established for the prevention of mutual crime and for the exchange of goods.[3] Great and excellent virtues and creations make their appearance in a contracted society, but it should not be understood as established for their sake.

Indeed, as I have said earlier, I believe that an immensely impressive fact about modern constitutional democracy is the culture that the spirit of its procedures and processes helps to foster. But I would not want this moral glory to be turned into a way of subverting the originating reason for its existence, which lies in necessity. Valuable effects and conse-quences must not be invoked as a justification for dying and killing. Actually, once modern democratic culture is thought to be so precious as

[3] Aristotle, *Politics*, bk. 3, chap. 9, 1280a.

to deserve armed defense, it betrays itself. It sacrifices the most basic right—the right to life. The sense of the social contract does not allow life to be sacrificed to something not indispensable to life; it certainly does not allow compelling such a sacrifice. At the same time, the disposition to defend it by violence taints or tinctures a way of life devoted to individual rights by making an idol of society or the state. The realization of a culture that is more fully in the spirit of constitutional democracy is permanently obstructed.

Let us not flinch when we articulate the barest meaning of the social contract. In a properly constituted political society, each person is to see and feel that the society owes its existence to necessity. The necessity is defined by each person's wish to live, to stay alive; and that wish must include the desire to stay alive free of enslavement and degradation, because to be a slave (or nearly so) is to have no security for one's life. This is the first consideration, and it is a consideration of self-interest. All other considerations that emerge when life is safe must be compatible with the continued safety of life. Society exists fundamentally to protect the self-interest each person has in staying alive, unenslaved and un-degraded. The proper social contract converts everyone's native interest in staying alive into an equal right which government must recognize and protect. (Immediately joined to that right and partly in its service is the claim of each person to other rights, personal and political.)

How much should be said to defend the right to unenslaved life? Should we try to prove that every human being has an equal entitlement? Then, how much should be said in behalf of being alive rather than dying before your time? Should we try to estimate the worth of being alive? It is probably best to say next to nothing. The burden of argument must be on those who want to spend lives. But anyone can just say, with Aristotle (not otherwise a friend of this chapter's argument), that people live together for various reasons but also "for the sake of mere life (in which there is possibly some noble element so long as the evils of existence do not greatly overbalance the good) . . . we all see that men cling to life even at the cost of enduring great misfortune, seeming to find in life a natural sweetness and happiness."[4]

At the other extreme, and in a more metaphysical mood, one can say for people (what they are not likely to say for themselves): a human being

---

[4] Aristotle, *Politics*, bk. 3, chap. 6, 1278b; trans. Benjamin Jowett.

is an infinity of possibilities and needs earthly immortality to realize them; but each life, being mortal, deserves at least not to be wasted. The question then is, How is it possible to move from the idea of the social contract to mandatory self-sacrifice, the sacrifice of one's life? How can I be treated as if I were obliged to die for you while at the same time you are supposed to be obliged to die for me? According to the constitutive theory, each is allowably self-interested and all are equal. How therefore can anyone morally accept anyone else's self-sacrifice? Further, how, under contractarian principles, can a number of us be thought obliged to die for something not ourselves—some idea or ideal, some abstraction or reification?

Consistently with the idea of the social contract, I think that conscription is justifiable only when it is a mere implementation of the rational wish of each to be preserved. Provision for "the common Defence" can properly mean only the effort to save lives unenslaved, undegraded. Conscription would be the way to organize the effort of everyone's self-defense. It would not rest on a claim to enforce a lethal other-regarding obligation; instead, it would give effect to the rational desire of each. It would come into being only when it would not likely be felt as an imposition or obligation at all, even if the temptation to shirk it may be strong. To be sure, the temptation to shirk is condemnable on grounds of its unfairness. The wish to benefit while leaving the cost to others is unfair. Fairness here is a subsequent circumstantial moral element, not a constitutive one; but it is important. The administered system of conscription is needed not only for the sake of efficiency but also to prevent free-riding. It is not possible within the contractarian framework, of course, to condemn the free-rider utterly: to claim, that is, that it is worse to be unfair than dead.

In any case, if we begin with the individualist premises of the U.S. Constitution, we seem to have no warrant to say that a person has a moral obligation to risk his or her life for any purpose; he or she certainly has no moral obligation to die so that another may live or enjoy some benefit. This is the case as between citizens impersonally bound together as equals and strangers—to leave aside some possible moral obligation to sacrifice oneself for a child or a defenseless loved one. In this latter sort of case, it is more than likely that the deed would be done not out of a sense of obligation but done reflexively. Indeed, to conceptualize this situation by reference to obligation is to denature it, to cheapen it. What of those—sick or old—too weak to defend themselves? All I can say is that they should be unresented free-riders. None of this argument denies that we may admire heroism at the risk of self-preservation. But the question is not what is admirable but what is obliged. There can be no valid legal command of complete self-sacrifice, the sacrifice of one's life, when there is no moral obligation to it.

Let us try to fill out the notion of self-interest or prudence involved. In the contractual theory most directly relevant to the U.S. Constitution— say, that of the Levellers and Tom Paine—the individual is understood as essentially defensive in aspiration, seeking not to invade or oppress others but rather to avoid being invaded or oppressed. The self-interest is not predatory or indefinitely acquisitive. The individualist and democratic idea of the social contract attributes that kind of modesty and mildness and moderation to most people abstractly which it already finds in the common people, in ordinary persons, when they live in social conditions that do not degrade or corrupt them. Only the few, or a few, crave the power to oppress, and would almost as soon be oppressed as oppress as long as the system by which some oppress and others are oppressed is maintained intact.[5] For ordinary persons, however, society is not a truce between the megalomaniacal (as that aristocratic hedonist Glaucon suggests in Plato's *Republic*) but an arrangement for certain security, a way of avoiding the worst condition in which our most creaturely potentiality, or savage concern for self-preservation, would be brought out, though reluctantly and as it were innocently. Self-interested people of a moderate disposition want to be left alone in peace, and want to leave others alone.

What is more, the democratic contractarian expectation is that democratic government, formed as an entailment of the agreement to live together bound by laws of political right (mutual respect for one another), does not exist in order to be continuously active. It does not exist for the sake of multiplying opportunities for decisions to be made and for socioeconomic interventions, or for the sake of multiplying offices to be filled democratically so that political experience may be widely disseminated. The modern democratic aim—as distinct from either the demotic

[5] Compare Aristotle on the general tendency to settle for a choice between domination and submission in *Politics*, bk. 4, chap. 11, 1296a–b; and Rousseau on "ambitious and cowardly souls, always ready to run the risks of fortune, and to dominate or serve almost indifferently, according to whether it becomes favorable or adverse to them." Jean-Jacques Rousseau, *Discourse on the Origin and Foundations of Inequality*, in Roger D. Masters, ed. and trans., *The First and Second Discourses* (New York: St. Martin's, 1964), 173.

aim or the democratic polis aim—is to limit and neutralize power, not to allow a sense of political legitimacy to embolden power and make it more self-confident and more pervasive, much less to violate individual rights under some specious pretext or other.

The theoretically attributed motive for one's general agreement to obey the laws may be prudence: self-interest "rightly understood," in Tocqueville's phrase about the American disposition.[6] This is the foundational motive; and if a desperate condition (the occurrence of a desperate state of nature) supervenes on normality, then the prudential motive is allowed to become actual, by most moral views. Nevertheless, the sustaining motive of the social tie will normally be moral. This is the temporally prior and personally deeper motive. After all, children are raised to be good as much as, or more than, they are raised to be prudent. A thought-out prudence is an adult acquisition (if then), but always mixed (in a necessarily confused way) with the moral motive.

Living a normal, undegraded life, each person will have the security needed for the individualist morality of respect for the equal claims of others to develop. It will develop on the basis of childhood training in goodness of the sort that takes its coloration from a society's commitment to rights. And adherence to such morality commits a person to protest when asked to be an agent of the government's attempt to violate rights at home or abroad. But, again, we must notice that though the prudential motive is normally constrained or even displaced by the moral motive, the *content* of the contractarian theoretical expectation does not substantially change. The impersonal morality, the justice, looked for is mostly negative: to abstain from wrongdoing. It is not the more activist, the more solicitous or benevolent, sector of right conduct which citizens, bound together as strangers, are supposed to look for from one another or to practice toward foreigners. There is thus a near coincidence of prudence and abstentionist morality: the sector of moral conduct expected in impersonal dealings is, for the most part, what prudent forbearance already dictates. Whether you respect your fellows or fear the law, you will behave in the same way; but the heart of what can be validly expected is that you abstain from harming others, the motivation to which can remain a matter of legal indifference.

On the other hand, good works that cost a lot come as they can and are often done in secret: the Gospel says, Let not thy left hand know what

---

[6] Alexis de Tocqueville, *Democracy in America*, trans. Henry Reeve, rev. Phillips Bradley (New York: Vintage, 1959), 2: bk. 2, chap. 8, 129–32.

thy right hand doeth.[7] The only substantive element that basic morality adds to prudence, and makes socially obligatory on all, is some *unexorbitant* samaritanism (for example, paying taxes for the relief of misery), which is not the same as either obliged self-sacrifice or the free giving of oneself. All that is usually involved is, in the words of a Supreme Court opinion, nothing more substantial than "mere loss of money."[8] Yet such samaritanism may not be obligatory toward foreigners: a lack of indefinite obligation may be a benefit of membership in a particular contracted society. At the same time, one has an obligation, as I have said, to protest becoming an agent in the violation of those rights abroad that require only abstention from wrongdoing to be honored.

I would also suggest that good works that cost a lot, good works that express self-sacrificing love for particular individuals or groups, especially strangers or foreigners (those it is hardest, not easiest, to like or love), are more likely to appear when the social tie is understood as made necessary by prudence or self-interest. Only when the tendency to idolize the total social group or the state is avoided can the energies of self-sacrificing love flow undeflected toward particular individuals or groups, whether in one's own society or outside it. (I thus distinguish these energies from the various grades of military courage, whether conscripted or free, whether for the sake of the cause or of one's fellows.) There is of course no guarantee that they will flow: such love is always rare. But it is made more likely, not less likely, by the mentality that accompanies the social contract between individuals, prudentially understood. The model here is Thoreau, as he expresses himself in his essay "Civil Disobedience." His discussion is framed by the view that government and its policies belong to the realm of the "expedient." He is also intent on rejecting the idea that one lives to do good to others. But he has an exceptionally keen sense of what it means to exploit them, and he volunteers to endure a penalty in the hope that his example will be contagious to his fellow exploiters and that the exploitation will end.

In a remarkable passage, Tocqueville conveys the essence of the democratic mixture of prudence and sympathy, which is not noble like Thoreau's moral ambition but which has its own excellence nevertheless:

There is no wretchedness into which he [the American] cannot readily enter. . . . It signifies not that strangers or foes are the sufferers; imagina-

[7] Matthew 6:3.
[8] *Addington v. Texas*, 441 U.S. 418, 424 (1978).

tion puts him in their place. . . . In democratic ages men rarely sacrifice themselves for one another, but they display general compassion for the members of the human race. They inflict no useless ills, and they are happy to relieve the griefs of others when they can do so without much hurting themselves; they are not disinterested, but they are humane.[9]

All in all, then, the proper contractarian understanding is that people do their *principal* duty when they do not invade one another. When individuals join together to fight a war, it must be because some outside group is out to enslave or degrade or kill them; and by joining together—in an administered conscription, if that is called for—each increases his ability to stay alive or avoid enslavement, though, of course, some will die. But in risking death, each risks it for his own sake. As Rousseau phrases the ideal in one of his self-consistent moments: "a man cannot work for others without at the same time working for himself."[10] Unless, in grave situations of administered self-sacrifice, each is working for himself when he works for others, the principles of the social contract, the principles of the U.S. Constitution, are not met. Individualist premises are abandoned. We are able to add: common moral understanding, when it is free of mystification, also is abandoned, just because common moral understanding does not oblige grave impersonal self-sacrifice.

A further element in the theory of the social contract is that any particular social contract is incomplete. The logic of individualist premises is that all people in the world be bound together in one contract, so that none may have to die before his or her time—or, if not one universal contract, then some sort of universal federation. National self-determination is only instrumental to the preservation of universal individual rights. (From this perspective, the idea that one has a fundamental right to be governed by members of one's race or ethnicity is grotesque.) Until such time as there can be one contract or one federation, there must be a will to peace. It would be absurd to see society as held together by a contract based on individualist premises and then think that the point of the contract was and is to create a more effective war-making machine, permanently disposed to look on the rest of the world as enemies, or potential enemies, and welcoming, if not actively seeking, occasions for war. This idea is alien to the rights and to the psychology of both prudent

[9] Tocqueville, 2: bk. 3, chap. 1, 176.
[10] Jean-Jacques Rousseau, *The Social Contract*, trans. Maurice Cranston (Baltimore: Penguin, 1968), bk. 2, chap. 4: 75.

184 The Inner Ocean

individuals and moral individuals. Even the doctrine of the so-called just war is pernicious because it assumes with little or no examination that political communities or nation-states have an absolute right to existence (and that therefore individuals do not). The so-called just war is sometimes indistinguishable from a holy war. The doctrine of the just war, therefore, need not tend to make war in general less likely, even though it may oppose any use of nuclear weapons and hence any nuclear war. I wish it were possible, in any event, not to associate the honorable name of justice with the deliberate infliction of pain and death, whether as a system of punishment or the practice of even strictly defensive war. Such infliction does not come from the best part of human nature.

The international logic of the idea of the social contract is understood best by Kant in his essay *Perpetual Peace* (1795) and also in "Idea for a Universal History from a Cosmopolitan Point of View" (1794). His understanding should be canonical and not, as is now the case, lost in obliviousness for the most part. His understanding should be part of our understanding of the Constitution. (But, alas, even he speaks of the absolute right of a contracted society to permanent existence, as if a nation is a superperson.)

I shall not fill out the treatment that conscription has received from the principal theorists of the social contract, all of whom, one should remember, influenced the founding generation in America. My understanding of them is helped by Michael Walzer's *Obligations*, in particular the essay "The Obligation to Die for the State."[11] I wish to say only that Hobbes, Locke, and Rousseau all go beyond self-interested conscription to a legally enforced moral obligation to die for the sake of preserving the body politic. We find in them an uncongenial assortment of remarks or implications about conscription for this abstract aim.

To begin with Hobbes, I must first say that he is a matchless advocate of the right to life. His concept of the unrenounceable right to life is the crucial theoretical contribution.[12] (Obviously, I am trying to work with it in this chapter.) His teaching is that we live contracted so that we may

[11] Michael Walzer, *Obligations* (Cambridge: Harvard University Press, 1970), chap. 4. See also his chap. 8, "The Obligation to Live for the State," which is a guarded appreciation of the idea that to have something to die for may be "to have a reason for living" (188).

[12] Thomas Hobbes, *Leviathan*, ed. C. B. Macpherson (Baltimore: Penguin, 1968), chap. 14: 192, 199; chap. 15: 212; chap. 21: 268.

live at all, but that any agreement to die for some reason other than trying to preserve unenslaved life is void. Yet he tries to have it both ways: he grants the Sovereign (explicitly) the right to conscript, even while granting the individual (implicitly) the right to evade conscription.[13] He is torn. His doubleness is also reflected in the fact that he words the social contract in two ways: sometimes he speaks only of the mutual renunciation of the natural right to invade one another, but at other times he includes the provision that individuals pledge their mutual aid against foreign and domestic enemies.

Quite without wavering, without hesitation of any sort, Locke simply includes in the original social contract made after a successful and rightful revolution, as well as in the express consent pledged by later individuals as they come of age in a properly established society, the agreement to lend one's force to the executive to protect the body politic. He obliges self-sacrifice in society, even though he explicitly says that the law of nature never obliges anyone to prefer the life of another to one's own.[14] It is as if political society permanently repealed the law of nature rather than merely adapting it to social uses. Rousseau anxiously mixes the most prudential reasons with the most mystified ones, ranging in his defense of conscription from the view that the very idea of membership entails mandatory self-sacrifice, to the idea that one owes a debt of gratitude to the society that kept one alive until the day it asks one to die, to the idea that it is not a bad bargain to risk death for one's society because one would have perished even sooner if there had been no society. The worst moment comes when he declares that in the properly established society a man's life is "no longer the bounty of nature but a gift he has received conditionally from the state."[15]

In his noteworthy anti-individualist essay "My Station and Its Duties," F. H. Bradley says that no theory of the social contract "will explain except by the most palpable fictions" the right of the state to compel self-sacrifice, and to compel it on the basis of an already existing feeling of obligation.[16] The mistake in Bradley's statement is that

[13] Hobbes, *Leviathan*, chap. 21: 269–70; "A Review, and Conclusion," 718–19.

[14] John Locke, *Two Treatises of Government*, ed. Peter Laslett (New York: Mentor, 1965), Second Treatise, chap. 2, sec. 6: 311.

[15] Rousseau, *The Social Contract*, bk. 2, chap. 5: 79. For the views of another theorist of contract see Samuel Pufendorf, *On the Duty of Man and Citizen According to Natural Law*, ed. James Tully, trans. Michael Silverthorne (Cambridge: Cambridge University Press, 1991), bk. 2, chaps. 11, 12, 13, 16.

[16] F. H. Bradley, "My Station and Its Duties," in his *Ethical Studies*, 2d ed. (Oxford: Clarendon, 1927), 164–65.

Hobbes, Locke, and Rousseau do not resort to "palpable fictions" when defending conscription as mandatory self-sacrifice. They may be uneasy, but they are unmetaphorically straightforward. Without adequate theoretical justification they move from the duty of abstaining from harm to the duty of grave self-sacrifice, and thus disclose the true point of vulnerability in their political theories. And in Rawls's *A Theory of Justice*, the most profound contractarian work of this century, there is only one direct page on conscription. In a grant of wide latitude that Rawls thinks narrow, he says that despite the fact that conscription is "a drastic interference with the basic liberties of citizens," it is "permissible only if it is demanded for the defense of liberty itself, including here not only the liberties of the citizens of the society in question, but also those of persons in other societies as well."[17] I do not believe that this conclusion can follow from Rawls's favored maximin strategy—what I call prudence. Rawls does not even take up the right to life as such, though he provides a sensitive discussion of both pacifism and conscientious refusal.[18]

Apart from Rawls, the other principal theorists of the contract are held fast, I think, by an unexamined sense of nationhood, which means (with Hobbes and Locke) loyalty to their own country because their country is to them like their family, but larger; or it means (with Rousseau) the ultimate reason-for-being of society. They are all of them inconsistent with their own individualist premises: the idea of the prudential basis of the social contract. Their sense of nationhood is atavistic. The one mitigation we may introduce is to acknowledge that all three of them (though Hobbes equivocally) seem to counsel a sparing foreign policy: their individualism has some effect even on their atavism. Their best sense does not allow imperialist or global ambitions, even though their writing on the proper political system is too theoretically permissive toward conscription.

We must go to the Levellers to find the contractarian idea emphatically joined to a bar against conscription: "That the matter of impressing and constraining any of us to serve in the wars is against our freedom, and therefore we do not allow it in our representatives; the rather because money (the sinews of war) being always at their disposal, they can never want numbers of men apt enough to engage in any just cause."[19] Steadfast opposition to conscription in contractarian thinking appears only

---

[17] John Rawls, *A Theory of Justice* (Cambridge: Harvard University Press, 1971), 380.
[18] Rawls, secs. 56, 58.
[19] "An Agreement of the People," November 3, 1647, in A. S. P. Woodhouse, ed., *Puritanism and Liberty* (Chicago: University of Chicago Press, 1951), 444; see also 362.

when such thinking is steadfastly democratic and not, instead, either undemocratic or democratic in Rousseau's participatory sense. Only then is contractarian thinking straining to be consistently individualist, and only then do we find the moral interest needed to avoid the fatal move from the duty of abstaining from harm to the duty of total self-sacrifice. To be sure, the Leveller opposition to conscription is absolute and therefore goes too far. There may be times when conscription is necessary. On the other hand, John Lilburne (an armed revolutionary) may be too casual in accepting the occurrence of war. But his sentiment goes in the right direction.

What, then, of conscription under the Constitution? The Supreme Court has found it disingenuously easy to uphold conscription whenever the state imposes it. Though the legal challenge (on the state level) to the Civil War draft was never taken up by the Supreme Court, it upheld the World War I draft in *The Selective Draft Law Cases*.[20] It based its decision on an earlier case, *Butler v. Perry*, in which the issue was not military but Florida's conscription of uncompensated labor on public roads. The lawyers for the defendant presented arguments to protest this forced labor, including the prohibition against involuntary servitude (except as a punishment for crime) contained in the Thirteenth Amendment. The Court's remarks on this amendment are especially relevant: "It contained no novel doctrine with respect of services always treated as exceptional, and certainly was not intended to interdict enforcement of those duties which individuals owe to the state, such as services in the army, militia, on the jury, etc. The great purpose in view was liberty under the protection of effective government, not the destruction of the latter by depriving it of essential powers."[21] These sentences are symptomatic of the way in which the individualism of the social contract can be conveniently forgotten. Notice the untroubled equation of jury service and military service, and the careless way in which something called the "state" is set above individuals and made to be the beneficiary of their indebtedness. Notice also how the right to life is not even mentioned as part of "the great purpose in view," while the Court slides unreflectively from the concept of the state as something to which individuals owe

---

[20] *Selective Draft Law Cases*, 245 U.S. 366 (1918).
[21] *Butler v. Perry*, 240 U.S. 328, 333 (1916).

duties to the concept of government as a mere means to the end of protecting liberty. All this is not constitutional jurisprudence in the spirit of a social contract between individuals, but rather a state-serving ideology.

In the *Selective Draft Law Cases* the theoretical reasoning is unimproved. Chief Justice E. D. White's opinion, in its answer to the several arguments against conscription, is little more than an endorsement of the government's brief. The basis of the opinion is not the Constitution but English law, the law of other countries (many of them not then democratic), and Vattel's *Law of Nations*. The foreignness of the reasoning comes out in this remark: "It may not be doubted that the very conception of a just government and its duty to the citizen includes the reciprocal obligation of the citizen to render military service in case of need and the right to compel it." Quite forgetful of democratic contractarian theory, and quite attuned to a state-serving ideology, White wrote in the climax of the opinion:

> Finally, as we are unable to conceive upon what theory the exaction by government from the citizen of the performance of his supreme and noble duty of contributing to the defense of the rights and honor of the nation, as the result of a war declared by the great representative body of the people, can be said to be the imposition of involuntary servitude in violation of the prohibitions of the Thirteenth Amendment, we are constrained to the conclusion that the contention to that effect is refuted by its mere statement.[22]

Thus, the individualism of the social contract is often helpless in the face of hard feelings that it was supposed to abolish or mitigate. Then again, what could be reasonably expected of a court in such a time? Even if it wanted to, it could not get very far by insisting, against the time, that the people not forget the meaning of their charter. In several cases the assumption is manifest: the power of Congress to raise and support armies entails the power to conscript.

In time of peace, the most we can find in Supreme Court opinions, and that in a dissent in 1931, is an implied distinction between wartime conscription (deemed unarguably valid) and peacetime conscription (deemed perhaps arguable).[23]

[22] *Selective Draft Law Cases*, 378, 390.
[23] See the dissent by Chief Justice Charles Evans Hughes in *United States v. Macintosh*, 283 U.S. 605, 631 (1931).

Mention should be made of the way in which the Supreme Court once upheld denial of naturalization to pacifists. The oath to support and defend the Constitution was read to mean readiness to bear arms, freely or under conscription, for men and women alike: ". . . we are a Nation with the duty to survive," said Justice Sutherland.[24]

It is also noteworthy that in his standard and splendid treatise *American Constitutional Law*, Laurence H. Tribe discusses conscription only briefly, and only in connection with conscientious objection, and with the requirement that young men register for the draft if they wish to receive financial assistance for college.[25]

To repeat: I am not saying that conscription is always wrong in theory, only that it is very narrowly permissible. A much more strenuous case for its use in any particular situation has to be made than the Supreme Court has ever made.

I here take up briefly a few matters implicated in the government's relation to the right to life.

If public policy is to be as unsamaritan as the Supreme Court allowed it to be in a case dealing with the failure of officials to prevent preventable child-beating (*De Shaney v. Winnebago County Department of Social Services*), then it becomes all the easier to say that the Constitution gives no unqualified power to government to mandate the possible loss of life by way of conscription. (I apologize for finding even a provisional use for this horrifying opinion.) Even though the case involved not death but profound injury, Chief Justice Rehnquist's words reached to the right to life. That is the relevance of the case here. The Court held that "the due process clauses generally confer no affirmative right to governmental aid, even where such aid may be necessary to secure life, liberty or property interests of which the government itself may not deprive the individual."[26] (By implication, neither does any other provision of the Constitution confer such a right to governmental aid.) In Foucault's terms: by exempting government from the duty to promote life, the Court under-

[24] *United States v. Macintosh*, 625. See also *United States v. Schwimmer*, 279 U.S. 644 (1929). These decisions were qualified in *Girouard v. United States*, 328 U.S. 61 (1946): compulsory noncombatant or civilian service could replace compulsory military service.

[25] Laurence H. Tribe, *American Constitutional Law*, 2d ed. (Mineola, N.Y.: Foundation Press, 1988).

[26] *De Shaney v. Winnebago County Department of Social Services*, slip opinion, 6 (1989).

mines government's authority to waste life, for what government does not actively bestow it cannot freely take back.[27] We are rid of a proprietary relationship. We are free because we are free of an amorphous gratitude. A potentially sinister connection is broken. But I think that Rehnquist's words are morally wrong: despite the risks of encouraging feelings of gratitude to government, a society is not allowed to be as unsamaritan as he says. As society's agent, government cannot remain idle in the face of a preventable and involuntary loss of life—to leave aside the complexities of the "affirmative right to governmental aid" necessary to secure liberty and property. The point is that the Court would never draw the life-saving inference that if there is no governmental duty to save life actively, there is no governmental authority to impose conscription for any reason it chooses. In fact, in several other opinions, the Court has further weakened the right to life, and has done so by damaging the idea that one owns one's body because one owns oneself.

It is important to insist that the right to life unparadoxically includes a right to suicide. To criminalize suicide or attempted suicide is to say that one's life is not one's own but is rather the property of the state or of society. If, however, my life is my own, I may end it prematurely, and I alone. I may not alienate my right to life except to myself. (I can never morally alienate my right to liberty because it can be actually alienated only to another, and no one has the right to use me as a slave.) The agency that condemns and punishes my will to die is claiming to own me. Relatedly, if it tries to keep me alive against my will, it is also claiming to own me. One result, in the words of Justice Stevens's dissent in a "right to die" case, may be as follows: "Today the State of Missouri . . . [can] vindicate its general policy favoring the preservation of human life. Tomorrow, another state equally eager to champion an interest in the 'quality of life' might favor a policy designed to ensure quick and comfortable deaths by denying treatment to categories of marginally hopeless cases."[28] There can be even worse results, more wasteful results, than the one Justice Stevens envisages, when the state's abstract claim of

[27] Michel Foucault, *The History of Sexuality*, vol. 1, trans. Robert Hurley (New York: Vintage, 1978), pt. 5. See also Foucault's remarks on the tension between the state's demand for military service and its inability to provide expensive life-prolonging medical technology for all people, in an interview titled "Social Security," trans. by Alan Sheridan, in Lawrence D. Kritzman, ed., *Michel Foucault: Politics, Philosophy, Culture* (New York: Routledge, 1988), 171–72.

[28] *Cruzan v. Missouri*, 58 *Law Week* 4840 (1990). See also the instructive discussion in David A. J. Richards, *Sex, Drugs, Death, and the Law* (Totowa, N.J.: Rowman and Littlefield, 1982), chap. 5.

interest in life makes it nearly impossible to rid oneself of so-called life-prolonging treatment. To be sure, the Court in the Cruzan case affirmed that "the United States Constitution would grant a competent person a constitutionally protected right to refuse lifesaving hydration and nutrition." But this liberty "interest" must be balanced against "relevant state interests." Even more troubling, the Court—though it evades making any general statement on suicide—is prepared to say, "We do not think a State is required to remain neutral in the face of an informed and voluntary decision by a physically-able adult to starve to death."[29] Only Justice Scalia, however, is willing to see a person's refusal of life-prolonging measures as suicide and to argue that in accordance with "our constitutional traditions . . . the power of the State to prohibit suicide is unquestionable."[30] The active preservation of life by the state here reaches its ultimate life-denying conclusion: my life is not my own. This idea can be sustained by the usually unstated religious idea that living a life is punishment, and punishment should not be escaped, no matter what.

It is also worthy of notice that the right to an abortion can be conceptualized in a way that is substantively similar to the right to suicide. In his dissent in *Webster v. Human Reproductive Services*, Justice Blackmun derives the right to abortion from personal autonomy, and he defines autonomy, in the words of the Court's opinion in *Thornburgh v. American College of Obstetricians and Gynecologists* (1986), as "the moral fact that a person belongs to himself and not others nor to society as a whole." Tellingly, Blackmun goes on to say that the plurality in Webster "would clear the way again for the State to *conscript* a woman's body. . . ."[31]

In sum, my right to take my own life is linked to a woman's right not to become a mere instrument of Life, and both rights sustain the sense that my life is not owned and not to be used by others. This sense, in turn, sustains my right not to have my life wasted by others.

It seems to me that the same logic that defends the right to abortion defends also the legal right to practice homosexuality. The sexual lives of adults are not (only) in the service of the abstract interest of the state or society in preserving (that is, reproducing) Life. (A commitment to existence as such is not the same thing as an interest in preserving Life by certain regulations of personal conduct. Existence is not endangered by any kind of nonreproductive sex or by a life of voluntary sexual abstention.)

I also think that the institution of capital punishment strengthens the

[29] *Cruzan v. Missouri*, 4920.
[30] *Cruzan v. Missouri*, 4926.
[31] *Webster v. Human Reproductive Services*, 492 U.S. 490, 557 (1989).

sentiment that the state owns the lives of the people. Many things can be said against capital punishment, but one of the most relevant in our context is that the state's power deliberately to destroy innocuous (though guilty) life is a manifestation of the hidden wish that the state be allowed to do anything it pleases with life. The ruthlessness of capital punishment is of a piece with that of war.

My hope, so far, is to raise questions about conscription by having us look again at the social contract and the contractual nature of the U.S. Constitution. Even if war in our age did not include the possibility of nuclear devastation and even the further possibility of human and natural extinction, there would be reason enough to raise questions. If you have spent a lot of time trying to make sense of political life, past and present, a conviction of its stubborn wastefulness may sink in and, once with you, not leave you, as a mood leaves you. The supreme manifestation of waste is large-scale war. History is full of it.

In thinking of the waste of war—and, on this, Joseph Schumpeter in his essay of 1919, "The Sociology of Imperialism,"[32] is as good a guide as any—one has an impetus to think again about conscription—even though, of course, large-scale wars have sometimes been fought without conscription, at least in our modern understanding of it. And in thinking about the justifiability of conscription, one may be led back not only to restrictions on conscription which the idea of the social contract between prudent individuals may create; one may be led back also to the impediment of war itself that individualism as a general democratic idea creates. Individualism contains more than the idea of the social contract. Its sponsorship of rights is sponsorship of a culture, as I have said. It is an outlook on life. The heart of the matter, in my judgment, is that war is always made much more likely when a sense of group identity is strong; and that, therefore, one task of a cultivated and elaborated individualism is to weaken group identity, and to do so naturally in behalf of oneself, but also in behalf of everyone else equally. I believe, then, that a strong standing obstacle in the way of the waste of war as well as of the overall irrationality of political life would be the democratic affirmation of a general individualism, including its claims of prudence.

[32] Joseph Schumpeter, "The Sociology of Imperialism," in *Two Essays*, trans. Heinz Norden (New York: Meridian, 1955).

The case against group identity would have to be built up slowly and carefully. I can give only a sketchy account here. I would begin by noticing that group identity exists in various kinds and degrees, from an affectionate regard for what is most close and most familiar to the pathological intensities of folk mystique. I cannot imagine a life without some group identity altogether, just as I do not wish to imagine a life in which children are raised to put prudence ahead of goodness. Group identity is both inevitable and desirable: inevitable because group identity has its root in the fact that we are not born as adults, as prudent contractors, but as creatures who attach ourselves preverbally and nonrationally to those around us and hence insensibly develop the ability to live outside ourselves, so to speak; and desirable because the ideal of stoic selfhood in isolation turns out to be self-delusion, in that it shows such a great desperation to be rid of one's fellows that one becomes all the more obsessively tied to them. Yet the ideal of group identity must be submitted to criticism because it is the source of much—though not all—of the tendency of political life to waste the lives (and well-being) of individuals. Let us keep to mind that though the Constitution's first phrase is "We the people," that We does not suggest the formation of a group identity that effaces and transcends individual identity.

To identify with a group too dumbly or too passionately means that one does not think of oneself apart from it. This identification is not an instrumental relationship. Rather, what or who one is, is defined—consciously or not—by reference to the group. To identify with a group *totally* means to accept an identity derived from what is outside oneself. It also implies that one imagines the group as a person, an enlarged self. It is me, but larger. But it also has the reciprocal effect of making me larger. Group identity is therefore a vehicle for both diminishing and magnifying the self. What is involved is not simply diminishing the self in order to enlarge it: diminishment is itself desired along with enlargement.

From such an inevitable process of abstraction, of self-alienation, come the waste of war as well as many other political irrationalities. War may come *directly* from a pathologically exaggerated sense of group identity. But as Schumpeter's analysis suggests, this sense also permits those who have a permanent vested interest in the war system to keep that system going. In relation to this systemic interest, specific "concrete interests," in turn, are secondary, though not necessarily minor. Concrete interests take advantage of the opportunities exploited by the vested systemic interests, while the vested systemic interests—a martial power elite dominated by a heroic or a statist mentality—succeed because they can appeal to an underlying group feeling, which may be potent even though it stops short of folk mystique. They may manipulate or inflame it, but they do not implant it. Schumpeter says about every power elite: "Created by wars that required it, the machine now created the wars it required."[33] We can add another factor at work that he does not mention, namely, the existence of systemic interests vested in the structure of order which find in war a device to distract attention from inequalities and grievances at home.

In any case, he points to a pervasive tendency in political life, the tendency for the instruments to become the purpose, for agencies to convert a people into means for the ends of those agencies. This is the true political perversion. We see versions of it everywhere we look, in all fields of life, but most crucially in political life. The perversion is in the reversal of means and ends; this happens politically when many are sacrificed for the few, when agents become masters. (There are, of course, good ways of reversing means and ends: for example, prizing the intrinsic values contained in procedures, processes, and other activities above their goals. But persons are not thereby instrumentalized.) The perversion would not be possible, to begin with, without an irrational, imprudent popular consent. The means could not become the end in itself if people were not already in love with the personified group and had not displaced onto it an unmastered and primordial need to have a fixed identity, something one can never find in and for oneself but only outside oneself, and then only unreasonably and half-consciously. Surely, however, this popular consent is not compatible with another kind of consent, the underlying consent by individuals to live defensively, to live by the terms of a prudent and democratic social contract, as embodied, for example, in the U.S. Constitution. Individualism is meant to moderate the psychological displacement that permits the working out of that political perversion which, in turn, is a main cause of waste of individuals, whether in war or in other ways. It is therefore important to notice that recent defenses of patriotism (perhaps self-sacrificing) have been made by such communitarian opponents of individualism as John Schaar, Alasdair MacIntyre, and Charles Taylor.[34]

[33] Schumpeter, 25.

[34] John Schaar, "The Case for Patriotism," in his *Legitimacy in the Modern State* (New Brunswick, N.J.: Transaction Books, 1981); Alasdair MacIntyre, "Is Patriotism a Virtue?" Lindley Lecture, University of Kansas, Philosophy Department, 1984; Charles Taylor, "Cross-Purposes: The Liberal-Communitarian Debate," in Nancy L. Rosenblum, ed., *Liberalism and the Moral Life* (Cambridge: Harvard University Press, 1989).

To say it again, the passion for group identity is not the only feeling or susceptibility that facilitates the waste of individuals. I shall just mention three others that are mutually related. They are almost universal, yet each one offends against the spirit of individualism in a democracy, and hence against the spirit of the Constitution. This is to say that even without conscription, a tremendous amount of freely given popular energy awaits its use in war, and that conscription itself rests on much besides a reluctant sense of duty. What I offer here is, I grant, oversimple but not, I hope, a remote distortion.

First, there is *machismo*, the cultural elevation of masculinity, which divides the world into men and non-men and proceeds to inspire men to fight men so that all men can keep all women in their place, keep them down, keep them under. To exaggerate a bit: wars between armed groups are a tactic in the war between the sexes (the genders). "All wars," said Herman Melville, "are boyish and are fought by boys."[35] Yet it is amazing how thorough the cooperation of women with this system has been. Individualism is a force against machismo because it tries to refuse to put people in categories and assign them a categorial destiny. Individualism teaches that a man or a woman is a person first and, only after, a man or a woman.

Second, there is the related proclivity to imagine the world as naturally and necessarily divided into sides or teams: what matters to this mentality is that there be sides or teams so that there can be strife, not that there are real divisions that may necessitate strife. This is the *abstract agon*, and it is related to the elitist wish (referred to above) to keep intact the system in which some oppress others. The abstract agon shows the general psychological proclivity to convert means into ends by valuing destructive action for the sake of its aesthetic or cathartic effects. Many people think along these lines quite without realizing what they are doing. But, again, individualism in a democracy tries to combat this proclivity, and does so in two ways. It directs the strife back into each self and tries to make an individual self emerge out of internal struggle, the struggle of oneself with oneself, so that one becomes whole by becoming double, by becoming self-conscious and self-examined. Then, too, individualism prefers a playful and bloodless agon to literal war. The essence of the politics of the Constitution is to convert the lust for contest into a turbulent but peaceful domestic politics, in which no one at home loses

---

[35] Herman Melville, "The March into Virginia, Ending in the First Manasses (July, 1861)," in *Battle-Pieces and Aspects of the War* (1866).

badly and no one abroad is victimized by the projection of a literally murderous combativeness. As Whitman put it in "The Return of the Heroes," a post–Civil War poem, there must be "saner wars, sweet wars, life-giving wars."

Third, there is the *sense of country as territory*, as turf, which figures in our imagination as something to be protected against foreign invasion. The land is often imagined as a nurturant mother, which no foreign force must be allowed to penetrate. The land is also often imagined as a father, as a source not of life but of a substancelike identity, which is not to be effaced by foreign conquest. This sense of country is linked to machismo but is not exhaustively defined by it. I do not deny that though turf is an abstract idea, it is less abstract than some other war-inspiring supersti- tions: the core of its realism is the simple fact that the land is the place, the scene, of one's life, not merely the place of one's earning a livelihood. It is a site as well as a stake. Yet the idea is characteristically carried to self- destructive lengths.

In sum, the individualist spirit of the Constitution, its concern for human dignity, is strenuously at odds with machismo, with the desire to see others as natural enemies, and with the sense of motherland or fatherland.

I am aware that other and darker and more elusive feelings and suscep- tibilities dispose people (not only philosophers and poets) to accept war and its waste. I refer first to the sentiment that leads people to defend war (tacitly) on the grounds that war ultimately prevents more waste than it causes. The feeling is that unless life were risked, its value would remain poorly defined. Only something precarious can be esteemed. If war causes many deaths, it nevertheless enhances the sanctity of life in a roundabout way. Now I do not deny that risking something may indicate and contribute to a sense of its value. But for those who do not merely risk their lives but lose them (freely or by conscription), there is no psychological effect: the supposed benefit accrues parasitically to their fellows. The lives of the killed were used for them. And, in any case, many wars have been or contained massacres, and therefore could not produce this supposedly beneficial effect except for distant spectators.

Another sentiment is that war must be accepted because it helps to distinguish human beings from animals. Those who rationalize this sentiment hint that the secret of human nature is that human beings will do all they can to avoid thinking that there is a (common) human nature because every other animal species has a common nature. The effort to make human groups distinct from one another, almost like different species, therefore has a not-ignominious source and is well worth the price of war, which must result from group identity. The irony of this position, however, is that if each group easily thinks of itself as a distinct and homogeneous species (or almost so), it artificially reanimalizes itself. The only escape from the problem and the ravages of its solution is a cultivated sense of the vast potentiality and inwardness of every individual equally. That sense is expressed by Emerson in "New England Reformers": "no society can ever be so large as one man."[36]

There is one last turn in the argument, however. I think it plausible to say that though individualism can provide powerful resistance to the fantasy projects of waste, it may be prone to self-betrayal. I would mention two possible reasons, without developing them fully. First, when the individual is put at the center of moral thought about political life, the language of obligation immediately makes its appearance. A new prison must be found for the released individual. Even if one does not want to go back to Christian teachings, the writings of Hobbes, Locke, Rousseau, and Kant, in varying ways and degrees, show this tendency. It is as if the theorists of the social contract were not really inadvertent or reluctant in countenancing conscription. The political bond is so moralized that positive duty can come to outweigh rights. Membership, when voluntary, seems to entail unlimited risk. Such a thought is not far from Hannah Arendt's reflections on the political contract in *On Revolution* (1963) and the "horizontal" contract in "Civil Disobedience" (1970).

The way is prepared for the dissemination of the suggestion that the social contract, unlike other foundations, creates the perpetual possibility of dying before one's time. One is dying because one has *consented* to die; one has *promised* to die; one has *obliged* oneself to die, if need be. It is as if the logic of being a moral agent is to be prepared to sacrifice oneself: that alone is how one shows that one deserves being recognized as a moral agent and how one realizes one's dignity. One owns one's life so that one may offer it up. Of course it is undeniable that unless some people had been and are now willing to die or risk death many of the individual rights that contribute to human dignity would never have been or would cease to be established. But can one ever be *obliged* to give up the right to life (unenslaved and undegraded) in order to protect one's own other rights or the rights of others? It is admirable to do so; it may be morally allowable to do so; but I do not see that it is morally obligatory. I

[36] Ralph Waldo Emerson, "New England Reformers," in *The Complete Essays and Other Writings*, ed. Brooks Atkinson (New York: Modern Library, 1950), 456–57.

do not see how it can be properly made legally mandatory. In any case, perhaps the very idea of conscription as ultimately a moral obligation could arise only in an individualist moral universe. That would be a terrible irony; Foucault can sensitize us to it.

Second, it is well to remember that in *On War* (1832) Carl von Clausewitz welcomed the coming of modern democracy precisely because he thought that the most absolute wars, the most theoretically perfect ones, the most aesthetically satisfying ones, could be fought only on the basis of mass mobilization—the mobilization not only of large numbers of people but also of a re-created sense of group identity. When the people look upon society as theirs, the bellicose disposition, he thought, is strengthened. His will to define life as war found sustenance in the popular passion for self-sacrifice, democratically engineered. "Drum-Taps," the Civil War poems of Walt Whitman, the greatest poet (perhaps the greatest thinker) of democracy, perfectly reflect and encourage that passion with a guiltless intensity. One can learn from Clausewitz that, for one sort of elitist mind, all that democracy is good for is to strengthen the inclination, present in every kind of government, to believe that authority is only the permission for officials to engage in crime, or to lead others into it, if not with impunity then at least with confidence. To adapt a remark by Oscar Wilde: there is no essential incongruity between crime and politics—even apart from political corruption and literal political gangsterism. To ward off the worst that Clausewitz points to, we should be ready to admit that the political mentality can be worse than the criminal mentality, because it thinks itself right or burdened with superhuman responsibility. Only when the individualist basis of modern democracy is deeply felt and acted on can this dangerous tendency, sometimes made more energetic in a self-forgetful democracy, be blunted.

These two latencies, one in the theory of the social contract on an individualist basis and the other in the democratic society that has grown under it, must be considered seriously. We should want to be able to say, however, that the theory of the social contract is the theory of the U.S. Constitution and that when looked at again it may give us the best starting point for challenging complacent acceptance of conscription for abstract purposes and for objecting to war and its waste.

CHAPTER EIGHT

On Political Evil

I mention at the outset that my readiness, presumptuous in itself, to say something about evil comes from studying the work of Hannah Arendt. She wrote about political evil more powerfully, I think, than anyone else ever has, and did so because totalitarianism, its most vivid form, obsessed her. Most of what I say was either suggested or provoked by her, especially by two books, *The Origins of Totalitarianism* (1951) and *Eichmann in Jerusalem* (1963). I wish to go on with the effort of responding to Arendt's urgent attempt to understand the phenomena that most need understanding. I must add, however, that my defense of individualism in a democracy provides an independent reason for my effort. In my judgment—a judgment I doubt Arendt shared—a cultivated and seriously meant individualism can provide obstacles to political evil.

People often recoil at the word "evil." Arendt herself recoiled, and she devised the notion of "the banality of evil" in the effort to correct herself. She wanted to make the doers of evil unglamorous and without even a perverse stature. Yet she retained the word. Many think, however, that practically any use of the word is an exaggeration, that it is melodramatic or lurid, that it always demonizes unfairly, and that it is best reserved for comic books and horror movies. But I find that attitude unacceptable in itself and useful only when construed as cautionary. I believe that we are right to use the word but that we must use it as sparingly as the facts allow. The word expresses the utmost condemnation. Surely many deeds or policies or conditions or systems deserve the utmost condemnation. If they are not wrong, nothing is wrong. Evil is the worst wrong.[1]

---

[1] For a stimulating discussion of cruelty as the worst wrong, see Judith N. Shklar, *Ordinary Vices* (Cambridge: Harvard University Press, 1984), chaps. 1, 6. This chapter

When I speak of evil, I refer to the deliberate infliction (or sponsorship or knowing allowance), for *almost* any reason whatever, of suffering of great intensity, whether on a small or large scale, and of death, whether on one, few, or many. The only infliction of suffering and death I think I would not consider evil is that done (by victims or their allies) in resisting those who kill or enslave or make miserable, or try to. These aggressions are as it were capital offenses, the only ones, even if they are usually committed not by criminals but by ordinary persons, organized and led. (Capital punishment, in the usual sense, is evil; it has nothing to do with self-defense.)

If strict self-defense against attack is not doing evil, even though it is the deliberate infliction of suffering and death, what is its moral status? Is it only like the morally allowable suspension of morality, the morally allowable prudential self-preferment that is granted guiltless people in a condition of scarcity who must struggle against one another for the means of survival? Or can deliberate infliction in a case of self-defense actually be thought morally right, a policy of justice?

I am not sure of the answer: the teachings of Socrates and Jesus against self-preferment inhibit easy acceptance of either possibility and seem to insist that deliberate infliction, even in strict self-defense, is evil, and therefore not to be done. Meeting these teachings half way means calling strict self-defense evil, but necessary and hence allowable evil. I incline to think, however, that from an individualist perspective, it may be better to call strict self-defense neither necessary evil nor justice, but a morally allowable suspension of morality. Self-defense against the guilty is not radically different from self-defense against the guiltless. In any case, the historical norm is evil done for the sake of advancing purposes and defending commitments that have nothing to do with strict self-defense, that is, with the preservation of people in unenslaved and undegraded conditions of life. My subject is the historical norm.

The subject in its fullness is evil that is deliberately inflicted by people (by governments or by persons in everyday life), not the intense suffering or premature death that accident or nature may cause. I include within deliberate evil the suffering and death that are expected and brought about, even if they are inflicted with regret and a sense of necessity. Of

began as a response to the second of Irving Howe's Tanner Lectures, "The Concept of Totalitarianism," delivered at Princeton University, March 1990. In it he discusses "abstract rage." For a critical discussion of the concept of group identity but one that is more sympathetic than my own in this chapter, see William E. Connolly, *Identity/Difference* (Ithaca: Cornell University Press, 1991), especially chaps. 1, 3, and 4.

course, human activity can result in unforeseen and hence indeliberate (or unintended) suffering and death, but this is not part of my subject.

The initial interest of a student of politics will be in political evil, in the evil that governments (or political movements) do or sponsor or knowingly allow, rather than in what individuals do as individuals. I would distinguish political evil from two related political phenomena: oppression and injustice. Kinds of political *evil* include almost all wars, specific deeds or policies in wars, slavery, deliberate impoverishment or neglect of correctable misery, deliberate moral and mental degradation, torture, judicial murder, capital and corporal punishment, slaughter, massacre, and genocide. In the language of rights, which I believe is the proper moral language to use when thinking about the relation of the political sphere to people, evil is the obliteration of personhood and hence the deprivation of all the personal and political rights of one, few, some, or many. Contrastingly—but I do not want to make the contrast excessively sharp because the boundaries are sometimes indistinct—political *oppression* takes such forms as tyranny, despotism, and dictatorship; systematic intolerance; and systematic discrimination. Oppression is thus the denial of many or most personal and political rights; but some rights are still respected, even if precariously, and not acknowledged as rights; for example, the right to life, and the right to lead a life in a family, at work, and in some privacy. (But suppose oppression causes reduced life expectancy in multitudes? Is that not evil?) Political *injustice* is the denial of one or a few personal or political rights—say, the denial of the right to vote or to publish without prior restraint or to remain silent when standing accused of a crime.

If, at home, modern constitutional democracies often do or allow injustice, whether in episodic acts or in sectors of social life, their policies abroad may sustain or perpetrate not only oppression but also evil.

I shall confine myself to political evil *on a large scale*. I want to insist that political evil matters radically if it is done to only one person, as oppression and injustice also matter; but for now my interest is in evil as policy (which I mean to include evil as condition or system), evil on a large scale.

I have already granted that the boundaries between the categories of evil, oppression, and injustice are not always clear. Other problems with my approach arise; for example, the language of rights may sometimes sound artificial or not weighty enough, especially when what is involved is not injustice but oppression or evil. I must also notice that until the seventeenth century the world did not speak about individual rights, and thus in thinking about evil in the more remote past we must see evil as it was seen then. In support of my approach I would say that over time there has usually been fairly steady agreement on what counts as the worst pain and suffering: unwanted, dreaded, to be resisted if possible. There has also been agreement that it is better not to die before one's time. The theory of rights universalizes this agreement, makes it reciprocal and egalitarian, promotes it insistently, examines other political values and purposes for their compatibility with rights, and consigns these values and purposes to a subordinate status. The whole world now says that it accepts this codification of long-standing attitudes. The whole world now uses the language of rights.

Despite all difficulties, therefore, I think that, on balance, distinctions can be made between evil, oppression, and injustice and that the idea of rights can provide both a standard for distinguishing them and the basis on which to protest them. Roughly and selectively put: what Hitler, Stalin, Mao, and Pol Pot did was evil; the untouchables in India, the blacks of South Africa under apartheid, and the peasants of most of Central and South America endure oppression; and the condition of the British colonists in America before the Revolution was in my judgment—which is based on the primacy of preserving life, innocent and guilty alike—one of injustice. My belief is that only evil certainly justifies violent resistance; oppression may or may not; and injustice does not. Violent resistance to injustice may arouse our sympathies, but it may have to be condemned as evil.

Why do governments or political movements inflict or permit evil on a large scale? As a student of political theory I was disposed for a long time to think that the great or good texts that I teach—the canon that academic political theorists teach and that goes from Plato to Marx and Nietzsche—must throw light on this question. But since I started thinking about political evil I have been struck by how little help the canon of political theory gives. That is why I claim so much for Arendt, and why I would also single out another contemporary who has done invaluable work: Tzvetan Todorov in *The Conquest of America* (1982). (Yet maybe the argument I will develop is taken mostly from Plato's *Republic*, or Rousseau's *Discourse on the Origins of Inequality*, but I am not sure that it is.) A further point is that much of this canon often ends up on the side of evil without quite knowing it—siding with intense suffering and premature death on a great scale, the scale of action that usually only political agencies and forces are capable of. (Plato himself makes war intrinsic to the just social order, which would lack an organizing, disciplining, and justifying principle unless it had foreign enemies to fight.)

I therefore argue for two main points. First, much of the time the canonical political theorists do not worry about the evil that governments do—to leave aside other political forces. They may have a keen sense that governments can be oppressive or unjust, but not that they do evil. To the contrary, many political theorists see in government a remedy for evil, face-to-face or small-scale evil: the actual or potential crimes and transgressions of individuals (and sometimes small groups or factions) against each other. Often they ignore the greater evil for the smaller. They tend to be on the side of order rather than peace, and call it justice. They then proceed to explain evil by reference to human nature, suggesting that the explanation of evil as such is to be found in the basic instinctual and appetitive endowment of human beings or the wickedness or depravity of the human heart. All deliberate evil is explained by human nature. Pessimism is the truth, many theorists say, that makes sense of the whole range of suffering and wrongdoing. I believe, instead, that pessimistic analyses do explain a great deal about face-to-face and small-scale evil—the immediately dramatic kinds, political and private—but not enough about political oppression and injustice on a large scale and too little about political evil on a large scale.

When I say, second, that the writers in the canon often end up on the side of evil, I mean more than one thing, but especially that they assume without examination the validity of the idea of the group or they actively defend it. In both cases the idea of strong group identity is promoted. They assume or defend the priority of the group over the individual, and the defensiveness or assertiveness of one's group in relation to other groups. They subtly or unconsciously encourage individuals to live outside themselves and to regard outsiders as alien. My contention is that much of political evil on a large scale is intimately connected to deep belief in the group and in its identity. By group I especially mean the armed national group in a world of armed groups, but also the armed revolutionary group or the armed and dominant group that victimizes other groups in its society.

As is obvious, my two points are aimed against one of the most influential and standard accounts in the literature of political theory. Human beings are supposedly ravenous beasts. In general, unless they are reined in they would destroy one another. By this account, the task of political theory is to show the need to disarm individuals and clusters of individuals and make them civil. Uniting them against the outside world keeps them better behaved at home. Worrying about the power of government is less important than worrying about the multitudes of ordinary persons.

Suppose, however, that this account—versions of which are found in all the Western traditions of political theory, and from the start—may not say enough of the truth and may even deflect our attention from the matter of political evil on a large scale? I do not deny—how could anyone?—that human beings need both restraint and habituation to right conduct. All I wish to propose is that the seemingly inevitable accompaniment to making people better and less prone to evil in everyday life is making them, at the same time, parties to evil on a large scale. The everyday evils of violent crimes and other transgressions are reduced; and by that reduction, political evil is enabled and facilitated. Social order is, among other things, a device for producing political crimes on a large scale. I do not mean that society sends some of its wickedness outward and thus reduces it at home. Rather, the attempted solution of the problem of wickedness at home allows the creation of other sources of evil than wickedness. That inference suggests that there may be some difference between what causes individuals and clusters of them to commit face-to-face and small-scale evils and what allows governments (and movements) to do evil on a large scale. Let me add that it is a rare generation in which the amount of large-scale political evil is less than the amount of murders, beatings, and other violent crimes in everyday life.

Political societies are—at least intermittently—engines of evil, not only of oppression or injustice. Governments of all forms (like armed movements of all tendencies) do or allow evil *as a matter of policy*—that is, in cold blood, not hot blood. Actually the mentality is bloodless even when murderous. They do or allow it at home in regard to sectors of their population, or they do or allow it in regard to other societies. And because evil is policy, I find it impossible simply to say that only the basic human instinctive or appetitive endowment is needed to account for evil's occurrence. Policy is not merely instinct or desire. To a significant extent, it is impersonal. It is an artifice, an elaborate construction.

As I suggest later, the passions that initiate and help to sustain evil are abstract: unfelt, or if felt, then willed or adopted or put on or experienced in a dreamlike way. This abstraction leads me to believe that political evil is much more a product of human susceptibilities than of inherent substantive nature, of specific dominating urges. No straight road leads from human wickedness to political evil, from individual crime to official or partisan crime, whatever the bulk of the canon of political theory says or implies. Even if everyone is, by nature, aggressive or transgressive, that fact still does not explain political evil. Political commitments transform human beings, making them capable of acting more terribly (in methodical, detached, even self-sacrificing ways) than wickedness ever could. On the other hand, those who lead blameless everyday lives can be transformed into unreluctant agents of political evil.

Those thinkers who attribute innate innocence to humanity get in the way less, when we try to understand political evil on a large scale, than do those who attribute depravity. If you will, political evil on a large scale arises from the psychology of Adam and Eve before the Fall rather than after (if human creatures who were never children can be said to have a psychology).

I grant that if the relevant susceptibilities are universal (or nearly so) and irresistible (or resistible only with great effort and, even then, rarely with complete success), then evil as policy must be produced as regularly as it would be by innate viciousness. By neither hypothesis would political evil be a mere deviation or circumstantial happening. Nevertheless, we can at least say that the susceptibilities reveal not an innate inclination to immorality but a disposition to fantastical excess (on the one hand) and to normality and the "human, all too human" (on the other). These susceptibilities implicate the student of large-scale political evil in the uncanny. Excess is manifestly uncanny and normality is uncanny in spite of itself.

If we start with the thought that power tends to corrupt, we still do not have an adequate account of why political agencies and forces do or allow evil. Lord Acton's phrase (echoing Mill) seems to lodge the explanation in the cruelty, arrogance, or pride of the powerful. Those personal vices must be part of the explanation, undeniably. But evil as policy requires other sources. In trying to explain it, I would, however, follow Acton in highlighting the difference in roles between leaders and people, even though they share some decisive traits. Now, I do not mean to put all the blame on leaders or to claim dualistically that leaders are radically worse than ordinary persons. Differences in position and hence in the opportunity to act do, however, matter greatly. In every case of evil policy, evil on a large scale, we can therefore ask these questions: First, what were the susceptibilities and what were the purposes of the leaders that inspired or instigated it? Second, what were the susceptibilities and what were the feelings in ordinary persons which were necessary to carry it out? (These include susceptibilities and feelings that leaders can take as already reliably present when they initiate evil.) Third, what were the susceptibilities and what were the feelings in ordinary persons which, though not necessary to carry out the policy, made it easier to do so? The three questions are not sealed off from one another. Sometimes discussion of one question involves reference to the other two because of shared traits. I must also say from the start that I do not think that one account can trace all political evil on a large scale to a single ultimate cause. But some elements do stand out.

We should begin an account of political evil on a large scale with an effort to understand the characteristic *susceptibilities* of the powerful. After all, they are the ones who initiate evil. A preliminary generalization is that those in or with power—whatever the form of government or nature of the armed movement—are especially prone to fantasy projects and to thinking on a large scale (to use the phrase "on a large scale" again). They are tempted by the grandiose. They are prone to a special kind of abstraction: those in or with power tend not to perceive human beings as individuals. They tend to convert their own people into ingredients or resources or instruments, or to gather them up into various categories, or even to see them all as just one disposable or usable mass. Correspondingly, they also tend to see people in other societies, or certain groups in their own, abstractly, though not as means but rather as "other" or, in the extreme, as necessarily enemies (as necessary enemies).

Political abstractness takes a second form among the initiators of evil. Those who design the policy, provide the inspiration, give the orders, often can literally see only some details or incidents in their policy. They literally see only little. Hence the evil they initiate is largely invisible (until of course the suffering and destruction rebound on them, if it does). I do not wish to assert, however, that leaders would inevitably end their policies if they could see the full effects up close. But frequently leaders not only have abstract projects, they also experience their projects abstractly—that is, invisibly, impalpably, in a manner that is absent to the senses. Relatedly, many of those who sustain the policy by administering it, or by carrying it out every day, may literally see what they do, but the division of labor separates some people from all visibility and parcels out visibility to others who do literally see. It is as if the epitome of evil on a large scale is raining bombs from a great height. No one engaged in a policy of evil, on any level, can see or feel the whole policy. (Of course, combatants in war often see more than a little.) Only an individualist imagination could dissolve the fantastical abstraction. The crucial role of invisibility is one of the considerations that lead me to say, therefore, that human depravity counts for little in the production of evil as policy, and abstraction for a great deal.

Woven in with the tendency to launch abstract projects and to experience them abstractly is the habit of personifying one's society or state: to make it a unity and a person and then to attribute to it moral existence and moral rights by analogy to those of individuals. Just as leaders convert persons into useful or noxious quantities, so they also convert a legal fiction into a person. But though they imagine the society or state as an individual, they imagine it as an individual vastly more significant and dignified than any real individual. It is a person, but a superperson. Its existence is its interests, which it may do anything to preserve, protect, and defend. The activities, the wrongs that the state denies to individuals in pursuit of their own individual interests, the state allows itself, on behalf of the fancied interests of the totality of individuals. The state kills, maims, coerces, and deceives, and does so almost never to ensure the literal unenslaved survival of the population. This personification is also a kind of abstraction to which those in power tend as by vocation, even though it is not confined to them. (Comparable phenomena are at work in the minds of leaders of armed movements.)

I think that Hegel articulates and glorifies what many in power feel at least dimly but rarely voice. In the Introduction to his *Lectures on the Philosophy of World History*, he says:

> For world history moves on a higher plane than that to which morality properly belongs. . . . Whatever is required and accomplished by the ultimate end of the spirit . . . and whatever providence does, transcends the obligations, liability, and responsibility which attach to individuality. . . . The litany of private virtues . . . must not be raised against them [world-historical deeds and those who perform them]. . . . World history might well disregard completely the sphere to which morality . . . belongs . . . by ignoring individuals altogether . . . for what it has to record is the activity of the spirit of nations.[2]

It is hard to imagine a greater license for evil than these words. They consecrate the tendency to all the sorts of abstraction which I have just mentioned.

I believe that these susceptibilities help to make much of even usual politics, "superficial and inhuman," in Thoreau's phrase in "Life without Principle." They are part of the ground of evil, but only part, because leaders are helpless without multitudes of followers, of ordinary persons.

Some ordinary susceptibilities are another part of the ground because

---

[2] Georg Wilhelm Friedrich Hegel, *Introduction: Reason in History*, 2d Draft (1830), trans. H. B. Nisbet (Cambridge: Cambridge University Press, 1975), 141.

they embolden the initiators of large-scale political evil. I revert to the suggestion I made earlier, that there is an intimate connection between evil as policy and deep belief in group identity. I mean to distinguish this belief from the sorts of abstraction to which I have just said that leaders are prone. It is belief in something seemingly real and tangible—say, a way of life—but belief normally carried beyond the bounds of good sense to the point of superstition. Belief in group identity is usually shared equally and intensely by leaders and people alike. I admit that ordinary persons routinely lend themselves to political abstraction, to personifying the society and attributing extraordinary rights and powers to its government; and they may vicariously enjoy the fantasy projects of government and the thinking on a large scale that goes with it. By sharing these traits with their leaders, and yet remote from power, people live twice removed from reality. But, more directly, ordinary persons everywhere do more than lend themselves to deep group identity: they embrace it no less fiercely than their leaders. Even more decisive in the production of evil as policy than the abstractionist or statist (or partisan) mentality of those in or with power is the strong susceptibility of people, leaders and ordinary persons alike, to lose themselves in the group, to forget themselves in it, and to sacrifice themselves (freely or half-freely, not only under compulsion) in its worship. There is a kitschy ecstasy in being able to say We. One feels enlarged, but also gratefully reduced, by identifying oneself with the group, by imagining that one's identity is not one's own merely, but necessarily created by the group and expressed most significantly in what the group does and endures as a group.

Identifying with a group is the polar opposite of the democratic idealist effort to identify with other individuals for the sake of understanding and sympathizing with them. In the former case, the difference between oneself and one's fellow citizens is suspended, not as in empathy but for the sake of what has only an imaginary reality. Collectivized strangers deceive themselves into thinking that they are so much alike in the most important respects that they do not have to make an effort to know one another and that outsiders are known well enough just because in their difference they seem inferior. When group identity is strong, group members feel themselves as a solid and repellent mass, not as a society held together by a contract.

Even when a leader manages to make a whole society an instrument of his will and a means to his megalomania, he is likely to be consumed by an inability to imagine himself as himself. He must incorporate a group into himself before he can feel that he has being. He can exist only inflatedly. This irrationality is far removed from naked self-seeking.

I cannot imagine human life without some measure of group identity, but I also cannot imagine a comparatively decent life (at least internationally) unless group identity is mitigated considerably by the doctrine of individual human rights—by the conviction, that is, that other people are as real to themselves as I am to myself or we are to ourselves. I am not saying that each of us should live for oneself alone, only that we should not be crazy while thinking that we are being only social.

So far, then, I have introduced two susceptibilities, two considerations that prepare the way for evil on a large scale: first, the abstract quality of political calculation made by leaders, which is a kind of half-thinking; second, the deep belief in group identity, shared by leaders and people alike, which recurrently turns extreme or pathological and which is another kind of half-thinking. But I emphasize that in regard to both leaders and people the heart of the matter is deep belief in group identity. Without this universal susceptibility, oppression and injustice would still exist, but probably not evil on a large scale. I think that it is, in one form or another, significantly implicated in the initiation of evil as a policy, and then in its maintenance, its normalization or systemization. If groups are imagined too vividly, individuals lose sight of themselves and are lost sight of. Ordinary persons thus cooperate with their undoing and the victimization of other ordinary persons. That is what evil as policy often amounts to.

The question I raise now is whether there are formulations that capture the essential purposes of leaders who initiate evil. What are the dominating aims that seem recurrently to take advantage of the susceptibilities in leaders to which I have just referred? The first thing to say is that almost never do the practitioners of evil say or admit that evil (or some kind of wrong) is their purpose, that evil is their good, as Milton's Satan says. It is hard enough to find them saying or getting them to admit that they do evil incidentally, or that they even do some wrong, in the course of achieving some purpose. The political pursuit of evil as evil—evil for the pleasure of doing evil—is almost nonexistent. Perhaps particular individuals, acting officially or in private life, pursue evil as evil. We say of them that they are sadists; or that they are driven by an insatiable longing for retribution or compensation; or that for obscure reasons they are in the hold of malignant envy, spite, or malice; or that they are mad with vainglory. Famous literature contains impressive depictions of such characters. But I do not believe that the initiation of political evil on a large scale can be explained by reference to such considerations.

The reason is that the feelings or passions behind the purposes are abstract passions; they are not like everyday passions, even the most intense of them. They are no mere sublimations or "desublimations" of everyday passions. Leaders are vocationally impelled to create the objects that create the passions. The politics of evil is only the hideous exaggeration of normal politics and it is not best understood as the exaggeration of everyday evil. Woven into abstract passions, of course, are personal passions; but these are enclosed by or dispersed in or energized by or given form or coherence or meaning by abstract passions. A war, for example, consists in the motions of hatred—violence intent on at least the partial destruction of another group. But war is initiated not because of hatred like everyday hatred but because of abstract hatred or some other abstract, depersonalized feeling or passion like abstract envy or jealousy or pride or anger. You do not need even abstract hatred to start a war. The sporting spirit, or the spirit of playing a game to win, may be enough.

Thinking on a large scale, which is abstract, is accompanied by the appropriate feelings that are also abstract: the unaware imitation of feelings that deserve to be called real or true only when, because of real genuine psychological processes, private individuals have them and act on them, that is, when private individuals act criminally. The normality of armed groups is analogous to the condition of individual madness: extreme paranoia and monomania. Those who have abstract feelings lead a vicarious life without knowing it: the life leads them. They also feel obliged to have or simulate certain feelings. Not quite voluntarily, leaders imagine the feelings that the group would have if it were a person, even though it is not a person, and then act on them for the group, in a volatile combination of feeling nothing and having deluded feelings. This mentality is similar to but much less real than the intense group loyalties connected to localities, institutions, games, and sports. Leaders (and followers) transfer these harmless or invigorating (if somewhat abstract) passions to a murderous plane. They are constantly taking an invented group reality for a natural reality and allowing it to impose itself, to dictate a logic or pattern that must complete itself.

Yet, though abstract, these passions are often stronger than personal ones, just because their abstractness tends to make them unsatisfiable and hence limitless. Supposedly devoted to a higher level of reality or seriousness, abstract political passions, but especially those productive of evil, are actually more nearly dreamed or endured deliriously than experienced in an awakened state. Apparently more rational in a gamelike way because unaffected by unconscious personal urges, these passions are perfectly irrational because they are systematically insulated from the reality of individuals. The group-objects cherished or loathed are cartoons or caricatures; they provide no objective correlative for any honest feeling. True or unabstract feelings figure importantly in the maintenance of evil by ordinary persons, not in its instigation by leaders. Part of what I mean when I call evil an artifice is that the instigating passions are abstract: they are, in part, considerations formed automatically by the mere possession of political power (on the one hand) and by deep belief in group identity (on the other). (In a moment I will discuss the contribution that ideology makes to the creation of objects that elicit the abstract passions of evil.) If I seem to be speaking too much of the abstract, then let us use such cognate terms as the imaginary or the symbolic.

In short, abstract passions lie behind the abstract projects or purposes that leaders develop and then experience abstractly. This unreality tends to pervade all politics; it surely characterizes the initiation of evil as policy. And because ordinary persons, not just leaders, deeply feel group identity, they too share in abstract passions.

I have so far traced political evil to the unreality that adheres to all political activity. Suppose, however, that someone says, invoking Plato, that the everyday life of individuals is itself full of unreality—full of abstract or imaginary feelings and of desires for what is only symbolic—and is spent in bondage to what is nothing more than the play of shadows on the cave's wall. Indeed, Plato taught that private unreality creates and sustains political abstraction, fantasy, and superstition, and hence evil. To this Platonist view I would say only that small-scale and face-to-face experience, visible experience, routinely provides its own checks on the destructive effects of everyday irrationality. There is greater sanity in private life, even in its insanity. When the checks fail, the effects are nevertheless confined—a cold thing to say, I grant.

Further, I have been trying to suggest that political activity, whether evil or not, is no mere emanation of private feelings and desires but to an appreciable extent creates a world that is discontinuous with everyday life. I acknowledge this fact with dismay, not with Hegel's reverence. The discontinuity is a sign of the political sphere's moral inferiority and the repugnance of even its necessity. It is inferior even though characteristically it is inwardly innocent or like innocence, while private life shows more than traces of inner wickedness; and even though face-to-face evil comes out of the worst feelings and impulses, while political evil has other sources.

Elements of the Platonist view, however, can be insistently put forward. Someone can say that even if the notion of an abstract passion (in the twofold meaning of simulated feeling and deluded feeling) makes sense, there is an analogy or continuity between real passions and abstract ones. Real ones prepare the way for abstract ones by providing everyday language for them and by making them feel familiar. Then, too, abstract hatred or abstract pride, for example, is still in some sense hatred or pride. The same psychic disposition is there; the will to hate or feel pride is there, or at least to fantasize hatred or pride. Attention should be paid to the passion, not to whether it is abstract or genuine, and it should be called the vice it is. Indeed, it is better to say that the passions behind political evil are real, not abstract, even though they may be triggered or accompanied by confused or displaced mental processes. The traditional account of evil as stemming from innate human vice is, after all, on the right track.

All I can do in answer is to concede the plausibility of this view but then try to go on thinking that the passions of political evil—the passions that instigate it and are necessary to maintain it—are not real as everyday passions are.

Can we generalize, then, about the content of the projects of evil, the essential purposes of evil as policy? What crystallizations of abstract passions does the historical record show? I offer only a short and selective sampling. My formulations are obvious. First, governments and armed movements do evil in fighting against it. (I acknowledge, however, that there must be an appreciable moral difference between doing evil while resisting it and instigating the evil that is then resisted.) Second, they do evil in trying to achieve a positive moral good. Third, they do evil in fighting against something that they call evil but that they see not as morally evil but as worse than morally evil. Fourth, they do evil in trying to achieve a positive good that is claimed to be greater than moral goodness. It may be that evils on the greatest scale come about when governments or political groups believe and persuade people to believe that there is evil worse than moral evil, or good greater than moral goodness, and act with a total lack of scrupulousness on that belief. When morality is dislodged from its supremacy, terrible evils result. This statement is platitudinous, but it needs repeating. On the other hand, the production of evil on behalf of fighting moral evil or trying to achieve a positive moral good has also been undeniably enormous.

All in all, it is hard for me to judge where the larger perplexity is found: whether in the fact that evil can come from moral sources or in the fact that transmoral ones can produce moral indifference. A way out of perplexity may be found if we go on the assumption that ideology is close to indispensable. In just about every case, I think that we will find that political evil on a large scale is instigated when the normal abstract mentality of power holders is inflamed by an ideology that simultaneously inflames group identity (in leaders and people) and ties that identity to a moral or a transmoral purpose. Inflamed identity pursues its purposes without regard to moral limits: I mean respect for individual human beings, for what we now call human rights. And where evil is done while resisting it (and hence not instigated, properly speaking), the resistance often takes on the qualities of what is resisted.

Thus ideologies (and I include religions) have a peculiar ability to make leaders and people impersonally ruthless and merciless. The energies for deliberate evil on a large scale could not get going without ideology in either of its two basic forms: cheap ideas or noble ones drastically simplified.

The great danger comes when ideology is starkly dualistic. Dualism is the essence of most of the ideologies that help to initiate (as well as maintain) evil on a large scale. One group attributes a range of inferiorities to other groups, claiming that these others are uncivilized or incurably lower and, even more deadly, unclean or unredeemably impure or untouchable or subhuman or morally monstrous or ontologically evil. We all know the whole range. Perhaps the normal condition of group identity is derangement, or nearly so, because stark dualism is never very far away.

I have no general theory to account for the emergence or success of particular dualistic ideologies. But we all love the supposed clarification that dualism gives life. It is awfully hard to fight that love. We are fatally susceptible to bad aestheticism. We succumb to the religious or metaphysical untruth contained in many ideologies. Or we fail to cure that blindness that will not see that most groups, so different from one another in beliefs and practices, are nevertheless the same in the sorts of claim they make about themselves: that they are better or best, special, distinctive, or unique. (A person feels that a loved one is unlike anyone else in the world. But such a feeling has a reality that group self-love does not.) Groups love untruth; they love themselves in the same ways. Dualistic ideologies intensify such love. Social Darwinism in its dualism of the fit to live and the unfit, and dualistic ideologies of faith, gender, language, race, ethnicity, class, and nation have made all the difference in modern life, and a huge difference throughout all history. They have been sincerely believed by leaders, not only by followers. They are not mere rationalization of interests. Indeed, interests are often a rationalization of ideological passions, rather than the reverse, as if interests could lend some realism or reality to abstract purposes. Nor are group ideologies merely the convenient vehicle for raw, preexistent passions or desires or impulses. Ideologies create passions and the rest—though, to be sure, they take advantage of what I have been calling susceptibilities. Man is an ideological animal and becomes truly moral only in the effort to resist ideology.

The critique of dualistic thinking owes much to Nietzsche. It is a shame that in the course of rejecting the dualism of good and evil he inconsistently retains a commitment to another charged dualism, that of good and bad.

Let me now give some illustrations of each of the four essential purposes of evil as policy. The Northern states in the Civil War and the allied countries in World War II did great evil in fighting against great or greater evil. In fact, I think that the prosecution of any war, whatever the cause, always involves evil on all sides. Evil is evil even if it is part of the effort to repel evil, and even if it is less than the evil resisted. Whenever the better side inflicts suffering and death beyond strict defensive necessity, it does evil. Sometimes, who knows, the better side may do more evil than it remedies. The Northern states in the Civil War and the Allies in World War II were not (at least initially) debauched by an ideology. But once they began to react to evil, once they stood up for human rights, they disregarded bounds, they acted unconditionally. Some of their deeds showed an abstract rage to punish which was dualistically inspired. And what of the evil done those who, as conscripts, suffered or died in fighting an evil system though they themselves were not originally threatened by it with the death, enslavement, or degradation it inflicted on others?

Second, revolutionary governments, like revolutionary movements, characteristically do evil in behalf of creating a new society, a claimed positive moral good, not only for the sake of destroying the evil old order. Doubtless the two aims are intertwined: destruction must precede attempted reconstruction. The worst of such cases are all in this century: the regimes of Stalin, Mao, and Pol Pot all help, in fact, to define evil in this century.

Third, the conquest of the Americas by Europe, the enslavement of African blacks, and Nazism are prime examples (at least in part) of

governments doing or allowing inconceivable evil in the name of overcoming some evil ideologically imagined to be worse than moral evil.
Here we will find that a recurrent aim is to rid the world of what is found
or designated as unclean or to subdue and cleanse it.

For cases of governments or movements that did or allowed evil for the
sake of achieving some positive good claimed to be greater than moral
goodness, we may instance the Crusades, the so-called civilizing mis-
sions of European imperialism, holy wars of forced conversion, the
promotion of culture by exploiting others, and many projects in the West
that seek to conquer new worlds, to adventure beyond the limits, to
withstand or overcome the nature of things in the spirit of Machiavelli, or
to master nature and human nature technologically.

I grant that I give in a schematic way the four essential purposes in the
initiation of evil and that any given case can probably be looked at in
more than one manner and hence classified in more than one way. There
are mixed cases. Doubtless there are usable general descriptions other
than those I have given. But to repeat the main point: ideologies are
recurrently available to draw out to the uttermost the leaders' susceptibilities, which are always present, to engage in grandiose and abstract
calculations and to imagine themselves as being at one with the group,
and the group as one, and the group as superior. Of course, ideologies
also seduce ordinary persons into acceptance of the leaders' purposes.
The susceptibility to half-thinking is universal, not confined to either the
people or their leaders. But the point to emphasize is that leaders are not
cynically free of ideological commitments.

I now return the focus to the susceptibilities and feelings of ordinary
persons which are necessary to carry out and sustain evil as policy. I have
insisted that they share the most important one with their leaders: a
constant disposition to see the world as necessarily divided into groups
and to think that one's life is inseparable from one's group. Even if one
thinks at all of oneself as one self, as a self, as having an identity, one finds
it hard or impossible to conceive of that identity except by reference to
the group. That is the normal condition; indeed, it is claimed to be the
condition of normality. Individualism is the exception. Group identity is
not the result of deliberate ideological creation. It is created indeliberately. Groups secrete it. Ideologies, however, can inflame it to the point
where ordinary persons come to think that their group is innately better

than other groups. In turn, this inflammation or exaggeration, already on the way to derangement, turns absolutely pathological in its effects when other groups are seen as so different as to be not human or less than human. If politically instigated or allowed evil lasts over a period of time, we can be almost sure that the sense of group identity is ideologically exacerbated.

But no matter how strongly group identity is ideologically reinforced, it cannot work alone to sustain evil. Once evil is launched, and in a situation where exacerbated group identity can be taken for granted, other ordinary susceptibilities offer the necessary assistance. For example, we all have a general tendency to conform, whatever it is that we seem moved to conform to, even evil. We imitate what is around us, no matter what. Also, the capacity to see clearly, when what is before us is disturbing, is easily lost. And habituation to evil can make it ungraspable. But there are other human proclivities that help to sustain evil, and they, too, are all necessary to it; yet most are otherwise innocuous, and none is certainly malignant. Instances are: a wish to be left alone and not to be bothered, a conviction that all orders should be obeyed, a wish to be loyal, a wish to perform a function skillfully, a wish to get ahead. Normal life—that is, the unexamined life—often goes on nicely, though insensibly framed by a system that does evil to others. Arendt went so far as to say that the good family man "is the great criminal of the century."[3] Passive acceptance is as potent as active cooperation.

Beyond that, even a kind of conscientiousness may be indispensable to evil on a large scale. In regard to the institution of slavery, Thoreau said in "Civil Disobedience," "The broadest and most prevalent error requires the most disinterested virtue to sustain it. The slight reproach to which the virtue of patriotism is commonly liable, the noble are most likely to incur. Those who, while they disapprove of the character and measures of a government, yield to it their allegiance and support are undoubtedly its most conscientious supporters, and so frequently the most serious obstacles to reform."[4]

Thus, out of our very ordinariness, evil gathers its necessary support; also from even some otherwise admirable traits. On the other hand, a universal human deficiency must be mentioned. It, too, is not a wicked

[3] Hannah Arendt, "Organized Guilt and Universal Responsibility" (1945), in Ron H. Feldman, ed., *The Jew as Pariah* (New York: Grove, 1978), 232.
[4] Henry David Thoreau, "Civil Disobedience," in *Walden and Other Writings*, ed. Brooks Atkinson (New York: Modern Library, 1950), 643.

impulse or instinct. Rather, it is a shortcoming: our obtuseness, really the almost invincible stupidity of our common humanity. This is the worst side of our ordinariness. I mean that unless we take exceptional care we easily forget that everything we condemn we may already be guilty of, or that we are or have been guilty of something not unlike what we condemn. We are usually not different, not better, but just the same, whatever the appearances or surface contrasts. Yet we strike out punitively, perhaps all the more so because we suspect ourselves. The profoundest epistemology is found in Jesus' parable of the mote and the beam.[5] Forgetfulness of its lesson—the most common occurrence in the world— helps to maintain many wrongs, including political evil on a large scale, especially when evil is done in the fight against moral evil or in the attempt to achieve a positive moral good.

I shall now make just a few remarks on those susceptibilities and feelings that, though not necessary for carrying out evil as policy, make it easier to do so. If anywhere, it is here that plain human wickedness and obscure human depravity have a place. I mean that though the love of inflicting pain, the urge to be cruel, is not at all necessary for the initiation or maintenance of evil on a large scale, the adherence of some people to evil is gained. Evil as a system provides them with greatly enhanced opportunities to inflict pain face to face or on a small scale. In a population of millions you can find thousands like this. Systems of cruelty need ideologies, as Arendt tirelessly insisted; but as she also showed, they do not need cruel persons. Orwell's explanation, in *Nineteen Eighty-four*, of totalitarianism as motivated entirely by personal sadism is terribly misleading. (His "Notes on Nationalism" [1945] is a better guide.) Still, if there are a good number who love cruelty, they help to keep evil going. They do their bit. Ideologies give them cover and may even reduce their inhibitions.

I do not mean to dualize—to divide the world into the cruel and the uncruel—or to be casually cruel to the cruel. It is entirely possible that a person is cruel only because he or she was treated with cruelty, especially early in life. It is also possible that persons would not show their cruelty unless the political chance came along. Nevertheless, some people act sadistically when they are given a chance, and some do not.

[5] Matthew 7:3–5.

One further point, the most general one, is that just about any susceptibility or feeling can attach someone to evil as policy. Ordinary persons
find in such evil numerous occasions for satisfying one or another desire,
for acting out all of the vices with impunity and some of the virtues with
honor. They therefore may find their lives enhanced by their participation in the evil; and they, enough of the time, just forget or overlook or
ignore the evil nature of that to which they contribute by their participation. They do not think; that is, they do not conceptualize or imagine the
totality (the system or condition or process) of which they are a part. This
general proclivity is not exactly necessary for the maintenance of large-
scale evil. But evil is certainly helped when the lucky ones find it possible
to victimize without being victims. This consideration reinforces the
Arendtian point I have been trying to promote: evil persons are not
needed to sustain evil as policy. The great strength of evil is normality:
unself-examined, and inclined to the imaginary, and hence devoid of real
imagination, the imagination that is needed for sympathy or empathy.

Correspondingly, if in some sense those who initiate evil must be
regarded as evil, it is not in the usual sense. Zealous—one might almost
say religious—devotion to ideological half-thinking, whether in the form
of bad aestheticism or moral fanaticism or religious or racial intoxication,
is much more salient in the instigators and inspirers of large-scale evil
than are sadism, depravity, or even the seven deadly sins; though of these
sins, clearly pride or vanity or vainglory in all its vagueness and un-
boundedness will always be found mixed in with all the considerations
I have tried to adduce. But it is pride in the group or pride of the group
that is, shall we say, more than half of the problem of evil, not egotism.
From such pride, whether tending toward arrogance or toward humiliation, the other deadly sins of leaders—such as hatred or envy or jealousy
or anger—emerge, and do so in the abstract form to which I earlier
referred.

My last point has to do with one's attitude toward political evil on a large
scale. Suppose that, following Arendt's suggestions, we say that at least
some occurrences of political evil are of a special heinousness and hence
that the leaders and auxiliaries are unforgivable.[6] She had the Nazis in

6 Hannah Arendt, *The Origins of Totalitarianism*, 2d ed. (New York: Meridian, 1958),
459. See also her discussion of forgiveness in *The Human Condition* (Chicago: University of
Chicago Press, 1958), 236–43.

mind. But I doubt that the Nazi extermination of the Jews is altogether distinct from some other occurrences of evil; certainly it is not unique in scale, though it is probably distinct in other respects, such as concentrated legal and official deliberateness, and the will to impose a completely fictional group identity on a population that was objectively unthreatening and then destroy that population. Nevertheless, if the Nazis are unforgivable, then so are the regimes of Stalin, Mao, and Pol Pot. Is the concept of the unforgivable appropriate for the formation of a right attitude toward political evil on a large scale?

A lot depends, I think, on whether one has been a victim, or has a personal connection to the victimized, and therefore feels as a victim through that connection. Any victim's perspective will likely be personal, and rightly. The experience of victimization can feel like subjection to the cruelty of persons who act as if they enjoy cruelty, even though they may not. During experienced cruelty, and afterward if he or she has survived, a victim surely can, with justice, be unforgiving. To expect otherwise is to expect sainthood of everyone; this is impossible. It is best not to advise victims. If, however, we are lucky enough to be untouched, but are still compelled, how should we think and feel? The spirit of the Gospels, at its best, explicitly or indirectly, seems to place no wrong or wrongdoer beyond forgiveness. (I here exclude the unforgivable sin of blaspheming against the Holy Ghost,[7] because I really do not know what the sin is and cannot work it into any meaning that interests me.) In the Sermon on the Mount, Jesus says not to resist evil and to love our enemies.[8] Even if we personally have had no evil done us to forgive, we can imagine suffering evil and should be able to imagine the suffering of others which goes on all around us. Should an observer become able to regard evil on a large scale in the spirit of the Gospels at its best? Is the spirit of the Gospels right for oneself not only as an observer but also as a potential sufferer trying to ready his or her perception and will for any eventuality?

Notice the considerations that figure in, or that may be elicited from, the Gospels and that are supposed to mitigate our hatred of wrongdoers and incline us to love them, even. On the cross, Jesus said, "Father, forgive them; for they know not what they do."[9] A way of reading the general sense of these words is that those who do terrible wrong never know what they do; they are too caught up in motion or action to stop

[7] Mark 3:29.
[8] Matthew 5:39, 44.
[9] Luke 23:34.

and think; they are blinded or numbed by either too much desire or too little feeling. Another thought suggested in the Gospels is that no matter what people do they always think that they are doing the right thing; even those who do the worst sincerely think that they are doing the right thing, or at least a most valuable thing. In his remarks in "Experience" about sin or wrongdoing, Emerson says, "The conscience must feel it as essence, essential evil. This it is not; it has an objective existence, but no subjective."[10] Then there are some other considerations. Those who make others suffer, themselves suffer; with more love or forgiveness shown them, now or in their past, they would have been or will be better. And, people who make others suffer may be inwardly divided and act reluctantly and, even as they act, or soon after, may feel regret or remorse. And, in their place, the victims would act in the same way because the victims have the same victimizing desires. And, in other circumstances—and the circumstances people find themselves in are a matter of contingency—the wrongdoers would act better.

All these considerations form the stuff of Christian charity and therefore the stuff of modern democratic moral sense. Are these considerations properly applied to the leaders and auxiliaries of evil on a large scale—such evil as the Spanish destruction of the native peoples of America; the European enslavement of African blacks; the Nazi extermination of Jews, Romani people, gays, and disabled people; and Stalin's, Mao's, and Pol Pot's extermination or allowed slaughter of whole categories of people? Should the dispassionate student contemplate such evil, and then forgive the leaders and auxiliaries in the sense of trying to avoid condemning them and hating them? I cannot believe that Jesus had such a scale of evil in mind when he taught forgiveness and love. I do not know what a true adherent to the Sermon on the Mount must or can feel about evil as policy. The relation between the Sermon on the Mount and political life, scarcely touched on in the Gospels, is a subject that has engendered a vast and contradictory literature. Even if one wants to begin thinking about the moral life by reference to the Sermon on the Mount, as I do, one may nevertheless think that the words of Jesus do not offer enough help. The abstractness I have made so much of does not figure as a problem in his thinking.

If what I have been suggesting about the sources of the worst political wrongs—of evil as policy—is on the right track, the moral judgment of

[10] Ralph Waldo Emerson, "Experience," in *The Complete Essays and Other Writings*, ed. Brooks Atkinson (New York: Modern Library, 1950), 361.

the leaders and auxiliaries of political evil may become a bit tricky. Activities that seem easiest to condemn turn out to originate in and to be largely sustained by common susceptibilities that are not intrinsically vicious, and that furthermore encourage an inwardness that is not vicious but either empty or fantastical or, in a way, innocent. How does one morally judge (and judge one must),[11] murderous impersonality, murderous delirium, murderous innocence? Those who do political evil are often not even sinners, but they are worse than sinners.

In any case, each of us must stand in a personal relation to the questions of evil. No one can presume to legislate the proper attitude.[12] All I would say is that if the word "unforgivable" is too strong to describe the way we should judge the practitioners of evil on a large scale (and I do not think it is), then, at the least, we could agree that to become reconciled to the occurrence of evil is a disaster, even though its occurrence is inevitable.

[11] Despite Matthew 7:1.
[12] See Arendt's effort to provide a way of judging Adolf Eichmann in *Eichmann in Jerusalem*, rev. ed. (New York: Viking, 1964), 277–79.

CHAPTER NINE

Individualism, Communitarianism, and Docility

In this chapter I look at the recent communitarian critique of liberalism from a certain perspective. My interest is in the tendency of both communitarianism and liberalism to contribute to docility, in Foucault's sense, which is, roughly speaking, a condition in which people unreluctantly accept being used, and do so because they have been trained to do so. A delegate to a Soviet congress spoke of the majority's "aggressive obedience," a fine near synonym for docility. The concept of docility is meant to point to a great question about modernity: Is the liberation of the individual only a new servitude, and perhaps a worse one than that endured in the old order? I believe that communitarianism is theoretically more favorable to docility than liberalism is. There is a further complication I would like to deal with, which is that Foucault, the profound recent theorist and critic of docility, is also a critic of (what we call) liberalism, precisely on the grounds that liberal society is largely, and more than any other society, the scene of docility. I shall subject his critique of liberalism to some scrutiny, with the hope of suggesting that he takes a wrong turn in single-mindedly associating docility with it.

It is not certain that the recent communitarian critique of liberal society will turn out to have made a permanently valuable theoretical contribu-

I thank Maurizio Viroli for his generous criticism. I also refer the reader to Richard Poirier's excellent discussion of Nietzsche and Foucault in relation to Emerson in *The Renewal of Literature: Emersonian Reflections* (New York: Random House, 1987), especially 185–96.

tion. A good deal of that critique seems to be dominated by an anxiety about cultural conditions that may be only brief but vivid fashions. To be sure, the recent communitarian critique has antecedents that go back to the early nineteenth century and perhaps before that. Insofar as that is the case, the recent critique may sometimes tend to be unoriginal and repetitious. Some part of what is good in the critique may be old; what is new, at best iridescent. Still, if one is concerned about docility, there is advantage in taking a brief and general look at what some recent critics have been saying. I have in mind such writers as Benjamin Barber, Sheldon Wolin, John Schaar, Alasdair MacIntyre, Christopher Lasch, Michael Sandel, Charles Taylor, and Michael Walzer (some of the time), among numerous others.

When the communitarians attack liberal society they are really attacking individualism. For them individualism is the heart of liberalism. Though the communitarians differ among themselves on important issues, they share a common aversion to at least some of the tendencies of individualism.

More exactly, the liberal individualism they criticize is positive individuality or the individual assertiveness and expressiveness that grow out of rights-based individualism in a representative democracy with capitalist institutions. The United States is held up as the principal example of an individualist society because it is the purest case, the least mixed with preindividualist elements—as it is the least mixed with predemocratic and precapitalist ones.

What do the critics claim to see in liberal society? I shall take a bird's-eye view and offer a few generalizations. A distinction may first be useful, however. We can distinguish between what the critics believe that people need in a liberal society but fail to get (on the one hand) and what the critics themselves need and fail to find (on the other hand). The latter consideration is as important as the former, but it is not frequently explicit.

Let us turn first to what the critics believe that people need. Naturally, the critics differ among themselves in their emphases, inclusions, and omissions, but I think that they would be likely to agree on the following critique. First, it is said that people need more *togetherness* than the individualist institutions and practices and general spirit of liberal society provide. Liberal society is "atomistic"; it cuts or weakens the habitual and unrationalized ties among people; it is indifferent or disrespectful to the past and to tradition; it fosters little or no attachment to anything outside oneself and one's circle; it makes personal identity a burden by making it paramount and by forcing it to be the willed creation of each individual; it makes people lonely and hence prone to alienation and to all the pathologies that alienation engenders.

Second, it is said that people need more *discipline* than liberal society provides. In such a society, people are too self-absorbed, and self-absorption too easily passes into selfishness, while selfishness expresses itself in the limitless pursuit of goods that do not gratify because they have no relation to any desire but the unappeasable desire for prestige and status—unappeasable, because prestige and status constantly fluctuate. Liberal society thus makes people anomic. The discipline of virtuous restraint is disregarded, with the result that the encouragement to individualism is paradoxically the encouragement to self-dispersal. If people were taught to care for themselves less and for others more, they would be happier. Greater discipline leads to greater contentment. Boundedness is necessary for happiness. Just for the well-being of the individual, greater discipline is called for.

Third, people need greater encouragement to share their lives with others, to care about others for the sake of others, and to cooperate in the attempted solution of common problems and dangers. People should have greater *mutuality* than they are conditioned to have in liberal society. Liberal society allows people to think that they owe little if anything to others, that they are self-made, that all they are and do derives strictly from their own merits or lack of them. The result is unacceptable cruelty to, or neglect of, the less fortunate, who are seen as undeserving rather than unlucky, and insidious condescension toward all those who do not succeed brilliantly. Another result is an accumulation of social and cultural problems that threaten to engulf everyone, no matter how fortunate or unfortunate.

Fourth, it is said that people need greater encouragement to think of the flourishing of their nation or group in a hostile world and to think less of their individual successes and failures. Liberal society makes people narcissistic. It weakens the natural human tendency to acquire a *group identity* vis-à-vis other groups. Liberal society imprisons people in their individual identities and thus denies them the release into something larger than themselves, while also weakening their will to make the inevitable patriotic sacrifices that a hostile external world unexpectedly but regularly calls for.

There is no doubt that this line of critique captures some part of life in a liberal society. Whether or not it is intrinsic to human nature to need what the communitarians say that people need, and whether or not societies always need to encourage what the communitarians say they must, there are serious troubles that may be plausibly attributed to liberal individualism in a context of representative democracy and capitalism. The question is whether communitarian thinkers offer a remedy that would have the result of inducing greater docility in society, apart from other possible bad consequences. Perhaps one can say that the wish for more mutuality is the only one of the four aspirations which is devoid of a strong initial affinity to the practices of docility.

Let us say that there is a need for greater mutuality. I believe, however, that liberal individualism does not theoretically preclude a fair amount of it. One of the sentiments needed for greater mutuality is a heightened feeling of the finitude of the individual. Does liberal individualism theoretically exclude this feeling? I do not think so. The sense of oneself and one's existence as an accident; of one's place and time as crucial in one's formation, though not all-determining; of the role that good luck and bad luck play in one's endowment and circumstances; of the unrequited contribution of countless people (most of them nameless), dead and living, near and remote, to one's well-being; and of the vulnerability of any life to being derailed or overwhelmed—this compound sense of finitude is not only consistent with liberal individualism but part of the energy behind its emergence.

When, on the other hand, Emerson, a principal theorist of the moral and existential potentialities of rights-based individualism, speaks of the "infinitude" of the individual, he is not disagreeing. Infinitude is experimental self-reliance, not literal self-creation. It is catching up with some of one's unused potency. In theorizing self-reliance he is opposing (in our terms) togetherness, discipline, and group identity, not mutuality. By his question, in "Self-Reliance," "Are they *my* poor?" he wants to transmit the shock of Jesus' saying, "The poor you have always with you"; no more than Jesus is he counseling indifference to the disadvantaged. He does not want guilt to sicken charity; rather, he wants respect to inform compassion. He does not want assistance to become a mutually degrading routine. I think that Emerson's attitude, because of its complexities, is a good guide to thinking about what individuals owe one another as strangers and fellow citizens in a liberal democracy. Thoreau's reflections in *Walden* on philanthropy, and afterward on his encounters with involuntarily poor people, like John Field's family, promote Emerson's attitude powerfully.

For all that I have said, however, I must grant that espousing mutuality as a constant guide to public policy does not come easily to proponents of liberal individualism. When mutuality passes beyond relief of the needy to a greater effort to persuade or entice people to care actively for one another's well-being, individualists bridle. An individualist must find distasteful and unreal the abstract impersonation of feelings that have their original reality in face-to-face relationships. Even worse, the tendency of such guided or administered or engineered mutuality is to work with the same effect of docility as those things individualism fears precisely because they are immediate sources of docility: greater togetherness, greater discipline, and greater group identity. Some of this tendency is already present in the work of such social liberals as T. H. Green and John Dewey, both of whom urge so much mutuality that they betray the very idea of rights. They make rights merely instrumental to a society-wide and abstract mutuality. Liberal individualism can have no difficulty with measures to alleviate suffering: it does not aspire to repeal basic morality, which mandates such alleviation. Beyond the relief of misery, however, social projects often appear to promise more docility, whatever else they may achieve.

But even if we grant the need for greater mutuality, we do not grant the heart of the communitarian case. For one thing, the communitarian critics may fail to see that liberal society contains individualist revisions, new versions, of all the desiderated elements, and all these revisions work to reduce the tendency to make people docile rather than to increase docility. Communitarians are usually reluctant to take in the fact that individualism redefines human bonds; it does not foolishly try to eliminate them. In a liberal society, ideally, the state is changed into government, and ruling into governing; society ceases imagining itself as a natural growth or cyclical process and becomes more consensual and voluntary; and the people becomes an entity held together by agreement rather than religion, ethnicity, a long and unforgiving memory, or the mimesis of traditional roles and customs. Love and friendship, marriage and the family, are also transformed. A liberal society is explicit, to an unusual degree, in its transactions and therefore in its bonds. People are connected, yet in a new way. There is a second point: intensities of connection are made local or temporary in a liberal society. Episodes characterize an individualist life. The assumption of permanence is disparaged as false to the feelings. Merely episodic involvement may be seen as superficiality, but it may also be seen either as playfulness or as attempted sincerity, and in both cases as a flight from false solidity.

As Robert Frost teaches in "The Tuft of Flowers," people work together "Whether they work together or apart." The essence of all these individualist revisions of human ties is a movement toward allowing individuals to make up their world as they go along. That is a principal aspect of individualism, and the hidden spring of self-centered behavior. The alternative is prescriptive prearrangement, that is, submission (whether conscious or habitual) to the given. To a defender of liberal individualism, such submission in itself diminishes the people who endure it, by weakening the self-dissatisfaction intrinsic to the effort to make up the world as one goes along. Beyond that, the communitarians may not have pondered other implications of this submission and hence of their claims concerning what people need or should be encouraged to acquire. The problem is docility (mobilized docility, aggressive obedience), which is distinct from submission and to which I shall return.

Let us now turn to what the communitarian critics themselves need and fail to find in liberal society. Here I propose an interpretation of the mentalities that appear to underlie, in part, the criticisms that these writers offer. Only to some small degree—if at all—do they acknowledge directly that such mentalities inspire their writings. Nevertheless, their writings leave certain impressions on some who have tried to understand the communitarian critique, and to do so with fairness if not with sympathy. At the same time, it is doubtless true that these mentalities are not peculiar to the critics but will be found throughout liberal society. Nevertheless, these mentalities help to account for the fact that the critics see liberal society so selectively and harshly and offer the sort of remedies they do, remedies that would promote docility.

Two mentalities make their presence felt. The first is religious in nature, the second is aesthetic. Let me admit that I speak as one who is not religious and is also afraid of some of the effects a passionate religiousness has or can have on liberal society and on human affairs in general. Then, too, though I know and do not regret the major role that aesthetic considerations play in human life, even apart from erotic desire, and even though in an often unrecognized manner, it is certainly possible to distinguish between kinds of aestheticism. As Emerson suggests in "The Poet," bad poetry (so to speak) is part of the fabric of ordinary—that is, unreflective—life. In every society, ordinary life is full of bad displacements and condensations, of unintentional metaphorization and shadowy symbolism. Worse, some kinds of socially exaggerated aestheticism are hideous in their perverse beauty. I find that communitarianism is often an encouragement to bad poetry, to a heightened conventional aestheticism that in modern circumstances can be satisfied only with mischievous or even pernicious results.

Concerning the religious mentality, I would say that some of the critics desire to live in a society that is religiously grounded, organized, and sustained. Some may be genuine believers, others may think that without transcendent belief no society can last. The latter often speak of the need for a basic myth to hold society together, while the former insist that worship of the true God is indispensable to the life of an incorrupt society. Both sorts of critics find the secularism of liberal society— despite or because of its toleration of plural religions—unendurable. And both sorts are guarded in their expression of religious views, especially in the United States, where the Constitution separates church and state and disallows any religious test for holding public office. The implicit communitarian sense is often that the only real community is a society pervaded by a common religion because a real community must have a well-defined and particular way of life, and only a ritualized or sacramentalized way of life can be well defined and particular. Liberal individualism is death to a ritualized or sacramental order. It is death to God. It kills a properly rooted life.

The aesthetic mentality is, in some respects, closely related to the religious one but may stand on its own separately. Some communitarian critics long for a society whose customs, manners, visible surfaces, and daily transactions (public and private) all seem designed or composed and therefore seem to have strong and unmistakable meanings and to fit together to create one great composition, one great meaning. That is, a good society should seem to be the emanation of one superior, controlling intellect that may surpass the actual intellects of the human individuals involved in the life they enact and carry forward. In effect, the communitarians ask us to give up the will to have moments of transcendence in which one tries to see one's society as from a distance or a height, or in which one tries to see it as an alien or an enemy does or could. Instead, one should treat society as prior, that is, as always prepared to receive everyone, as all-enclosing and wiser than oneself. Every society provides the script, and in good societies all play their parts and say their lines unselfconsciously. The model is the ancient polis—at least as imagined by contemporary communitarians—or Rousseau's city. This aestheticism can take an even worse turn: into tribalism, the most odious of all aspirations. To such aesthetic critics, tribalist or not, liberal society appears formless, unintegrated, unskillfully improvisatory, incoherent, slovenly, and often downright ugly. That aesthetic judgment is, however, narrow, almost incurious. It does not allow for the possibility that beauty has more than one way of appearing in the world, a way peculiar to modern democracy and radically different from the classical or the aristocratic.

From the perspective of liberal individualism, both what the communitarian critics say that people need and what the theorists themselves appear to need are retrogressive. Communitarian views give the impression of being inspired by a longing for a lost world (that is, a world that never existed except in misinterpretation). Communitarianism is nostalgic, antimodern. Common to what the critics say that people need and what they themselves appear to need is the message that, above all, people cannot be trusted—especially with freedom. The critics say or imply that if people are allowed to live more or less as they please, within the limits of respect for the claims of others, they will lead lives that are not only unhappy but also wasted. Not that the majority are throwing their lives away in drugs, drink, gambling, circuses, and casual sex. Rather, they seem to live to no purpose. The majority don't do or enjoy, in T. H. Green's formulation, "something worth doing or enjoying, and that, too, something that we do or enjoy in common with others."[1]

For people to lead worthwhile lives they must be enlisted in projects that are not merely their own, that do not come merely from their unmobilized choices, and that unite them with one another. The tendency of thought is Aristotelian or Rousseauist: the more that people must act together in order to act at all, the better. The communitarian critics want people to be led by, and thus to be more deferential toward, either personal or impersonal authorities. Their views can suggest only that they want people to be made happy and useful by being made more docile. I do not see what word captures their drift better. I do not intend to exaggerate when I say that communitarianism shows too many affinities to fascism, either in fascism's corporatist or in its ritualist and

[1] T. H. Green, "Liberal Legislation and Freedom of Contract" (1881), in John R. Rodman, ed., *The Political Theory of T. H. Green* (New York: Appleton-Century-Crofts, 1964), 51–52.

spectacular aspect. Recent communitarianism is yet another reactionary response to modernity, though, of course, still innocent of any direct baleful influence. Hatred of modernity promotes docility, either directly or indeliberately.

Some of the leading nineteenth-century theorists of individualism were profoundly worried about the urge to make people docile. One has only to read the powerful pages of Mill's *On Liberty* (especially chapters 4 and 5) and *Auguste Comte and Positivism*, and of Herbert Spencer's *The Man versus the State*, to see that significant expressions of liberalism are devoted to blocking the urge to treat people as objects in need of repair, or as well-tended animals prepared for burden or slaughter, or as forces in need of enlistment in projects that are not spontaneously their own. This great liberal contribution is maintained and sometimes enhanced by American rights-based jurisprudence, especially during the time of the Warren Court (1953–69). One can even say that the primary element in rights-based individualism is negative: to try to avoid not only the more blatant kinds of oppression which ensue when government fails to respect (or even acknowledge) the rights of individuals but also to avoid the more subtle kinds of oppression which ensue when government engages in soft or even unfelt oppression that does not seem to abridge rights (spying, monitoring, inspecting, testing, advising, and acting paternalistically) or in continuous activism that seems to enhance or enrich life but that weakens the desire and ability of people to respond to life as they please and to initiate projects on their own. Theorists of individualism detect in the communitarian critique a grave threat to human dignity, precisely because its hostility to rights opens the door to every sort of oppression, and its positive aspirations radiate a sense of mistrust of people and hence the desirability of gathering them up in patterns of supposedly useful or beautiful or pious activity.

Fairness requires, however, that a defender of liberal individualism acknowledge that some among the communitarians are appalled by passivity and claim to see its prevalence in liberal society. To be sure, passivity is not the same as docility: docility, as I have suggested, shows itself in strenuous exertion. But the two conditions may be inwardly related, and may have some of the same practical effects. For example, Sheldon Wolin and Benjamin Barber believe that the moral emphasis on the individual is a way of privatizing people and leaving them in an unprotesting or complacent condition of mind. Wolin and Barber, among others, are trying to remain faithful to the idealism of the New Left. I find much to sympathize with in their attachment to the hopes and insights of the 1960s.

Nevertheless, I am struck by the way in which Wolin (in the powerful writing he did for his journal, *democracy*), imparts the sense that the effort to attain a more decentralized and participatory society requires the sort of militancy which penalizes diversity and disagreement in its ranks. Both single-mindedness and like-mindedness are needed. Historical experience indicates, however, that such militancy prefigures a reformed condition that will be oppressive. It turns out that the society in view is also inhospitable to diversity and disagreement. Wolin is generally disposed to criticize rights when they lead to bad results. In "What Revolutionary Action Means Today," he specifically asks: "How could a democratic conception of citizenship be said to be fulfilled—as a liberal conception would be—by having rights exercised for antidemocratic ends, as the KKK choice would be?"[2] He then offers an ideal of good citizenship which, in modern conditions, can only be a recipe for the enlistment of the energies of people who think themselves free when they are more likely to be subtly intimidated into a common enthusiasm. "The citizen, unlike the groupie, has to acquire a perspective of commonality, to think integrally and comprehensively rather than exclusively." Despite his endorsement of situational activism Wolin goes on to chide those who practice interest-group politics. Yet what other modern way is there of normally breaking up massification and homogenization? Acting on self-interest or on particular moral interests is, except in times of constitutional or other crisis, the only form that participatory politics can take. To discredit such action is not to hasten the end of passivity. And to idealize a situation in which all the citizens of a large society are constantly mindful of society as a whole is to favor increased docility, despite one's theoretical intentions. The "perspective of commonality" entails a politics in which leadership is essential, and along with it, the trained disposition to be led.

Barber, in his *Strong Democracy*, makes a strenuous effort to avoid nostalgia for the polis and to think of methods for introducing a greater degree of popular participation in modern large-scale democracy.[3] He

[2] Sheldon Wolin, "What Revolutionary Action Means Today," *democracy* 2 (Fall 1982), 17–28.

[3] Benjamin Barber, *Strong Democracy* (Princeton: Princeton University Press, 1984).

relies heavily on the use of "interactive" television for registering immediate popular opinion on the issues presented to it for decision. One
wonders, however, whether this sort of democracy actually avoids passivity, because of the conversion of significant questions of public policy
into a video experience. He also says that all his proposals must be
accepted together, and such acceptance turns out to mean that greater
popular participation is desirable only if there is at the same time the
universal requirement of periods of compulsory military or civilian service. One tendency in recent theories of citizenship like Barber's is to
yoke citizenship to legally mandatory self-denial. Participation is paid for
by conscription, by involuntarily living for others or for an abstraction.
So that the fear of passivity, once again, can lead to proposals that work,
on balance, in the direction of increased popular docility.

At this point, it may occur to someone to say that I have coopted
Foucault's word "docility" and some of his thoughts for the purposes of
defending the very viewpoint he attacks so mercilessly—individualism.
He is not a communitarian, but he surely is a critic of individualism.
How then can I find in individualism the defense and the remedy against
docility and the disciplinary society, while a great modern theorist of
these undesirable social conditions blames individualism for them? The
matter deserves long and close attention. I can say only something
sketchy.

It may be well to notice first that whether or not Foucault studied
Tocqueville, our thinking about him is enhanced if we attend to *The Old
Regime and the French Revolution* and the second volume of *Democracy in
America*. In particular, Tocqueville's discussions of individualism in an
age of democratic equality, and the causally connected condition of
democratic despotism, are especially relevant. Now Tocqueville does not
believe that the individualist individual, so to speak, is a fabrication, and
this fact establishes a tremendous difference between him and Foucault.
The initiating agency of individualism in Tocqueville's analysis is not
power/knowledge but the intimidating pressure of modesty, which each
individual feels in the face of all the others, his equals, and which issues
in private retreat and self-absorption. This kind of individualism causes
an expansion of the tutelary activism of state power. Despite all differences, however, Tocqueville does illuminate Foucault's theme of the
emergence of what Tocqueville conceptualizes as the minute regulation

of daily life. Particularly relevant are Tocqueville's analysis of the individualist absention from citizenship; the democratic substitution of lenient for brutal regimentation, with a consequent increase of effectiveness and extent of control; and the insensible transformation of much control into a "pastoral" (to use Foucault's word) or therapeutic solicitude by those in power toward the many, who seem to crave it as solace for the rigors of an economically competitive life. Reading Foucault is all the more advantageous when one keeps Tocqueville by one's side, especially in regard to the subject of individualism. Yet neither sees enough of the picture, ungrateful as it may be to say so.

At various places in his work, Foucault alleges that modern individualism is, appearances notwithstanding, the result of techniques of discipline. The more each person regards himself or herself as distinct from others, as special, as acting spontaneously, as living in response to the deep promptings of one's unique inner life, the more one is being victimized by the disciplinary and docility-inducing techniques of modern power (especially decentered institutional power). In his Preface to Deleuze and Guattari, *Anti-Oedipus*, he therefore says, "Do not demand of politics that it restore the 'rights' of the individual, as philosophy has defined them. The individual is the product of power. What is needed is to 'de-individualize' by means of multiplication and displacement, diverse combinations. The group must not be the organic bond uniting hierarchized individuals, but a constant generator of de-individualization."[4] I suppose that the sort of group he wants is a passionate but temporary affinity group. Each person will belong to many groups, serially or concurrently. Actually, Foucault is affirming the version of group life which grows most hospitably in an individualist culture, but he is not disposed to make this point.

Let us notice two of his main lines of critique. In *Discipline and Punish*, he tries to show how techniques of modern power in such institutional settings as prisons, mental asylums, schools, armies, and hospitals all tend to individuate the person by treating him or her as a special case in need of reformist or therapeutic attention. The techniques are not physically brutal but all the more rigorous for being lenient, or at least sparing in their violence. But the result is the creation or "fabrication" of an individual identity, an identity acquired by docile absorption of the habits and, above all, of the words and meanings implanted by techni-

[4] Michel Foucault, Preface to Gilles Deleuze and Felix Guattari, *Anti-Oedipus*, trans. R. Hurley, M. Seem, H. Lane (New York: Viking, 1977), xiv.

cians, not (as it is claimed) by one's natural unfolding. On the other hand, in *The History of Sexuality*, volume 1, Foucault tries to show that modern society systematically induces or exaggerates sexual desires and then guides their satisfaction. Modern culture creates an obsession with sex just as it creates the whole artifice of sexuality, of sexual roles and assignments. Such incitement is also a technique apt to make people docile. The key to this strategy of docility is also the fabrication of an individual identity—here, a distinctive sexual identity that is supposedly the locus of one's deepest secret and hence one's truest self. Modern culture then encourages the struggle to learn and express the secret, the self. But, again, one has been given a secret or a self to express; one has had a project thrust on one, which is only a trap.

The two lines of critique come together in a passage in *The History of Sexuality*, when Foucault refers to the two modes of individualization as "not antithetical" but rather "two poles of development" of the "power over life."[5] In both lines, Foucault is trying to suggest that individuality is an artificial production undertaken (let us say by dominant interests) so that people may be more easily controlled and used. Trained to become self-conscious and differentiated selves, people are forever tied to external encouragements and disciplines that keep them manageable even when (especially when) their lives are self-consciously experimental or exploratory or rebellious.

A passage in Nietzsche's *The Gay Science* throws light on Foucault's enterprise. Nietzsche highlights the perils of finding one's individuality in one's expanded or deepened consciousness. He says:

> My idea is, as you see, that consciousness does not really belong to man's individual existence but rather to his social or herd nature; that, as follows from this, it has developed subtlety only insofar as this is required by social or herd utility. Consequently, given the best will in the world to understand ourselves as individually as possible, "to know ourselves," each of us will always succeed in becoming conscious only of what is not individual but "average." Our thoughts themselves are continually governed by the character of consciousness—by the "genius" of the species that commands it—and translated back into the perspective of the herd. Fundamentally, all our actions are altogether incomparably personal, unique, and infinitely

[5] Michel Foucault, *The History of Sexuality*, vol. 1, trans. Robert Hurley (New York: Vintage, 1978), 139.

individual; there is not doubt of that. But as soon as we translate them into consciousness *they no longer seem to be.*[6]

This is a brilliant passage, but maybe not altogether right or in line with other equally great passages in Nietzsche about man's depth. (Think only of the discussion in *The Genealogy of Morals* [First Essay, sec. 6; Second Essay, secs. 16–18] on the way that induced "bad conscience" creates the soul but, in doing that, deepens individuals and fits them eventually for some otherwise unattainable unherdlike greatness.) Of course, Foucault does much more than repeat Nietzsche; and Nietzsche's suggestiveness spreads out in many directions, not all of them followed by or of interest to Foucault. But evidence of a basic similarity between them is striking when this passage is read after one has read Foucault. In one sector of his motivation, each aims to deliver people from all the vanity that grows from thinking about the distinctively human and that leads to the prison of docility, of self-expanding and therefore self-mutilating moral or social responsibility. With the concept of docility, Foucault ruthlessly develops Nietzsche's insight, even as he revises it.

What Foucault says is immensely instructive. He forces us to reconsider the fact that one outgrowth of rights-based individualism is a heightened concern to express one's being. His critique of expressive or assertive individuality is more valuable than that of the communitarians, and more must be conceded to it. It is undeniable that a good deal of what one struggles to express has not only been culturally implanted (that implantation is, in every society, necessary and inevitable), but, in addition, some of it has been thoughtlessly acquired from the ministrations of modern technicians of soul-making who are active in the media and in practically every institutional setting. Spontaneity often is unconscious mimesis. The rhetoric of the flowering personality contains some nonsense. Even Emerson, who began the theoretical effort to move rights-based individualism in the direction of a distinctive democratic individuality, has moments when he indulges in this rhetoric. In "Self-Reliance" he holds up the rose as a model for human being: "they are for what they are . . . there is no time to them. There is simply the rose." We are here too close to the dangers of wanting to be *en soi*, whole and stable like a thing; too close, also, to the dangers of bad faith, of clutching to an aspect of one's life as if one had an essence and that aspect were the essence.

[6] Friedrich Nietzsche, *The Gay Science*, trans. Walter Kaufmann (New York: Vintage, 1974), bk. 5, sec. 354, 299.

Emerson, however, corrects himself; he corrects the latency in rights-based individualism to make too much of oneself. The nobility of the Emersonian aspiration lies in transcending the ideal of individualism understood as the cultivation and expression of personality, precisely because Emerson, like his colleagues Thoreau and Whitman, knows how social, and not individualist, such an ideal is. They all go in the direction of self-abandonment, away from egotism, even away from self-expression, and do so as proponents of individualism. They encourage a more intense awareness of everything outside oneself, an awareness each individual owes to all persons as equal individuals, and to all creatures and things just for being what they are. This awareness is the democratic ecstasy. The Emersonians are sure that such awareness is dimmed by the essentially social desire to express oneself. Awareness is a more heroic aspiration than expressiveness, also more heroic and more sane, perhaps, than the aristocratic project urged in Pindar (Pythian II), "O find, and be, yourself," and perhaps intended in Nietzsche's admonition to become who you are. Thus the theory of democratic individuality distinguishes between the expressive self and the cultivated inward self and judges the former to be much less significant than the latter, while making the latter an opening onto the reality of the world.

It does not seem to me that Foucault allows for the possibility that this distinction can be made. His analysis has great power when it challenges the expressive self. It gives much less trouble to those who prize the cultivation of greater inwardness, the effort to explore the self's cave. Human depth is not always *trompe l'oeil*. Unconscious motives; obscure motives, movements, and associations; the capacity to feign or to be double; the capacity to talk to oneself; the capacity to draw things out by thinking them over; and above all the capacity to surprise oneself and others in one's speech and writing as well as in one's action—all these things testify to depth, to depth of soul. Memory, forgetfulness, and repression are all manifestations of depth. Language is one great source of depth, and its sole guarantor. It would be impossible to imagine any society, except the most rudimentary, in which the phenomena of depth did not exist, and exist in large measure independently of techniques of power/knowledge, though not, of course, independently of acculturation. "What is life," asks Emerson in "Natural History of Intellect," "but what a man is thinking of all day?"[7] How could life be human without

[7] Ralph Waldo Emerson, "Natural History of Intellect" (1870), in *The Complete Works of Ralph Waldo Emerson*, ed. E. W. Emerson (Boston: Houghton-Mifflin, 1903–4), 12:10.

mental depth, whatever Nietzsche and Foucault may want to entertain and have us believe? The critique of the "subject" is too often at the service of the wish, in Burke's remarkable phrase about Voltaire and Rousseau, to "subtilize us into savages."

Another troubling tendency in liberal society is for people to fret endlessly about their symptoms—to have a lust for therapy. Unphilosophical self-absorption is not a pretty picture, and gives a foothold to power/knowledge, whether or not power/knowledge causes it. But it is too much to expect of people in an individualist culture not to be nervous about themselves. They have been taught to take themselves seriously, to take themselves as ends rather than as parts or means or tools or weapons or resources. To say it again, they have been encouraged to make up their world as they go along. The lust for therapy is a vice, but the vice of an essentially serious disposition.

In sum, Foucault's analysis, for all its power, is strategically incomplete. His partiality is all the more damaging, given his apparent endorsement of the Deleuzian project to "ferret out the fascism that is ingrained in our behavior." The reality of liberal society is much more complex than he allows. Democratic culture contains more than the effects of fabricated individuality, even in reactionary times. In fact, the techniques of fabrication—of encouraged avowal and disclosure, and of technical training and care—may help supply some of the resources that enable resistance to fabrication itself and that can also lead to advantages apart from resistance like greater refinement, even greater depth. Fabrication can help to create a condition far better than its practitioners intend.

If the Emersonian theory of democratic individuality is an aspiration, it nevertheless aspires to an intensification of what is already present, if often confusedly or usually intermittently, in a liberal society. Even if we confine ourselves to phenomena of self-expression or self-assertion, we find not only or mainly helplessly fabricated selves or souls but a more complex situation. Foucault does not deal adequately with the vitality and creativity of various popular movements of resistance which originate in the will to express something that is being blocked, shunned, or repressed, whether or not one wants to call it "real." It is really painful not to express it. Foucault does after all insist on saying (in *Discipline and Punish*) that the soul is no illusion; it has a reality. "The individual is no doubt the fictitious atom of an 'ideological' representation of society [the allusion is to Althusser's thesis in "Ideology and Ideological State Apparatuses"]: but he is also a reality fabricated by this specific technology of power that I have called 'discipline.'" Power "produces reality."[8] Foucault, however, is not historical enough. The liberationist movements of the 1960s and after were and are fighting against categorial oppressions that rest on a conventional aestheticism related to the bad aestheticism to which I referred earlier: I mean here the aestheticism of duality—whether Manichaean or an attitude a little less stark but still averse to nuance, hybrid, and indeterminacy.

The oppression is real, even if its foundation and pretext are not. There is a commendable individualism in the will to stop being ashamed of one's arbitrary or unchosen characteristics, either the most superficial (like skin color) or the most tenacious (like desire) or the most culturally variable (like one's place in the sexual division of roles). Obsession with these characteristics is as old as humanity; modern power/knowledge did not originate either the characteristics or the obsession with them. The liberationist movement in the 1960s was not merely a lightweight response to minor and short-lived complaints. And just as it grew in the soil of rights-based individualism, so it continues to disseminate its influence, despite its crudities and its defeats. Feminism, gay rights, certain racial assertions, and other social movements are faithful to the spirit of rights-based individualism, precisely because the will to end shame is more important than any further ideal aspiration. The group affirmation is an act of resistance to stigmatized identities and functions more than it is a claim to positive virtue or value. When, however, there is such a claim, it is best understood as compensatory and hence temporary. If the claim insists on being more, then is the time to think that victim-souls are cooperating to their hurt with their fabrication.

To discredit liberal individualism is necessarily to strengthen all those forces in modern life which work to render people docile. If, therefore, liberal individualism may, in some respects, cooperate with these forces, it holds within itself large resources to resist docility. Where else can those resources be found? To what can appeal be made if not to individuals? And surely the real paramount sources of modern docility are not found in individualist feelings and practices, but in anti-individualist ones: fascism, religious fanaticism, exclusive group identity, state socialism, and power-statism. Foucault does not make this point, and he discourages others from making it. He seduces some into thinking that fabricated individuality (if that is what it is) is yet worse than the collec-

[8] Michel Foucault, *Discipline and Punish*, trans. Alan Sheridan (New York: Vintage, 1979), 194.

tivist horrors, while he himself seems to hate modernity so much as to prefer (if only implicitly) the old underdeveloped order.

The last word on liberal individualism cannot be that it is implanted only by suggestion and manifested in confessional anxiety; or that it is induced only by indoctrination and then encouraged to manifest itself in safe and programmed ways; or that it is fabricated only in order to facilitate a deceived but eager subjection; or that it is fabricated only in order to be mobilized for systematic productive purposes and enlisted in the attempt to abort the formation of an insurrectionary group identity. Foucault's various theses catch aspects of the painful truth and comprise an invaluable cautionary doctrine. If insisted on exclusively, however, they turn into an ideological caricature. The fabricated individual is not merely fabricated; the "enslaved sovereign" is neither enslaved nor sovereign.

Defenders of liberal individualism must hold to the premise that there is something worse than the wrongs and the deficiencies that the communitarian critics point to, and that is docility. A docile people is a people fit for mobilization; and the purposes of mobilization in advanced countries tend to be destructive and irrational. Only rights-based individualism provides a steady perspective from which to protest this mobilization. On the other hand—contra Foucault—another premise is that liberal individualism is preponderantly in opposition to docility and not its best friend in disguise. Admirers of Foucault should worry more about communitarianism than individualism. Indeed, they should work to rehabilitate individualism.

CHAPTER TEN

Whitman and the
Culture of Democracy

I think that Walt Whitman is a great philosopher of democracy. Indeed, he may be the greatest. As Thoreau said, Whitman "is apparently the greatest democrat the world has ever seen."[1] To put it more academically, he is perhaps the greatest philosopher of the culture of democracy. He writes the best phrases and sentences about democracy. By democratic culture, I mean these things especially. First, democratic culture is (or can be) the soil for the creation of new works of high art—glorious poems and moral writings, in particular. Second, democratic culture is (or is becoming) a particular stylization of life—that is, a distinctive set of appearances, habits, rituals, dress, ceremonies, folk traditions, and historical memories. Third, democratic culture is (or can be) the soil for the emergence of great souls whose greatness consists in themselves being like works of art in the spirit of a new aristocracy. All these meanings are interconnected and appear in Whitman's writings throughout his life. Perhaps they receive their most powerful expression in *Democratic Vistas* (1871). But, in my judgment, the central meaning when we study Whitman is democratic culture as the setting in which what I have elsewhere called "democratic individuality" (a phrase close to Whitman's usage) is slowly being disclosed. I believe that the setting for democratic individu-

I thank Benjamin Barber for the invitation to present an early version of this essay at the Walt Whitman Center for the Study of Democracy, Rutgers University, and for his generous discussion of these issues. I am indebted to David Bromwich, Leo Marx, Michael Mosher, Nancy Rosenblum, and Alan Trachtenberg for their responses.

[1] Thoreau, quoted in F. O. Matthiessen, *American Renaissance: Art and Expression in the Age of Emerson and Whitman* (New York: Oxford University Press, 1941), 649.

ality is a much more powerful and original idea than any of the other ideas of democratic culture I have just mentioned.

I have already tried to suggest that working together with Emerson and Thoreau, Whitman tries to draw out the fuller moral and existential significance of rights. These are the rights that individuals have as persons. The political system of democracy exists in order to protect these rights and also to embody them in its workings. Democratic individuality is what rights-based individualism in a democracy could eventually become, once the political separation from the Old World was complete, and had already become, to some degree, in their time. I see the Emersonians as trying to encourage the tendency to democratic individuality, to urge it forward so that it may express itself ever more confidently and therefore more splendidly. In their conception of democratic individuality, I find three aspects: self-expression, resistance in behalf of others, and receptivity or responsiveness (being "hospitable") to others. My judgment is that for the Emersonians the most important aspect of democratic individuality, by far, is receptivity or responsiveness. An individual's insistence on first being oneself expressively is valuable mostly as a preparation for receptivity or responsiveness: behavioral nonconformity loosens the hold of narrow or conventional methods of seeing and feeling (as well as preparing a person to take a principled stand in favor of those denied their rights).

This responsiveness or receptivity can also be described as a way—a profoundly democratic way—of being connected to others and to nature. As Whitman says in "Song of the Open Road": "Here the profound lesson of reception, nor preference nor denial."[2] It is a way that deepens the sort of connectedness already present in rights-based individualism but that only time and a steady commitment to rights can call forth. Time is needed because rights-based individualism is such a strange idea, and so untypical of past human experience, that those who live it and live by it—even though imperfectly—have to keep remembering, or keep learning as if they never knew, both the basic meaning and the farther implications of what they profess and enact. And the steady commitment therefore turns out to be not so steady after all, but only as steady as the strangeness permits.

Here I explore the connectedness that emanates from democratic

---

[2] Throughout I have used Walt Whitman, *Leaves of Grass*, ed. Sculley Bradley and Harold W. Blodgett (New York: Norton Critical Editions, 1973); cited as Whitman. Section numbers of "Song of Myself" are given in the text.

individuality, as Whitman perceives and perfects it. He knows, let it be said immediately, the extent of the strangeness, and the steadiness for what it is, in democratic society. He says in the Preface, 1876, to *Leaves of Grass*, "For though perhaps the main points of all ages and nations are points of resemblance, and, even while granting evolution, are substantially the same, there are some vital things in which this Republic, as to its individualities, and as a compacted Nation, is to specially stand forth, and culminate modern humanity. And these are the very things it least morally and mentally knows—(though curiously enough, it is at the same time faithfully acting upon them.)"

In the Preface, 1872, he looks back on what he has been doing since he began writing *Leaves of Grass*: " 'Leaves of Grass,' already published, is, in its intentions, the song of a great composite *democratic individual*, male or female. And following on and amplifying the same purpose, I suppose I have in my mind to run through the chants of this volume, (if ever completed,) the thread-voice, more or less audible, of an aggregated, inseparable, unprecedented, vast, composite, electric *democratic nationality*." For me, Whitman's greatness does not lie in his pursuit of an image of a democratic American nationality, an image—in my phrase—of a particular stylization of life. Such a notion strikes me as being of secondary importance at best. Even more, I do not think that the notion is consistent with the project of proposing "a great composite democratic individual." Nationhood is too close to a conception of group identity, a shared pride in tribal attributes rather than in adherence to a distinctive and principled human self-conceptualization that may one day be available to persons everywhere in the world. As national poetry, "Drum-Taps" is full of a hateful belligerence: Whitman sees and exults in the indissociable bond between nationhood and war. No, Whitman's greatness lies in his effort, the best effort thus far made, to say—to sing—the democratic individual, especially as such an individual lives in receptivity or responsiveness, in a connectedness different from any other. Such connectedness is not the same as nationhood or group identity. (A later point in this chapter is that it is not the same as "adhesiveness.")

I would like to suggest that his individualist effort attains its greatest height in the poem "Song of Myself." This is not to deny that everywhere in Whitman's work we will find resources for enriching or refining the poem's teaching. It is also true that he is sometimes less programmatic in this poem than he is elsewhere and later. But "Song of Myself" is of supreme value; it can organize one's reading of Whitman's body of writing. In thinking about this poem as the central work, one can make discoveries about the culture of democracy.

The poem is full of complexities. This democratic poem, like all of Whitman's best work, is immensely difficult; it is only barely accessible. His characterization of his own poems (in "As Consequent, etc.") perfectly suits "Song of Myself":

> O little shells, so curious-convolute, so limpid-cold and voiceless,
>
> . . . . .
>
> Your tidings old, yet ever new and untranslatable.

And if "Song of Myself" said—like any major work—unexpected things in its time, it gives the impression—like any major work—of having just appeared unexpectedly. So let us try to see what "Song of Myself" teaches. I mean to treat this poem as a work in political theory, which is what Whitman himself encourages (to say the least). Now and then, it is wise, however, to recall a line from "Myself and Mine": ". . . reject those who would expound me, for I cannot expound myself."

Whitman makes major additions from version to version and omits a few lines here and there. We should be content, I think, with the last version, that of 1891–92, even though it is interesting to study Whitman's changes. One change, however, should be noticed. Whitman did not call the poem "Song of Myself" until 1881. In the first version of 1855, the poem, like all the poems in the first edition of *Leaves of Grass*, had no title. Thereafter, the poem is successively called "Poem of Walt Whitman," "Walt Whitman," and finally "Song of Myself."

All of its various titles are odd—as, indeed, the title of the collection (*Leaves of Grass*) is odd. The titles are odd because when we read the poem, we do not find it autobiographical, except in a few unimportant details. The egotistical titles are not the titles of an egotistical work. Nor is the work self-referring or self-revelatory in any usual sense. There is scarcely anything intimate in it. It tells no story about the writer. Perhaps it would be all the more odd if the poem were self-revealing: until rather late in life, Whitman had little fame. Why should anyone have cared to hear an account of his life in 1855?

In the very first section of the poem, Whitman says:

> . . . what I assume you shall assume,
> For every atom belonging to me as good belongs to you.

Notice the extreme rapidity of movement in mood in these two lines. "What I assume you shall assume" seems to indicate that the poet is demanding that his readers obey him in their thought: a sentiment worse than egotistical. But then, in the next line, he is telling us that the reason we are to assume what he assumes is that "every atom belonging to me as good belongs to you." It is not that we must obey him as we read him. Rather, if we understand the poem, we will see that the poet and his readers are alike, and therefore we will come to assume what the poet does. In telling of himself, the poet is telling us about ourselves; that is what is to be assumed. His words about himself are words about us. As he proclaims in the climax of one of his long and observant catalogues of expressive human roles and functions: ". . . of these one and all I weave the song of myself" (sec. 15). In a Notebook entry (1855–56), Whitman says: "I have all lives, all effects, all hidden invisibly in myself. . . . [T]hey proceed from me."[3] In fact, if luck had made any of his readers democratic poets (and contingency is the thing that makes the largest difference), we would have said or sung poems with the same purport as "Song of Myself":

> (It is you talking just as much as myself, I act as the tongue of you,
> Tied in your mouth, in mine it begins to be loosen'd.)
>
> (Sec. 47)

We are alike in a certain way: living in a rights-based democracy enables and encourages a certain recognition of likeness. What is the nature of this likeness? In reading Whitman's statement that "every atom belonging to me as good belongs to you," let us emphasize the word "atom." What does it mean in this poem? An atom is a potentiality, I think. Every individual is composed of potentialities. Therefore, when I perceive or take in other human beings as they lead their lives or play their parts, I am encountering only external actualizations of some of the countless number of potentialities in me, in my soul. These atoms are in everyone; hence "every atom belonging to me as good belongs to you." The difficult and important complication is that in one's experience of

[3] Whitman, 707.

others one encounters their personalities, not their souls. The world contains an amazing diversity of personalities. Contingency has a great share in the realization of any potentiality. Souls, however, are the same: infinite potentialities.

At this point, I should try to say something about the categories Whitman uses or suggests in speaking of the different (so to speak, structural) components of the individual. I am guided to some degree by Roy Harvey Pearce and Harold Bloom.[4]

The key term is "soul": it frequently occurs in "Song of Myself" and in all of Whitman's work. I attribute to it both a secular meaning and a religious one, while the boundaries of the two meanings are not always sharp. Whitman intends, I think, some fluidity of definition. In its secular meaning, the soul is what is given in the person, and in all persons the given is the same: the same desires, inclinations, and passions as well as aptitudes and incipient talents. The secular soul is made up of the unwilled, the unbidden, the dreamt, the inchoate and unshaped. It is the reservoir of potentialities. Its roots are wordless. It exists to be observed and worked on, to be realized. In its religious meaning, soul is unique and unalterable individual identity; one's genius or "eidolon"; the "real Me" (from "As I Ebb'd With the Ocean of Life"); the "actual me" (from "Passage to India"). It seems to be untouched by experience, and it survives death to find numberless incarnations. For me, the Whitman that matters is the one who believes in the secular soul, not the one who fancies he believes in the religious soul (toward which he does sometimes turn a skeptical glance).

The sharply contrasting term to "soul" is, of course, "body." Whitman sometimes speaks dualistically of the soul and the body. He means to proclaim that the rights of the body are as sacred as those of the soul. He celebrates not only sex but the senses, which take their turn in being praised in "Song of Myself." When he does this, he is defying those whose religious conception of the soul is more conventional than Whitman's own and who associate the body with sin and damnation. On the other hand, Whitman's secular soul is unthinkable without the body and conversely.

What, then, is the self, insofar as it is not a synonym for the whole individual?

[4] Roy Harvey Pearce, "Introduction" [to the Facsimile Edition of the 1860 text of], *Leaves of Grass* (Ithaca: Cornell University Press, 1961), vii–li, and *The Continuity of American Poetry* (Princeton: Princeton University Press paperback, 1977), 69–83; Harold Bloom, *Poetics of Influence*, ed. John Hollander (New Haven: Schwab, 1988), 297–307.

246 The Inner Ocean

In "Pioneers! O Pioneers!" he says:

> I too with my soul and body,
> We, a curious trio.

From this verse and others, I would infer that the self (the I, the ego) is active self-consciousness and disciplined creative energy. It is a purely secular category that Whitman does not want us to confuse with soul, especially in its religious sense. The self does its great work when it observes its soul and body as from a distance and exploits the faculty of speech to tell as much of the truth as possible about them. The self is power that draws on its given resources of soul and body to become a poet: everybody is at least a partway poet. It is with the poet's virtues of receptivity (in whatever way or degree possible) that each self democratically connects to the world of persons, creatures, and things. "You be my poem" (from "To You") helps to define connectedness.

The other work that the self does is to put together a social persona, a personality, and thus enable the individual to lead a life. The creative energy of the self realizes one or another potentiality of the soul (and body). The personality is what is immediately recognizable by others: one's characteristics as they flow to and from one's work and social relations. Personality has surface and depths.

"Song of Myself" begins with "I celebrate myself." What the poem celebrates is soul, body, and self, but especially the inexhaustibility of the soul and the power of the self to observe the soul and make democratic poetical understanding. The poem does not really celebrate personality or social persona; it merely admires and praises it. Whitman depends on it to keep things going: he does not love society as society. He is not a novelist or a sponsor of novelists whose ultimate reality is well-rounded characters that appeal to our sense that each person is what he or she is, just like that, and could only and must be only that.

One last point: the crucial meaning of Whitman's term "composite," is not the structural condition of having components (soul, body, self, and personality) but, rather, the indefinite multiplicity of the soul.

I have made Whitman's teaching cumbersome. Some less clumsy effort must nevertheless be faithful to its complexity. Whitman is not saying anything simple, and I think that despite occasional vagueness or inconsistency he sustains his distinctions concerning the components of the individual throughout his work. William James's marvelous writing in "The Consciousness of Self" bears some important resemblances to

Whitman's understanding of components.[5] The views of both stem from a will to democratize human self-conception.

In any case, Whitman is suggesting two main ideas. All the personalities that I encounter, I already am: that is to say, I could become or could have become something like what others are. This thought necessarily means, in turn, that all of us are always indefinitely more than we actually are. I am potentially all personalities and we equally are infinite potentialities. Whitman's poetic aim is to talk or sing his readers into accepting this highest truth about human beings. Democracy covers it over less than other cultures do. If people take thought, they will have to acknowledge, first, that they have all the impulses or inclinations or desires (for good and for bad) they see realized around them, even if they act on other ones, and consequently, second, that each of us is, in Emerson's word, an "infinitude," or has, in another formulation of Emerson's, a "populousness of soul." The deepest moral and existential meaning of equal rights is this kind of equal recognition granted by every individual to every individual. Democratic connectedness is mutual acceptance. Rejection of any other human being, for one reason or another, for apparently good reasons as well as for bad ones, is self-rejection. A principal burden of Whitman's teaching, therefore, is that the differences between individuals do not go as deep as the commonalities. Personality is not the (secular) soul. He explicitly says in "To You" that every endowment (talent) and virtue is latent in every individual, not merely every impulse or desire.

If I am right in the suggestions I am making concerning the poetic aim of "Song of Myself," the result is rather strange (to use that word again). The great poem of individualism in a democracy is not individualist in any conventional sense. After all, to be individual originally meant to be indivisible. Clearly, "Song of Myself" is not asking us to pretend that we are indivisible. It is more than a matter of having components: soul, body, self, and personality. The (secular) soul itself is a crowded house. (Later on, in "One's-Self I Sing" [1867], he can refer to each of us as "a simple separate person." If he is still consistent with his earlier teachings, "simple" would have to connote unpretentious, yet precious, but not indivisible.) I read the disorienting and funny line "It is time to explain myself—let us stand up" as a pleased reference to inner multiplicity (sec. 44). More famously, he says toward the end of the poem:

[5] William James, "The Consciousness of Self," in *The Principles of Psychology* (1890) (New York: Dover, 1950), 1: chap. 10.

> Do I contradict myself?
> Very well then I contradict myself.
> (I am large, I contain multitudes.)
> (Sec. 51)

Our potentialities are not only numberless but—and for that reason—conflicting. We are inhabited by tumultuous atoms. We are composite, not even composed. In "Crossing Brooklyn Ferry," he goes so far as to posit "myself disintegrated, everyone disintegrated." I think that Whitman would have admired Nietzsche's convolutedly Platonic saying that the body is "but a social structure composed of many souls."[6] Whitman's radicalism shows in his distance from Plato's dream of harmony among the components of the individual and of stillness in the house of the potentialities.

Yet, in abandoning in "Song of Myself" the idea that the individual is indivisible, he is not creating an altogether new sense of individualism. He sees that more than a few American individuals are aware of their own composite nature and of their own undefinability. The telling point is not so much that the United States is a pluralist society made up of all psychological and sociological types as it is that democratic individuals see (if only unsteadily) that each of them contains the raw material of all types, yet is more than any type or all types, and is even more than its special personality. (Of course, it counts for a good deal that the democracy is as expressively diverse as it is, and is so on a plane of equality rather than hierarchically.)

Let me now summarize provisionally what Whitman is doing in "Song of Myself." He is presenting a portrait of himself, but it is not a portrait of his social or everyday personality. It is not a story, either, of the things that he has done or of the particular experiences that have shaped his personality or even shaped the course of his life. To tell these things is not to tell of what is most important about himself. "Song of Myself" is not like a photo or realistic drawing; but it is, nevertheless, the best and fullest account of himself—and also, of course, of everyone else.

The question persists: Why does Whitman not give a conventionally realistic account of himself, on the assumption that somehow he could

---

[6] Friedrich Nietzsche, *Beyond Good and Evil*, trans. Walter Kaufmann (New York: Vintage 1966), sec. 19, 26.

have interested the world in his personality? The answer must be that the portrait he gives is more truly himself than any realistic account could ever hope to be. How, then, to describe this portrait? Whitman's phrase is best: it is a portrait of "a great composite *democratic individual*." Everyone is composite, and in a democracy each one can and should see himself or herself as a "great composite *democratic individual*." If the (secular) soul is potentiality, an honest portrait of oneself will register one's ability to perceive, and to identify or sympathize or empathize with, all the actualized potentialities one tries to take in, and will also impart the sense that no actualization is definitive of anyone. The net impression left by "Song of Myself" is oneself, as it were, simultaneously but vicariously actualized in all directions. Oneself democratically perfected is truly a collage; one is "stucco'd" all over with personalities (sec. 31). A person is also a Picasso-like concurrence of many perspectives within one frame. Whitman cannot talk about himself just by talking about himself, nor can anyone. If I talk honestly—that is to say, poetically—about myself, I must talk about others. Perhaps I must talk much more about them than about myself, as Whitman does. "Song of Myself" is—to use the title of one of Gertrude Stein's books—*Everybody's Autobiography*. As he put it in a draft, "I celebrate myself to celebrate you."[7]

Thus the poem seeks to teach that so far from being indivisible or even coherently multiple, one is, and should be glad to be, at any given moment, a composite—that is, ambiguous and ambivalent—and that in a timeless but mortal sense one is an immense and largely untapped reservoir of potentiality. D. H. Lawrence has referred to Whitman's attempt to articulate an "accumulative identity."[8] One lifetime is not enough for the realization of more than a few potentialities, so that one lives many lives (on earth) only through the ability to perceive and identify with others and thus, in an unarrogant sense, to become them, if only for a minute now and then. Whitman's emphasis on absorbing others is precisely, for him, the best way of letting them be, of not possessing them. In "A Song For Occupations," he provides a succinct account of what it means to connect to others by identifying with them:

Neither a servant nor a master I,

. . . . .

If you stand at work in a shop I stand as nigh as the nighest
    in the same shop,

---

[7] Whitman, quoted in Matthiessen, 555.
[8] D. H. Lawrence, "Whitman" (1921), in *Whitman*, 845.

>If you bestow gifts on your brother or dearest friend I demand as good
>   as your brother or dearest friend,
>If your lover, husband, wife, is welcome by day or night,
>   I must be personally as welcome,
>If you become degraded, criminal, ill, then I become so for your sake.

The individual demands to share the goods, the suffering, the fate of the stranger, and does so by imagining the stranger's life as a life he or she could lead and never feel out of place. As Whitman says in his earliest Notebook: "A man only is interested in anything when he identifies himself with it."[9] Whitman wants to coax us into thinking that we can identify with anything if we try, and that if we try we show not presumption but democratic honesty.

"Song of Myself" teaches its lessons about the individual not only in what it says directly. Part of Whitman's poetic subtlety consists in his saying much about himself and every person through the compositional and structural traits of the poem. The poet is talking about the nature of himself and of every individual in the formal qualities that he has chosen. I do not refer to the absence of rhyme, the uneven lines, or the variety of rhythms in "Song of Myself" (and almost all of his poetry). Free verse does, to be sure, make a cultural point. There can be beauty when the inherited forms are abandoned and new forms are created. New forms express a new sense of artistic beauty: the artistic beauty appropriate for a new world, for a democracy. On the other hand, it is undeniably relevant for understanding the meaning of self-disclosure that Whitman creates a poem that is made up of genres. "Song of Myself" contains, for example: anecdotes, not all of which lend themselves easily to emblematic uses; philosophical reflections on the nature of the person but also on a full range of other questions that are made existential; descriptions of particulars that are observed with an eerie closeness; epic lists of localities and of human types; and lyrical passages of adoration and despair. This assortment of genres is a way of saying that adequate speech about oneself cannot be confined to any one genre.

My main interest, however, is rather that the sequence of passages and the poem's texture reflect the nature of the individual. These are the

---

[9] Whitman, quoted in Matthiessen, 518.

formal qualities that especially matter because they conduce to the feeling that our nature is strange (to use that word yet again), that oneself is a strange place. I believe that Whitman means to teach the lesson that if we are poetically persuaded of this strangeness, we will grow more in mutual recognition, in democratic acceptance. Feelings of superiority and other discriminations will exist, even exist intensely, but their validity will be challenged by a poetically enhanced awareness of the vastness of every individual equally.

By sequence (not plot or progression) and texture, I mean such qualities as the poem's discontinuities, abrupt transitions, and sudden eruptions into different tones; its overall indifference to the demand that a story about oneself be a story; the seeming disproportion of attention accorded in it to small matters; its startling conjunctions and almost arbitrarily associated matters; the blank spaces in it caused by the many things left unsaid but that a reader could have expected; its occasional hallucinatory quality; the dreamlike suddenness of emergences and vanishings in it; and the poet's dreamlike mobility of identity which consists in mobilities of foci (both grand and microscopic) and of tense and perspective.

These compositional and structural traits are needed to provide an accurate portrait of the whole person. If the direct teaching of the poem is that one is multiple, that one will find, if one looks honestly, others inside oneself, the formal qualities of the poem teach a related lesson, that one is (or should be) mysterious to oneself, as others are (or should be) to themselves. Exploring or examining oneself makes one less familiar to oneself. Knowing oneself is therefore knowing that there is no single, transparent entity to know. Hence knowing oneself is coming to know that one cannot really know oneself—at least not fully and not definitely. "As if I were not puzzled at myself!" he says (in an untitled poem excluded from the final edition).[10] The Socratic paradox of knowledge as ignorance is transferred by "Song of Myself" to self-knowledge. What mistily emerges from democratized self-examination is not so much inhibition as surprise. Montaigne's identification of self-contempt as the fruit of self-knowledge suffers a partial rebuke. The limits of self-knowledge are the limits of poetical speech, and Whitman says that though speech is the twin of his vision, speech "is unequal to measure itself." At any given moment, there is always more to know about oneself than one can say. He addresses these unpoetical words to the faculty of poetical speech:

[10] Whitman, 595.

My final merit I refuse you, I refuse putting from me what I really am,
Encompass worlds, but never try to encompass me,

· · · · ·

Writing and talk do not prove me, . . .

(Sec. 25)

If honest, one becomes almost another to oneself. By far the most important result would be that the passion to judge, condemn, and punish others is reduced and replaced, to an appreciable degree, by the desire to accept or empathize or sympathize with them. If an individual is composite, it should become much more difficult to equate a person with any of his or her deeds, no matter how awful—perhaps, also, no matter how good. As he programmatically says in "Great Are the Myths" (a poem he dropped from the final edition):

> What the best and worst did, we could do,
> What they felt, do we not feel it in ourselves?
> What they wished, do we not wish the same?[11]

I believe that the direct and the indirect lessons of the poem are democratic lessons in connectedness. The ideas of the individual as composite and of the individual as honestly unfamiliar to itself are ways of awakening all of us to human equality on the highest moral and existential plane. To admit one's compositeness and ultimate unknowability is to open oneself to a kinship to others which is defined by receptivity or responsiveness to them. It intensifies the mutuality between strangers which is intrinsic to the idea of rights-based individualism in a democracy.

———————————

Whitman's work is to encourage us to become ever more consistent in living the life of equal rights. He admits everyone and everything into his poem. His mode is intensification. "I am a look," he says in a fragment.[12] He poetizes everyone and everything. He invests them with beauty so that we may look at them, look as if for the first time, or look again and not look away, and then to feel instead of freezing. He freshens the beauty of beautiful persons (and beautiful natural and manmade things).

[11] Whitman, 585.
[12] Whitman, 694.

He goes far—as far as Emerson and Thoreau go—in trying to connect us to the world through a sense of beauty which dares to limit the ravenous appetite of the sense of moral virtue, because it easily turns (and for good reasons) world-despairing or even world-hating. But he is not content with doing only that. Whitman poetizes what is not conventionally thought beautiful: he tries to make wondrous the common, the commonplace, the everyday, "the plain landscape" (as he puts it in a Notebook).[13] Even more, he tries to have us think it possible that what is cheap or coarse or ugly or artless has its own beauty also—the beauty that any person or thing has just by being there, or has just by force of wanting to be looked at rather than turned away from. Even when he calls ugliness ugly, as in "Faces," and parades it, the depiction is so vivid that ugliness becomes humanly indispensable. As he says in an excluded poem, "Thoughts—1: Visages": "Of ugliness—To me there is just as much in it as there is in beauty."[14]

Similarly, in order to encourage what he calls sympathy, or what we can also call empathy, he enhances the humanity of human beings, the creatureliness of animals, the quiddity of things. He shows poetically, and invites us to share, his sympathy with what is already quite sympathetic but what, in our hurry, we do not sympathize with enough. But, more important, he poetically conveys the need to sympathize with what is unattractive or even repellent. He makes poetic room for the homely, the unimportant, the obscure, the overlooked, the despised, the wicked, and the diseased.

And all the while, of course, his constant appeal is for us to exercise recognition: to recognize that when one learns to perceive more beauty and feel more sympathy one is only doing justice to *oneself*, to one's composite nature. Just as I am more than others can take in, so are they more than I can take in. It is especially important to feel that the unbeautiful are not just unbeautiful and that the wicked are not just wicked, and to do so, as Whitman does enough of the time, without depending on any religious conception of the soul.

To live democratically, to live receptively and responsively, is risky, and therefore the invitation to it is easily resisted. Whitman knows that. This

[13] Whitman, 672.
[14] Whitman, 597.

is why he understands life in a democratic culture as heroic. Intensified democratic connectedness is heroic. What makes it so is the extraordinary amount of self-overcoming it requires. Many things in oneself must be overcome. First is the disposition to think that one is one's personality and that therefore it is all right to live one's life solely dedicated to the prohibitions and allowances of one's role or function or solely devoted to cultivating one's peculiarities and differences—what Mill favorably calls "eccentricity." Also to be overcome is the inevitable desire to close oneself to experience by finding others, or aspects of nature, condemnable or horrible. The failure of recognition and hence of acceptance is a perpetual possibility and frequent occurrence. Self-overcoming as the overcoming of fear and disgust is the poet's constant message.

Unblinking attention to surfaces and depths is facilitated by the conviction that what one perceives or intuits or interprets is not exhaustively constitutive of the individuals one encounters or imagines. One can endure the surfaces and depths all the better when one knows that people could exceed, in all directions, the given, particular aspect we encounter. Or, one can exult in the surfaces or depths all the more when one knows that they are mere temporary manifestations of a residual and inexhaustible potentiality, that they are only promises. Whitman thus aims to attach us more tightly to others as they are, whatever they are, while, and because, he points to the undefinable soul which each is, to which we cannot attach ourselves, and which we can only revere.

In a very late poem, "Grand Is the Seen," his lines can be read, in spite of Whitman, in a strictly this-worldly and mortal way and given a general relevance:

> Grand is the seen, the light, to me—grand are the sky and stars,
> Grand is the earth, and grand are lasting time and space,
> And grand their laws, so multiform, puzzling, evolutionary
> But grander far the unseen soul of me. . . .
>   .   .   .   .   .
> More evolutionary, vast, puzzling, O my soul!
> More multiform far—more lasting thou than they.

The visible is inferior to the invisible, but Whitman manages to raise the inferior (mere personalities), yet make the superior (souls) appear real.

For example, the life of work elicits from Whitman, in "A Song for Occupations," the paradigmatic judgment that in it there is "far more than you estimated, (and far less also,)." His poetizing has thus a two-way motion. Life is poetically richer than is commonly assumed but also less real than the souls from which it emanates. Part of Whitman's mission is to awaken admiration of the surfaces and depths of social beings and their relations. But he wants admiration to be honestly aware of the contingent nature of actuality and the real nature of potentiality. This awareness can lead to a more poignant admiration of what is there and thus avoid the bad faith that makes the world falsely solid and falsely necessary. (I hope that I am not making Whitman too Sartrean.)

Of course, my reading of Whitman runs the risk of ending up in a paradox, namely that of suggesting that no single manifestation is good in itself but that an indefinite number of potential manifestations has infinite worth. In answer, I would say that Whitman builds the feeling that what gives indefinite potentiality its worth is precisely the reverence toward anyone which it may arouse and hence the acceptance of everyone which it should lead to. The doer is more than the sum of deeds.

Here I shall notice just briefly an essential difference between Whitman and Emerson in the strategies they adopt to overcome not only fear and disgust but also what Whitman calls, in "Song of the Open Road," "a secret silent loathing and despair." Both are troubled by the timidity and general melancholy they find in American life, and both seem to suggest at times that the explanation is found in the rigors of economic pursuits and in the failure of economic rewards to gratify or even to compensate for the rigors.

In *Nature* and elsewhere Emerson tries to effect a reconciliation between the despondent individual and what is outside him or her—the "NOT ME," he calls it—by endeavoring to show that the processes of Nature are the emanation of God's mind but that this mind is like our own and thus that whatever we see is only our intelligence projected and externalized. The proof of humanity's affinity to Divinity is that Nature supplies all sorts of humanly valuable lessons, practical and moral. It seems to have been designed by a mind intent on instructing other minds. Nature is God's language; we learn to read it when we learn to see correspondences between the natural and the mental. Emerson's ambition—some of the time, anyway—is similar to Hegel's: namely, to overcome alienation and achieve reconciliation by recognizing resemblance between the way in which one's mind works and the way in which natural processes meaningfully unfold. There are times, too, when Whitman follows Emerson in this design. Indeed, later on in life, Whitman pays tribute to Hegel.[15] There is actually a great Hegelian or Emersonian moment in "Song of Myself":

Dazzling and tremendous how quick the sun-rise would kill me,
If I could not now and always send sun-rise out of me.

(Sec. 25)

His sunrise is his power of poetical speech, a power to re-create the world as it is by articulating it. For all that, however, I think that he is doing something in "Song of Myself" that is divorceable from Emersonian metaphysics. Indeed, the preceding lines lend themselves to an existentialist rather than a transcendentalist reading.

It is not a matter of detecting similarity in the processes of mind and nature but of discovering kinship between oneself and others (and the rest of nature). The relationship is not analogical or symbolical, not a correspondence or reflection, but actual; it is independent of any reference to a Creator or to any assimilation to a Creator. I think that Whitman's general way in "Song of Myself" is much the better way of trying to effect reconciliation. Not only does it avoid theological metaphysics, it does not too insistently moralize. Whitman comes right out and says in the Preface, 1876, that "while the Moral is the purport and last intelligence of all Nature, there is absolutely nothing of the moral in the works, or laws, or shows of Nature." And Whitman's way expands the sense of strangeness while it expands the sense of sameness.

I do not deny that some of Whitman's beliefs ease the risk of accepting his teaching, that is, the risk of living democratically. He suggests now and then (especially in *Democratic Vistas*) that the person has solidity, that one is no mere composite. It is as if he thinks that he has to give a guarantee that amid all the operations of perception and sympathy he wants to encourage, and hence the connectedness of kinship he wants to encourage, he is not urging us to dissolution. Courage and generosity in perception and sympathy will be more possible if one thinks that one has a core and that it always remain intact.

[15] See especially the section "Carlyle from American Points of View," in *Specimen Days*, in *Leaves of Grass and Selected Prose*, ed. John Kouwenhoven (New York: Modern Library, 1950), 729–36.

Whitman is not content with the limited stability that comes from memory, from the precarious continuity of consciousness, and from the moments—moments only—of self-concentration. Nor is he content to tie a person's constant identity to the simple fact that one's stream of consciousness—the mingling of self and soul on the terms of neither—is one's own and no one else's; that one has sole access to it; that, because of it, only I can live inside myself and know that I am I and not another. Whitman wants to affirm his faith that deep down in the person is something both distinctive and unchanging. What is involved is a religious conception of soul as unique and unalterable identity, whether immortal or not. In *Democratic Vistas*, he refers to "that something a man is, (last precious consolation of the drudging poor,) standing apart from all else, divine in his own right, and woman in hers." He also says, "The quality of *Being*, in the object's self, according to its own central idea and purpose, and of growing therefrom and thereto— . . . is the lesson of Nature. True, the full man wisely gathers, culls, absorbs; but if, engaged disproportionately in that, he slights or overlays the precious idiocrasy and special nativity and intention that he is, the man's self, the main thing, is a failure, however wide his general cultivation."[16] These passages seem to threaten the radicalism of "Song of Myself." They seem to locate individuality in each person's profound and permanent difference rather than in the flight from fixed identity and toward the generosities of perception and sympathy.

Whitman had been reading Mill's *On Liberty*. The first paragraph of *Democratic Vistas* refers to it. I think, however, that Mill's grand (third) chapter on individuality may contaminate Whitman's thinking. He combines Mill's notion of the individual as exceptional, as eccentric (Whitman's word is "idiocratic") with his own belief in a substratum; but all the while he is doing his real work, which is to vivify the genuinely democratic idea that an individual should try not to acquire or retain an identity (in the wrong spirit). I mean that a democratic individual, if he or she is to be true to the spirit of democracy, should not (on the one hand) aspire to become a shaped presence, like a work of art, resplendent in its integrity and unmistakable in its attainment, or (on the other hand) try to disclose one's true "genius."

I think that such substantialist talk about the person or the soul gets in the way of Whitman's most democratic teaching. I much prefer to stay with his idea that what is left inside oneself when one is filling a function

---

[16]Whitman, *Democratic Vistas*, in Kouwenhoven, 471, 487. Compare the "Me myself" in "Song of Myself" (sec. 4), which is more impervious than receptive, perhaps.

or playing a part is an infinite reservoir or, better, repertoire. Unexpressed potentiality rather than an indestructible core (that must remain hidden or can show itself only specially) suits the idea of "a great composite democratic individual," which is the idea to be preserved.

It is undeniable that one cannot live on the heights of receptivity and responsiveness continuously. To put it clumsily, one must have a personality. That is, one must do a job, fill a function, play a part—probably more than one. One must live a life that is made up mostly of ordinariness. In the Preface, 1876, Whitman says, "To the highest democratic view, man is most acceptable in living well the practical life and lot which happen to him as ordinary farmer, sea-farer, mechanic, clerk, laborer, or driver." A person will perform his labors and also "his duties as a citizen, son, husband, father and employ'd person." Ordinariness becomes troubling only when it is rooted in unreflective conformity. Lines in "That Shadow My Likeness" tell us that Whitman wants us to be haunted by, and thus suspicious of, our conformity:

> That shadow my likeness that goes to and fro seeking a livelihood,
> chattering, chaffering
> How often I find myself standing and looking at it where it flits,
> How often I question and doubt whether that is really me.

Whitman's highest hope must be that there will be moods or moments in which an individual comes to and remembers or realizes the deep meanings of living in a rights-based democracy. These occasions of self-concentration may be rare, but they should have some pervasive and long-lasting effect, even if somewhat thinned out. Whitman's model for such moments is poetic inspiration, but his phrases about the mood of composition are interchangeable with those he uses in a Notebook to describe existential receptivity to the world: "the idea of a trance, yet with all the senses alert—only a state of high exalted musing—the tangible and material with all its shows—the objective world suspended or surmounted for a while and the powers in exaltation, freedom, vision."[17] The effect will show itself not only in solitary spiritual acts of perception or sympathy when "Appears aloof thy life, each passion, each

[17] Whitman, 672.

event,"[18] but also in democratically inspired deeds from the most casual to the most disciplined. Attentiveness and empathy, even if not continuously strong, gradually build up the overt connectedness of a democratically receptive culture: its tolerance, its hospitableness, and its appetite for movement, novelty, mixture, and impurity.

It is better, however, not to pretend that receptivity can be a direct and continuous principle of public policy. Once everyone's rights and minimal needs are guaranteed, the aim of political action will remain undetermined by Whitman's teaching, except indirectly. The image of such indirectness is given in Whitman's "By Blue Ontario's Shore," when he speaks of the influence of good poetry: "Will it absorb into me as I absorb food, air, to appear again in my strength, gait, face?" Another image of indirectness is given in his powerful catalogue of woe, "I Sit and Look Out":

> All these—all the meanness and agony without end
> I sitting look out upon,
> See, hear, and am silent.

Attention and silence are not the final deeds, only the indispensable preliminary to a sane, ameliorative response, the content of which is inspired but not specified by Whitman's ideal of receptivity.

I would also like to suggest that this overt, acted-out connectedness is not well illustrated by Whitman's notion of adhesive love, or love of comrades. This is, in my judgment, too literal an application of receptivity and responsiveness. It is equality made too literal: one is dissolved in the "en masse" rather than remaining connected to others as an equal. It promises to exceed sympathy but must fall short of it and become gregariousness. The line used in a war poem, "Over the Carnage Rose Prophetic a Voice," is false: "affection shall solve the problems of freedom yet." Adhesiveness threatens to suffocate the very individualism of personality which Whitman is trying to promote, while it despiritualizes and falsifies the superior idea of oneself as composite, and hence as indefinite, and hence not properly amenable to an all-enfolding merger. It does not go with the spirit of rights-based individualism. It also serves the sinister project of nationalism. The comradely side of Whitman is not his most attractive because it is not the genuinely democratic one. Comradeship in a struggle and comradeship as a consolation for the griefs of a

---

[18] An uncollected poem in Whitman, 672.

hierarchical or stigmatizing society are fine, but comradeship as the defining democratic bond is not good because it is not fine.

It is well to notice that adhesiveness does not figure in "Song of Myself" and that in "Song of the Open Road" (1856), close in time to "Song of Myself," Whitman does give, for once, a notion of adhesiveness which does not betray his most radical individualism:

> Here is adhesiveness, it is not previously fashion'd, it is apropos;
> Do you know what it is as you pass to be loved by strangers?
> Do you know the talk of those turning eye-balls?

The model is sexual cruising—momentary intensities, which are a sort of connectedness which is in the same family of sentiments as sympathy. If what I have just said is too glib, consider, instead, some lines (from "A Song of the Rolling Earth") that give one of Whitman's best definitions of sympathy:

> I swear I begin to see love with sweeter spasms than that
>   which responds love,
> It is that which contains itself, which never invites and never refuses.

Another lesson Whitman teaches is that the composite individual will live for itself in a manner greatly different from the self-absorption of nondemocratic cultures. First, all that Whitman says about the individual is an instigation to act out more and more of one's potentiality. "Once more I enforce you to give play to yourself," he says in "So Long!" (in a line dropped from the final edition).[19] That means to lead a more experimental life. It may also mean to seek a heterogeneous accumulation of experiences, as if only in that way can numerous yearnings of one's soul be accommodated. Whitman's hope is that with so much to gain there cannot be very much to lose. He says in "A Song of the Rolling Earth" that "undeniable growth" establishes the reality of soul. Second, and relatedly, in any given activity, the idea that one is always capable of more than what one is now doing should affect the quality of how one does what one is doing. Whitman's greatest formulation appears in the fourth section of "Song of Myself":

> Apart from the pulling and hauling stands what I am,
> Stands amused, complacent, compassionating, idle, unitary,
> Looks down, is erect, or bends an arm on an impalpable certain rest.

[19] Whitman, 638.

Looking with side-curved head curious what will come next,
Both in and out of the game and watching and wondering at it.

There is a whole ethic of action compressed in these five lines, and it is an ethic that peculiarly suits a democracy because of the consecration that democracy gives to the will to transform action into contentious play, to replace military combat by "saner wars, sweet wars, life-giving wars" ("The Return of the Heroes"). "In and out of the game" is democratic seriousness: "Nothing is for keeps" is a truth that should be embraced rather than resented.

Democracy has sometimes been associated with grossness, a plebeian, underbred grossness. Edmund Burke said in *Reflections on the Revolution in France* that under the system of aristocratic manners "vice itself lost half its evil by losing all its grossness." Well, Whitman is trying to suggest that democracy has its own grace, the grace of being "both in and out," hence the grace of unsolemnity, of looseness, and that this grace is enabled finally by the understanding that those toward whom one acts are one's equals, are oneself in the most important respects. This is no mere stylization. It is easier to be graceful if we never feel that we are in the presence of aliens. Democratic grace is caught in Whitman's almost rhetorical questions about the democratic individual:

The friendly and flowing savage, who is he?
Is he waiting for civilization, or past it and mastering it?
(Sec. 39)

The ethic of "in and out of the game" Whitman dares to apply even to suffering, whether one's own or that of someone else. He is suggesting that if I stop my own momentum in order to observe others their hurts can register more painfully on me than they had before. If I am not quite completely in my own game, I can have a chance to notice what is happening to others who may be caught up in my game or in some other. Also, if I am not quite completely in my own game, I am able, perhaps, to observe my own hurts rather than merely suffering them, and they may, therefore, register less painfully on me.

At this point, perhaps, even an appreciative reader of Whitman may think that his idealization of the composite individual asks too much and may, in addition, ask for the wrong thing. His poetic identification with all who suffer may seem forced. Here I take up sketchily some of the difficulties that the overall aspiration to an intensified connectedness may encounter.

To begin with, one can ask, are there not inevitable and desirable limits on the ability to perceive beauty? How far can one go in seeing beauty when, by conventional standards of both taste and decency, what presents itself is trivial or shameless or hideous? Why not rather encourage a greater effort at aesthetic improvement? Whitman himself is eager to see a more aesthetically accomplished and vibrant culture.

There is good sense in this complaint, as Whitman's own more conventional aestheticism, as found especially in *Democratic Vistas*, demonstrates. In response, I suppose one can say that what comes to characterize American art more and more in the twentieth century is the uncanny and persistent appetite to make art out of junk and thus to get us both to redefine what art is and to look again at what we are disposed to overlook or disdain or throw away as junk. This appetite is faithful to the spirit of Whitman's work. It is a democratic characteristic; it is radical; it is heroic in a new way. And, for these reasons, it is best not to establish too quickly the limits on generous perception and, instead, to anticipate that American art will frequently manage to redeem aesthetically the apparently unredeemable. What artists do professionally, others can do without planning. (This phenomenon exists apart from the insidiously attractive qualities of mass or popular art, attractive precisely to the well educated because they detect in some of this art a seriousness that repays generous perception.)

Greater difficulties are encountered in the matter of sympathy or empathy. Are there not both proper moral and inevitable mental limits to the ability to identify with human beings? Let us leave aside the admirable wish to establish kinship with animals and indeed with inanimate nature, as Whitman tries to do. Let us even grant Whitman the amazing mobility of identity that he poetically claims when, for example, he says:

> I turn the bridegroom out of bed and stay with the bride myself,
> I tighten her all night to my thighs and lips.
>
> (Sec. 33)

and then immediately goes on to say:

> My voice is the wife's voice, the screech by the rail of the stairs.
> They fetch my man's body up dripping and drown'd.
>
> (Sec. 33)

He moves from identifying with the bridegroom to identifying with the established married woman, that is, from consummation to loss. He is both sexes and many conditions. Let us allow that an individual, democratically prepared, can perform such feats of empathy, and should want to.

What does one say, however, when Whitman writes:

> I am the man, I suffered, I was there.
>
> .   .   .   .   .
>
> I am the hounded slave, I wince at the bite of dogs,
> Hell and despair are upon me . . .
> Agonies are one of my changes of garments,
> I do not ask the wounded person how he feels,
>   I myself become the wounded person,
> My hurts turn livid upon me as I lean on a cane and observe.
>
> (Sec. 33)

When encountering or imagining a hounded slave, what does it mean to become the hounded slave? Whitman amazingly says, "My hurts," not "His hurts." But is he encouraging us to feign transfers of identity? At the same time, one leans on a cane and observes. The extreme of empathy is claimed, and at the same time the extreme of detachment is being admitted, and not only admitted but insisted on. The question arises as to whether there are sufferings so terrible that the lucky unsuffering individual, no matter how intensely democratic in reception, cannot share them in imagination. Similarly, are there not acts of criminality so atrocious that one should not be encouraged to try to understand the person who is responsible for them? Can one find the serial killer in oneself, if one only tried? Whitman insists a number of times that he is as evil as the worst person. It is not possible to believe him. Do not even the greatest tragedians and novelists take shortcuts in their impersonations of madness and criminality, and have to?

Furthermore, is it not the case that when we encounter people performing their deeds, they are often simply acting according to rules? There is no personality to understand. All that needs to be understood are the rules that people are following. Such understanding may be hard to come by, but empathy or sympathy may have no place in the attempt to achieve it. More generally, may it not be the case that people, even in one's culture, are just too different from one another? Is not what is most important about all of us not our potentiality but our divergent personalities, the sum of what, in each case, our particular culture has made us?

Or, put more generously, what is perhaps best about us is the way in which we take one potentiality and realize or embody it fully and therefore achieve something definite and formed. What could be better than shaping a life by means of a voluntary and resourceful submission to a discipline or project? Sartre, the great theorist of bad faith, was also the great theorist of project. Is not reality found there and only there? Yet another question may arise. If Whitman means that one must try to see individuals from even the most dissimilar cultures as actualizations of one's own potentialities, is he not presuming to understand what he really cannot? Is not even the most democratically determined observer confined in his or her perspective?

To all these questions concerning moral and mental limits to sympathy or empathy (and there are more), one may be able to give only hesitant answers. I do not pretend to give any answers here. Is Whitman conscious of these problems? Does it matter whether we say that he is or is not? He certainly appears reckless. In "Song of the Answerer," he says, "Every existence has its idiom," but immediately insists that the poet "resolves all tongues into his own," without loss. Yet, in that remarkable poem "The Sleepers," Whitman raises the possibility that he understands that his radical empathy is only a dream, that mobile identity is only a dream (and that only in sleep or death are people alike and equal):

> I dream in my dream all the dreams of the other dreamers,
> And I become the other dreamers.
> I am a dance—
>
> . . . . .
>
> I am the actor, the actress, the voter, the politician,
>
> . . . . .
>
> I am she who adorn'd herself and folded her hair expectantly.

Does it help to enlist so austere a philosopher as R. G. Collingwood in defense of Whitman's effort at empathy? In *An Autobiography*, he characterizes the historian: "If he is able to understand, by rethinking them, the thoughts of a great many different kinds of people, it follows that he must be a great many kinds of man. He must be, in fact, a microcosm of all the history he can know. Thus his own self-knowledge is at the same time his knowledge of the world of human affairs."[20] Could it be that unless a claimed kinship is the basis of observation all appreciation of "otherness" tends to turn into a mere patronizing aesthetic of the picturesque or into a

[20] R. G. Collingswood, *An Autobiography* (London: Oxford University Press, 1939), 115.

paternalist anthropological solicitude? Human beings may be denatured, in either case, by being seen or imagined only as surfaces. More likely, otherness will arouse fear and disgust.

Finally, I would only say again that, at the least, it is democratic not to draw the limits too narrowly and not to give up too quickly or complacently in epistemological defeat. Whitman is straining to extend the limits of knowing, and it is democratically better to err on the side of presumptuousness than on the side of bafflement. Implied in Whitman's idea of the burden of perception and sympathy that the spirit of democracy means to impose is the will to activate the feeling of contingency: it is a matter of chance that any person has been born and then been raised in one way rather than another. Further, every life is interwoven with chance, with good and bad luck. Things could easily have turned out differently. The proper way of acknowledging contingency is to realize that the same biological being that I am could have been culturally situated in an indefinitely great number of places and acquired a different personality and outward life in each case. And all the time, if I look inward, I can see the beginnings of other possibilities that I do not act on or act out and that make me indefinitely more than my socially shaped personality.

Now, Nietzsche, the principal theorist of helpless and bounded perspective-seeing and of the pathos of distance, can nevertheless say, "To *want* to see differently, is no small discipline and preparation of the intellect for its future 'objectivity'—the latter understood not as 'contemplation without interest' (which is a nonsensical absurdity), but as the ability *to control* one's Pro and Con and to dispose of them, so that one knows how to employ a *variety* of perspectives and affective interpretations in the service of knowledge."[21] Or, as Wallace Stevens—heir of both Whitman and Nietzsche—says about the aim of poetical perception and feeling:

> It is a visibility of thought,
> In which hundreds of eyes, in one mind, see at once.[22]

Whitman has his own perspectivism, and it corresponds to a person's inner multiplicity in a double sense. On the one hand, the composite individual has many eyes with which to see diversity appropriately. On

---

[21] Friedrich Nietzsche, *On the Genealogy of Morals*, trans. Walter Kaufmann (New York: Vintage, 1969), essay 3, sec. 12, 119.

[22] Wallace Stevens, "An Ordinary Evening in New Haven," sec. XXX, in *The Collected Poems* (New York: Vintage, 1982), 488.

the other hand, he or she, like anything else, needs to be seen by many eyes—not only by the many sets of eyes of many individuals, but also by any one individual's many eyes.

But Whitman's final lesson is solitude, not the adventures of human connectedness. He would not be a defender of individuality if he taught otherwise. His work urges each of us back to a solitary relation with something unconceptualizable—perhaps the sheer fact of existence, of one's being and the being of anything else, even and especially when "cheaper, easier, nearer" ("A Song of the Rolling Earth"). What makes this solitude democratic—a democratic transcendence of democratic culture—is the, as it were, philosophical self-respect (what Tocqueville saw as natural Cartesianism) that democracy encourages in each person and that Whitman's work tries so profoundly and so desperately to make convincing. Democratic culture therefore opens the possibility for each to take himself or herself seriously as directly connected to whatever is irreducible, to that around which the mind can never close. In "Song of Myself," he gives a perfectly secular indication (induced by musical passion):

> . . . to feel the puzzle of puzzles,
> And that we call Being.
> To be in any form, what is that?
> (Secs. 26–27)

One's culmination is impersonal contemplation of the puzzle. For the sake of this, one must be one and only one. One's end is found alone.

As he puts it matchlessly, though still too religiously, in *Democratic Vistas*: "Alone, and identity, and the mood—and the soul emerges, and all statements, churches, sermons, melt away like vapors. Alone, and silent thought and awe, and aspiration—and then the interior consciousness, like a hitherto unseen inscription, in magic ink, beams out its wondrous lines to the sense . . . it is exclusively for the noiseless operation of one's isolated Self, to enter the pure ether of veneration, reach the divine levels, and commune with the unutterable."[23]

---

[23] Whitman, *Democratic Vistas*, in Kouwenhoven, 491.

Index

Library of Congress Cataloging-in-Publication Data

Kateb, George.
   The inner ocean : individualism and democratic culture / George Kateb.
      p.   cm. — (Contestations)
   Includes bibliographical references and index.
   ISBN 0-8014-2735-5. — ISBN 0-8014-8014-0 (pbk.)
   1. Individualism.   2. Democracy.   I. Title.   II. Series.
JC571.K344   1992
320.5′12—dc20   92-52764